SELECTIONS FROM MAJOR CANADIAN WRITERS

SELECTIONS FROM

MAJOR CANADIAN WRITERS

Poetry and Creative Prose in English

edited by

DESMOND PACEY

Professor of English
and
Vice-President (Academic)
in the
University of New Brunswick
Fredericton, New Brunswick

McGraw-Hill Ryerson Limited

Toronto   Montreal   New York   London   Sydney   Johannesburg
Mexico   Panama   Düsseldorf   Singapore   Sao Paulo   Kuala Lumpur
New Delhi

ISBN 0-07-077662-8

4 5 6 7 8 9 10 AP 3 2 1 0 9 8

Printed and Bound in Canada

ACKNOWLEDGEMENTS

EARLE BIRNEY: Poems on pages 62 to 67 from *Selected Poems* by Earle Birney are reprinted by permission of The Canadian Publishers, McClelland and Stewart Limited, Toronto.

ELIZABETH BREWSTER: Poems on pages 144 to 147 included in *Passage of Summer* by Elizabeth Brewster are reprinted by permission of McGraw-Hill Ryerson Limited. Poems on pages 148 to 150 from *Sunrise North* by Elizabeth Brewster, © 1972 by Clarke, Irwin & Company. Used by permission.

MORLEY CALLAGHAN: "Now That April's Here" from *Morley Callaghan's Stories* by permission of The Macmillan Company of Canada Limited.

BLISS CARMAN: Poems on pages 9 to 14 are reprinted by special permission of the Bliss Carman Trust, The University of New Brunswick, Canada.

LEONARD COHEN: Poems on pages 165 to 169 are all included in a collection of poems entitled *Selected Poems: 1956-1968* by Leonard Cohen. Copyright © 1964, 1966, 1968 by Leonard Cohen. A Bantam Book/published by arrangement with The Viking Press, Inc.

LOUIS DUDEK: Poems on pages 121 to 123 are from *Collected Poetry* (Delta Canada, 1971).

FREDERICK PHILIP GROVE: "Snow" reprinted by permission of Mr. A. L. Grove, Toronto, Ontario.

HUGH HOOD: "Flying a Red Kite" from *Flying a Red Kite* by Hugh Hood, reprinted by permission of McGraw-Hill Ryerson Limited.

ABRAHAM MOSES KLEIN: Poems on page 69 are from *Hath Not a Jew* by A. M. Klein. Poems on pages 70 to 77 are from *The Rocking Chair and Other Poems*. All poems are reprinted by permission of McGraw-Hill Ryerson Limited.

MARGARET LAURENCE: "The Loons" from *A Bird in the House* by Margaret Laurence reprinted by permission of The Canadian Publishers, McClelland & Stewart Limited, Toronto.

IRVING LAYTON: Poems on pages 94 to 95 are from *Lovers and Lesser Men* by Irving Layton. Poems on pages 88 to 93 are from *Collected Poems* by Irving Layton. All are reprinted by permission of The Canadian Publishers, McClelland and Stewart Limited, Toronto.

STEPHEN LEACOCK: "My Financial Career" from *Literary Lapses* by Stephen Leacock reprinted by permission of The Canadian Publishers, McClelland and Stewart Limited, Toronto.

NORMAN LEVINE: "The Cocks are Crowing" reprinted by permission of Norman Levine.

DOROTHY LIVESAY: Poems on pages 79 to 86 from *Collected Poems: The Two Seasons* by Dorothy Livesay are reprinted by permission of McGraw-Hill Ryerson Limited.

HUGH MACLENNAN: "Confessions of a Wood-Chopping Man" reprinted by permission of Hugh MacLennan.

PREFACE

This collection is intended primarily for those students who wish to learn something of the history of Anglo-Canadian literary development, but who prefer to study relatively few major authors in depth, rather than many in a more superficial way.

No doubt there will be some readers who feel that some authors that I have excluded deserve to be present, and that some that I have included do not justify their place. I myself have twinges of guilt about some of the very fine writers whom I have reluctantly excluded — poets such as W.W.E. Ross, Raymond Knister, Robert Finch, Roy Daniells, A.G. Bailey, John Glassco, Ralph Gustafson, Anne Wilkinson, Wilfred Watson, Anne Marriott, Douglas LePan, Patrick Anderson, Margaret Avison, Phyllis Webb, Jay Macpherson, Daryl Hine, Milton Acorn, Bill Bissett, b.p. nicol, Fred Cogswell, John Robert Columbo, George Jonas, Michael Ondaatje, Margaret Atwood, Gwendolyn MacEwen, Tom Marshall, George Johnston, John Newlove and Robert Cockburn; writers of short stories such as David Lewis Stein, Clark Blaise, Dave Godfrey, John Metcalf, and D. O. Spettigue; and critics or essayists such as Northrop Frye, Marshall McLuhan, George Woodcock and Robertson Davies.

To have included all or most of these writers, however, would have meant producing an altogether different kind of anthology, a collection of snippets. The twenty-one poets and twelve prose writers represented do seem to me to be the ones who, in the period since the Canadian Confederation of 1867, have most fully exhibited the development of a Canadian tradition.

The University of New Brunswick
March, 1973

Desmond Pacey.

TABLE OF CONTENTS

A.   Poetry

B. Short Stories and Prose Sketches

General Introduction

The very existence of English-Canadian literature is still occasionally debated — many would see it as merely a branch of English or American literature — and even those who admit its existence are often at a loss to define whereof its special identity consists. And yet the fact is that as early as the first half of the nineteenth century English-Canadian writers such as Thomas Chandler Haliburton and Major John Richardson were being eagerly read throughout the English-speaking world (and, in Haliburton's case, beyond) and that a large part of the reason for their popularity was that they were recognized to be dealing in material and attitudes that were new and distinctive. It is, admittedly, difficult to establish a distinctive literature in a relatively young country which uses the same language as two older and more powerful countries — Great Britain and the United States — but it would be foolish to deny that in Canada, as in Australia and New Zealand, this task is gradually being accomplished.

Because of its size, this anthology does not attempt to give a full historical survey of Canadian literature in English. To do so would mean going back, first of all, to the many books of travel and exploration written in the seventeenth and eighteenth centuries about the territory that is now known as Canada, and continuing indeed almost to our own day. Secondly, it would involve a sampling of those works of colonial literature, often imperfect in artistry but of great social and historical interest, which issued from the press in the period prior to the Confederation of the Canadian provinces into a federal state in 1867. There were, in the eighteen-twenties, -thirties, -forties, and -fifties, many books by early settlers which still command respect: Haliburton's *Sam Slick*, a series of brilliant sketches of character and humour; Richardson's *Wacousta*, a thrilling if somewhat melodramatic adventure story of the Indian wars; and Susanna Moodie's *Roughing It In The Bush*, a record of the hardships of pioneer settlement alternatively comic and pathetic, to name but three of the best.

This anthology concerns itself, however, exclusively with the literature of the post-Confederation era. It was with the coming of Confederation in 1867 that Canada began to develop a genuine sense of nationality and a literature designed to express it. The movement began in the eastern province of New Brunswick, in the poetry of Charles G.D. Roberts and Bliss Carman, but it quickly spread to Ontario, where the poetry of Archibald Lampman, Duncan Campbell Scott, Isabella Valancy Crawford and others soon began to command attention. During this first rush of more or less concerted literary activity, extending roughly from 1880 to 1910, poetry, mainly poetry of a romantic sort celebrating the spectacular qualities of Canadian landscape and climate, was the chief medium of expression. A certain amount of prose was also written — pioneer histories of Canada, historical novels attempting to stir up pride in Canada's past, a few regional novels and short stories designed to identify the kind of life characteristic of the various regions of the country — but, with few exceptions, it was of lower quality.

World War I provided the impetus for a second movement in Canadian literary development. The war gave Canadians a renewed sense of identity, a new pride of achievement, and the post-war period saw a remarkable efflorescence of art and literature. In poetry, E.J. Pratt and Dorothy Livesay in Toronto began to write of the Canadian scene with a new authority and energy, and A. J. M. Smith, F. R. Scott, and A.M. Klein in Montreal began to apply the techniques of modernist verse to a sceptical, witty examination of the contemporary scene. In prose, Stephen Leacock, who had begun to write his deftly humorous sketches just before the war, continued to delight readers throughout the world with his combination of subtle irony and broad farce, and there began to develop a school of realism in fiction which made the historical romances and regional idylls of the late nineteenth and early twentieth century seem highly artificial and irrelevant. In western Canada, Frederick Philip Grove applied his searching vision to the life of pioneer settlement on the prairies, and in the east Morley Callaghan began to produce his honest and subtle analyses of urban life.

WWII

The third major movement in Canadian literature in English came during and after World War II. This war, coming after the great depression of the nineteen-thirties in which the Canadian publishing industry had almost foundered, also gave to Canadians a renewed sense of national purpose and pride. Young poets such as Earle Birney, Irving Layton, P. K. Page, Louis Dudek and Raymond Souster exercised their talents in the close examination of Canadian society, mocking its pretensions, satirizing its inequities, but at the same time signalling their belief that it was a society worth struggling to save. Novelists such as Sinclair Ross, Hugh MacLennan and Ethel Wilson performed much the same function in prose: everywhere the emphasis was on seeing things as they really are, on stripping away the veils of illusion.

The movement towards social realism and commitment that so remarkably accelerated during World War II has continued with only minor modifications to the present day. For a period during the nineteen-fifties it began to appear that Canadian poetry was turning away from social realism towards fantasy and myth (in the work of James Reaney, Jay Macpherson, Eli Mandel and others) but it soon resumed what appears to be its main road in the realistic (but by no means unimaginative) poetry of Alfred Purdy, Alden Nowlan, John Newlove and others. Some poets, such as Leonard Cohen, Margaret Atwood and Michael Ondaatje, have proven their capacity to unite fantasy and myth with the stuff of everyday experience. A very similar development has occurred in prose fiction: Norman Levine, Hugh Hood, Mordecai Richler and Leonard Cohen have all given us critical, sceptical examinations of the basic nature of contemporary Canadian life, but have not hesitated to introduce humour and fantasy into their work on occasion, overlaying realism with symbolism. Richler and Cohen in particular, in their satirical passages, have frequently employed the satirist's technique of fantastic exaggeration.

The present state of English-Canadian literature is one of widespread experimentation. Poets in particular are trying out a great variety of techniques: concrete poetry, pop poetry, found poetry, psychedelic expressionism. The number of aspiring young writers, and especially writers of verse, is legion. What of permanent interest will emerge from this welter of activity it is still too early to say, but that there is and will be a vital Canadian literature in English is beyond dispute.

But in what sense is this literature distinctive? This, perhaps, is a question which can be more satisfactorily answered by readers outside Canada than by those within. I trust that the readers of this anthology will attempt to answer this question for themselves, so I will content myself with three suggestions: that the distinctiveness of Canadian literature in English consists in its attitude to the physical environment, to the social environment, and to the individual person.

The physical environment of Canada is one of extremes — extremes of heat and cold, of fertility and infertility, of assurance and apprehension. Reflecting this fact (symbolized most fully perhaps by the 150° temperature range of the country) Canadian writing swings between the dream and the nightmare: a sense of exultation and exhilaration on the one hand, and a sense of terror and despair on the other. In all our leading writers — in Lampman, Carman, Grove, Pratt and Cohen, for example — we find this violent oscillation between extremes.

The social environment of Canada is complex and difficult. Canada is not British, and it is not American — but it is partly both and always struggling to be something distinctively other. Hence, in much Canadian writing we find a strange sense of a tightrope walker. To relieve the tension we keep laughing at ourselves, mocking any tendency to fall on one side of the wire or the other. Haliburton ridiculed the inclination of his contemporary Nova Scotians to admire and imitate the Americans; F. R. Scott, in "The Canadian Authors Meet," made fun of our penchant for imitating the British by having a poet laureate, and in "Saturday Sundae" made fun of our readiness to appropriate the worst features of American civilization; and Irving Layton, in "Anglo-Canadian," scoffed at the value Canadian intellectuals attach (or did attach) to an Oxford education and an Oxford accent. Earle Birney, in "Canada: Case History," has perhaps given us the most comprehensive satirical account of this anxious Canadian quest for identity:

> His Uncle spoils him with candy, of course,
> yet shouts him down when he talks at table.
> You will note he's got some of his French mother's looks,
> though he's not so witty and no more stable.
> He's really not so much like his father and yet
> if you say so he'll pull a great face.
> He wants to be different from everyone else
> and daydreams of winning the global race.

The predominant tone in Canadian literature in responding to the facts of both the physical and social environment of Canada is, then, one of wry ambiguity. Snow is seen as at once beautiful and terrifying, Canadian society as groping uncertainly between the poles of Britain and America. Only in relation to the individual human being is there a straightforward, relatively unambiguous response. Canadian writers are, almost without exception, humanists, who see man as admirable in his persistence and his devotion. There are remarkably few villains in Canadian literature, and even for these few, abundant excuses are made. It is perhaps in this respect that our literature approaches the naiveté which we might expect to find in a young country.

Thomas Chandler Haliburton's Sam Slick is vain, tricky, selfish and devious — but he is fundamentally admirable, even lovable. Stephen Leacock's townsmen in *Sunshine Sketches of A Little Town* are parochial, petty and prejudiced — but they are human beings in whose variety we delight. Frederick Philip Grove's prairie dwellers are often ignorant, headstrong and passionate — but we admire them because, even in the face of storms and other hardships, they persevere. Ethel Wilson's women have much the same quality of heroic persistence despite seemingly insurmountable obstacles.

To sum up, it seems to me that the dominant image which emerges from reading Canadian literature in English is of modestly heroic individuals who manage to endure in a society which is ambivalent almost to the point of confusion and in a climate and landscape which alternately threatens and cajoles. "Look — in spite of all, we have survived" — that, over and over again, seems to be the theme of the selections which follow.

Desmond Pacey

A Brief Chronology of Canadian Literature in English

1749	Founding of Halifax, Nova Scotia
1752	Establishment of the Halifax *Gazette*
1763	Treaty of Paris Pontiac's Conspiracy
1769	Publication of Frances Brooke's *History of Emily Montague* — "the first Canadian novel."
1774	The Quebec Act
1776	The American Declaration of Independence
1783	The coming of the United Empire Loyalists, fleeing the American Revolution
1791	The Constitutional Act, separating Upper Canada (now Ontario) from Lower Canada (now Quebec)
1812-14	American-Canadian War. Deaths of Brock and Tecumseh
1823	Establishment of *The Canadian Magazine* in Montreal
1824	William Lyon MacKenzie's *Colonial Advocate* (1824-1834) Founding of the Literary and Historical Society of Quebec
1825	Publication of Oliver Goldsmith's *The Rising Village* — first book of poems by a native English-Canadian
1827	Joseph Howe purchases the *Nova Scotian*, the magazine in which Haliburton's *Sam Slick* was to appear
1832	John Richardson's *Wacousta*
1836	Catherine Parr Traill's *Backwoods of Canada* Thomas Chandler Haliburton's *The Clockmaker*
1837	Rebellions (in favour of responsible government) in Upper and Lower Canada

1838	Anna Jameson's *Winter Studies and Summer Rambles in Canada*
1852	Susanna Moodie's *Roughing It in the Bush*
1856	Charles Sangster's *The St. Lawrence and the Saguenay*
1857	Charles Heavysege's *Saul*
1864	E.H. Dewart's *Selections from Canadian Poets* — the first anthology
1867	The British North American Act (Confederation)
1877	William Kirby's *The Golden Dog* (historical romance)
1880	Charles G.D. Roberts' *Orion and Other Poems*
1882	Foundation of the Royal Society of Canada
1884	Isabella Valancy Crawford's *Old Spookses' Pass, Malcolm's Katie, and Other Poems*
1886	Completion of the Canadian Pacific Railway Charles G.D. Roberts' *In Divers Tones*
1888	Archibald Lampman's *Among the Millet*
1889	William Douw Lighthall's *Songs of the Great Dominion*
1893	Bliss Carman's *Low Tide on Grand Pré* Charles G.D. Roberts' *Songs of the Common Day* Duncan Campbell Scott's *The Magic House and Other Poems* Establishment of *Queen's Quarterly*
1894	Bliss Carman's *Songs from Vagabondia*
1895	Bliss Carman's *Behind the Arras* Archibald Lampman's *Lyrics of Earth*
1896	Bliss Carman's *More Songs from Vagabondia* Charles G.D. Roberts' *The Book of the Native* Duncan Campbell Scott's *In the Village Viger*
1897	Bliss Carman's *Ballads of Lost Haven* William Henry Drummond's *The Habitant and Other French Canadian Poems*

1898	Ralph Connor's *Black Rock* (regional novel) Charles G.D. Roberts' *New York Nocturnes* Duncan Campbell Scott's *Labour and the Angel*
1899	Archibald Lampman's *Alcyone*
1900	Archibald Lampman's *Poems* (D.C. Scott, ed.)
1901	Bliss Carman's *Last Songs from Vagabondia*
1902	Bliss Carman's *From the Book of the Myths*
1903	Bliss Carman's *From the Green Book of the Bards* Charles G.D. Roberts' *Book of the Rose*
1904	Bliss Carman's *Songs of the Sea Children* *The Friendship of Art* *The Kinship of Nature*
1905	Bliss Carman's *Sappho* Duncan Campbell Scott's *New World Lyrics and Ballads*
1906	Duncan Campbell Scott's *Via Borealis*
1907	Robert Service's *Songs of a Sourdough*
1908	L.M. Montgomery's *Anne of Green Gables*
1910	Stephen Leacock's *Literary Lapses*
1911	Stephen Leacock's *Nonsense Novels*
1912	Stephen Leacock's *Sunshine Sketches of a Little Town*
1913	Stephen Leacock's *Behind the Beyond, and Other* *Contributions to Human Knowledge*
1914	World War I (1914-1918) Stephen Leacock's *Arcadian Adventures with the Idle Rich*
1915	Stephen Leacock's *Moonbeams from the Larger Lunacy*
1916	Stephen Leacock's *Further Foolishness* Duncan Campbell Scott's *Lundy's Lane and Other Poems*
1918	Stephen Leacock's *Frenzied Fiction* *The Hohenzollerns in America*

1919	Charles G.D. Roberts' *New Poems*
1920	R.P. Baker's *English-Canadian Literature to the Confederation* — first literary history Stephen Leacock's *Winsome Winnie* Establishment of *The Canadian Forum*
1921	Duncan Campbell Scott's *Beauty of Life* Establishment of the Canadian Authors Association Establishment of *Dalhousie Review*
1922	Frederick Philip Grove's *Over Prairie Trails* Stephen Leacock's *My Discovery of England*
1923	Frederick Philip Grove's *The Turn of the Year* E.J. Pratt's *Newfoundland Verse* Duncan Campbell Scott's *The Witching of Elspie Pierre*
1925	Frederick Philip Grove's *Settlers of the Marsh* E.J. Pratt's *The Witches' Brew* Establishment of *The McGill Fortnightly Review* (1925-1927)
1926	E.J. Pratt's *Titans* *The Poems of Duncan Campbell Scott*
1927	Frederick Philip Grove's *A Search for America* E.J. Pratt's *The Iron Door* Charles G.D. Roberts' *The Vagrant of Time* Mazo de la Roche's *Jalna*
1928	*Canadian Short Stories* (Raymond Knister, ed.) Morley Callaghan's *Strange Fugitive* Frederick Philip Grove's *Our Daily Bread* Dorothy Livesay's *Green Pitcher*
1929	Morley Callaghan's *A Native Argosy* Bliss Carman's *Sanctuary* Frederick Philip Grove's *It Needs to be Said* Raymond Knister's *White Narcissus*
1930	Morley Callaghan's *It's Never Over* Frederick Philip Grove's *The Yoke of Life* E.J. Pratt's *Verses of the Sea* *The Roosevelt and the Antinoe*
1931	Establishment of *The University of Toronto Quarterly*

1932   Morley Callaghan's *A Broken Journey*
      Dorothy Livesay's *Signpost*
      E.J. Pratt's *Many Moods*

1933   Frederick Philip Grove's *Fruits of the Earth*

1934   Morley Callaghan's *Such Is My Beloved*
      Charles G.D. Roberts' *The Iceberg and Other Poems*

1935   Morley Callaghan's *They Shall Inherit the Earth*
      Dorothy Livesay's *The Outrider*
      E.J. Pratt's *The Titanic*
      Duncan Campbell Scott's *The Green Cloister*
      Initiation of annual "Letters in Canada" in the
       University of Toronto Quarterly

1936   W.E. Collin's *The White Savannahs* — first collection of
       critical essays
      New Provinces (poems by A.J.M. Smith, F.R. Scott,
       A.M. Klein, Leo Kennedy, Dorothy Livesay, E.J. Pratt)
      Morley Callaghan's *Now That April's Here and Other Stories*

1937   Morley Callaghan's *More Joy in Heaven*
      E.J. Pratt's *The Fable of the Goats and Other Poems*
      Establishment of Governor General's Literary Awards

1939   World War II (1939-1945)
      Frederick Philip Grove's *Two Generations*

1940   A.M. Klein's *Hath Not a Jew . . .*
      E.J. Pratt's *Brébeuf and His Brethren*

1941   *Contemporary Verse* (British Columbia, 1941-1951)
      Hugh MacLennan's *Barometer Rising*
      E.J. Pratt's *Dunkirk*
      Sinclair Ross' *As For Me and My House*

1942   Earle Birney's *David and Other Poems*
      Ralph Gustafson's *Anthology of Canadian Poetry*
      Stephen Leacock's *My Remarkable Uncle*
      Establishment of *First Statement* (1942-1945)
      Establishment of *Preview* (Montreal)

1943   E.K. Brown's *On Canadian Poetry*
      Archibald Lampman's *At the Long Sault and Other Poems*
       (E.K. Brown, ed.)
      E.J. Pratt's *Still Life and Other Verse*
      A.J.M. Smith's *Book of Canadian Poetry*
         News of the Phoenix

1944	Frederick Philip Grove's *The Master of the Mill*
	A.M. Klein's *The Hitleriad* and *Poems*
	Dorothy Livesay's *Day and Night*
	P.K. Page's *The Sun and the Moon*
	E.J. Pratt's *Collected Poems*
	A.W. Purdy's *The Enchanted Echo*
	Unit of Five (poems by Souster, Dudek, Wreford, Page, Hambleton)

1945   Earle Birney's *Now Is the Time*
Irving Layton's *Here and Now*
Hugh MacLennan's *Two Solitudes*
E.J. Pratt's *They Are Returning*
F.R. Scott's *Overture*
Miriam Waddington's *Green World*
Establishment of *The Fiddlehead* and *Northern Review* (1945-1956)

1946   Louis Dudek's *East of the City*
Frederick Philip Grove's *In Search of Myself*
Stephen Leacock's *The Boy I Left Behind Me*
P.K. Page's *As Ten, As Twenty*
Raymond Souster's *When We Are Young*

1947   Frederick Philip Grove's *Consider Her Ways*
Dorothy Livesay's *Poems for People*
Malcolm Lowry's *Under the Volcano*
W.O. Mitchell's *Who Has Seen the Wind*
Desmond Pacey's *Book of Canadian Stories*
E.J. Pratt's *Behind the Log*
Duncan Campbell Scott's *The Circle of Affection*
Raymond Souster's *Go to Sleep World*
Ethel Wilson's *Hetty Dorval*

1948   Earle Birney's *The Strait of Anian*
Morley Callaghan's *The Varsity Story*
A.M. Klein's *The Rocking Chair and Other Poems*
Irving Layton's *Now Is the Place*
Hugh MacLennan's *The Precipice*

1949   Earle Birney's *Turvey*
Hugh MacLennan's *Cross Country*
James Reaney's *The Red Heart*
Ethel Wilson's *The Innocent Traveller*

1950   Dorothy Livesay's *Call My People Home*
Norman Levine's *The Tightrope Walker*

1951	Elizabeth Brewster's *East Coast*
	Ernest Buckler's *The Mountain and the Valley*
	Morley Callaghan's *The Loved and the Lost*
	Irving Layton's *The Black Huntsman*
	Hugh MacLennan's *Each Man's Son*
	Marshall McLuhan's *The Mechanical Bride*
	A.M. Klein's *The Second Scroll*
	Raymond Souster's *City Hall Street*

1951
Elizabeth Brewster's *East Coast*
Ernest Buckler's *The Mountain and the Valley*
Morley Callaghan's *The Loved and the Lost*
Irving Layton's *The Black Huntsman*
Hugh MacLennan's *Each Man's Son*
Marshall McLuhan's *The Mechanical Bride*
A.M. Klein's *The Second Scroll*
Raymond Souster's *City Hall Street*

1952
Earle Birney's *Trial of a City and Other Verse*
   Cerberus (poems by Dudek, Layton, Souster)
Louis Dudek's *The Searching Image*
   Twenty-four Poems
Norman Levine's *The Angled Road*
Desmond Pacey's *Creative Writing in Canada*
E.J. Pratt's *The Last Spike*
Ethel Wilson's *Equations of Love*

1953
Raymond Souster's *Shake Hands with the Hangman*

1954
Elizabeth Brewster's *Lillooet*
Louis Dudek's *En Mexico*
Irving Layton's *In the Midst of My Fever*
   The Long Pea-Shooter
Hugh MacLennan's *Thirty and Three*
P.K. Page's *The Metal and the Flower*
Mordecai Richler's *The Acrobats*
F.R. Scott's *Events and Signals*
A.J.M. Smith's *A Sort of Ecstasy*
   Poems: New and Selected

1955
Earle Birney's *Down the Long Table*
Irving Layton's *The Cold Green Element*
   The Blue Propellor
Dorothy Livesay's *New Poems*
The Selected Poems of Sir Charles G.D. Roberts
   (Desmond Pacey, ed.)
A.W. Purdy's *Pressed on Sand*
Mordecai Richler's *Son of a Smaller Hero*
Miriam Waddington's *Second Silence*

1956
Leonard Cohen's *Let Us Compare Mythologies*
Louis Dudek's *The Transparent Sea*
Irving Layton's *The Bull Calf and Other Poems*
   The Improved Binoculars
A.W. Purdy's *Emu, Remember*
Raymond Souster's *Selected Poems*
Ethel Wilson's *Love and Salt Water*
Establishment of *The Tamarack Review*

1957	Elizabeth Brewster's *Roads*
	Northrop Frye's *Anatomy of Criticism*
	Dorothy Livesay's *Selected Poems 1926-1956*
	Mordecai Richler's *A Choice of Enemies*
	The Blasted Pine (F.R. Scott and A.J.M. Smith, eds.)
	F.R. Scott's *The Eye of the Needle*
	Establishment of The Canada Council

1958
Louis Dudek's *Laughing Stalks*
Ralph Gustafson's *Penguin Book of Canadian Verse*
Irving Layton's *Music on a Kazoo*
                A Laughter of the Mind
Norman Levine's *Canada Made Me*
Alden Nowlan's *The Rose and the Puritan*
                A Darkness in the Earth
Desmond Pacey's *Ten Canadian Poets*
E.J. Pratt's *Collected Poems* (second ed.)
James Reaney's *A Suit of Nettles*
Sinclair Ross' *The Well*
Raymond Souster's *Crepe-Hanger's Carnival: Selected
                Poems, 1955-1958*
Miriam Waddington's *The Season's Lovers*

1959
Morley Callaghan's Stories
Irving Layton's *A Red Carpet for the Sun*
Hugh MacLennan's *The Watch That Ends the Night*
A.W. Purdy's *The Crafte So Longe to Lerne*
Mordecai Richler's *The Apprenticeship of Duddy Kravitz*
R.E. Watters' *Check List of Canadian Literature*
Establishment of *Canadian Literature* and *Prism*

1960
Margaret Avison's *Winter Sun*
Morley Callaghan's *The Many Coloured Coat*
Margaret Laurence's *This Side Jordan*
Hugh MacLennan's *Scotchman's Return and Other Essays*
Eli Mandel's *Fuseli Poems*
Brian Moore's *The Luck of Ginger Coffey*
Alden Nowlan's *Wind in a Rocky Country*
A.J.M. Smith's *Oxford Book of Canadian Verse*
Robert Weaver's *Canadian Short Stories*

1961
Margaret Atwood's *Double Persephone*
Morley Callaghan's *A Passion in Rome*
Leonard Cohen's *The Spice-box of Earth*
Irving Layton's *The Swinging Flesh*
Norman Levine's *One Way Ticket*
Malcolm Lowry's *Hear Us O Lord from Heaven
                Thy Dwelling Place*

Hugh MacLennan's *Seven Rivers of Canada*
Alden Nowlan's *Under the Ice*
Ethel Wilson's *Mrs. Golightly and Other Stories*

1962   Earle Birney's *Ice Cod Bell or Stone*
Hugh Hood's *Flying a Red Kite and Other Stories*
Alden Nowlan's *The Things Which Are*
A.W. Purdy's *Poems for All the Annettes*
James Reaney's *The Kildeer and Other Plays*
                     Twelve Letters to a Small Town
A.J.M. Smith's *Collected Poems*
Raymond Souster's *A Local Pride*
                     Place of Meeting

1963   Morley Callaghan's *That Summer In Paris*
Leonard Cohen's *The Favourite Game*
Margaret Laurence's *The To-Morrow Tamer and Other Stories*
                     The Prophets' Camel Bell
Irving Layton's *Balls for a One-Armed Juggler*
A.W. Purdy's *The Blur in Between*
James Reaney's *The Dance of Death at London, Ontario*
Mordecai Richler's *The Incomparable Atuk*

1964   Earle Birney's *Near False Creek Mouth*
Leonard Cohen's *Flowers for Hitler*
Hugh Hood's *White Figure, White Ground*
Margaret Laurence's *The Stone Angel*
Irving Layton's *The Laughing Rooster*
Eli Mandel's *Black and Secret Man*
F.R. Scott's *Signature*
Raymond Souster's *The Colour of the Times*

1965   Adoption of Canadian Flag
C.F. Klinck *et al., Literary History of Canada*
A.W. Purdy's *The Caribou Horses*
A.J.M. Smith's *The Book of Canadian Prose*
Raymond Souster's *The Elephant on Yonge Street*

1966   Margaret Atwood's *The Circle Game*
Earle Birney's *Selected Poems, 1940-1966*
Leonard Cohen's *Beautiful Losers*
                     Parasites of Heaven
Margaret Laurence's *A Jest of God*
F.R. Scott's *Selected Poems*
New Wave Canada (Raymond Souster, ed.)
Miriam Waddington's *The Glass Trumpet*

Sinclair Ross' *Whir of Gold*
Made in Canada; New Poems of the Seventies (Douglas
Lochhead and Raymond Souster, eds.)

1971   Margaret Atwood's *Power Politics*
Earle Birney's *Rag & Bone Shop*
Louis Dudek's *Collected Poetry*
Frederick Philip Grove's *Tales from the Margin*
Hugh Hood's *The Fruit Man, the Meat Man and the Manager*
Irving Layton's *Selected Poems* (enlarged ed.)
Norman Levine's *I Don't Want to Know Anyone Too Well
and Other Stories*
Dorothy Livesay's *40 Women Poets of Canada*
Alice Munro's *Lives of Girls and Women*
Alden Nowlan's *Between Tears and Laughter*
James Reaney's *Colours in the Dark*
Mordecai Richler's *St. Urbain's Horseman*
Raymond Souster's *The Years*

1972   Margaret Atwood's *Surfacing*
Survival
Elizabeth Brewster's *Sunrise North*
Leonard Cohen's *The Energy of Slaves*
Hugh Hood's *You Can't Get There from Here*
Dorothy Livesay's *Collected Poems*
Eli Mandel's *Poets of Contemporary Canada, 1960-1970*
A.W. Purdy's *Selected Poems*
Hiroshima Poems
James Reaney's *Listen to the Wind*
Miriam Waddington's *Driving Home*
Establishment of *The Journal of Canadian Fiction*

1973   Irving Layton's *Lovers and Lesser Men*

POETRY

Charles G.D. Roberts
(1860—1943)

Charles G.D. Roberts has sometimes been called the "father of Canadian literature" since it was he who led our first significant poetic movement in the eighteen-eighties and -nineties. In those two decades Roberts himself, his cousin Bliss Carman, Archibald Lampman, Duncan Campbell Scott, William Wilfred Campbell, George Frederick Cameron, and Pauline Johnson were publishing regularly in the leading magazines of the English-speaking world. The poetry they produced was romantic in attitude, strongly influenced by such English romantic poets as Wordsworth, Keats, Shelley, Coleridge, Byron and Tennyson, but it brought this attitude to bear upon distinctively Canadian matters: the natural environment, the climate and weather, the native inhabitants, the pioneer settlers, the beginnings of a national consciousness.

Born and brought up in the eastern seaside province of New Brunswick, and a graduate of the University of New Brunswick, Roberts became editor of *The Week*, a literary magazine in Toronto, then a professor of English at King's College, Windsor, Nova Scotia. From 1897 to 1925 he spent most of his time outside of Canada — in New York, in Paris, and in London. During this period of exile he wrote mainly prose fiction, and most successfully, animal stories which brought him a wide reputation. After his return to Canada in 1925 he reverted mainly to the writing of verse. He was knighted in 1936 by King George V, he died in Toronto on November 26, 1943, and was buried in Fredericton, New Brunswick.

The poems which follow are taken from the *Selected Poems of Sir Charles G.D. Roberts*, edited by Desmond Pacey, Ryerson Press, Toronto, 1955.

TANTRAMAR REVISITED[1]

Summers and summers have come, and gone with the flight of the swallow;
Sunshine and thunder have been, storm, and winter, and frost;
Many and many a sorrow has all but died from remembrance,
Many a dream of joy fall'n in the shadow of pain.
Hands of chance and change have marred, or moulded, or broken,
Busy with spirit or flesh, all I most have adored;
Even the bosom of Earth is strewn with heavier shadows,—
Only in these green hills, aslant to the sea, no change!
Here where the road that has climbed from the inland valleys and woodlands,
Dips from the hill-tops down, straight to the base of the hills, —
Here, from my vantage-ground, I can see the scattering houses,
Stained with time, set warm in orchards, meadows, and wheat,
Dotting the broad light slopes outspread to southward and eastward,
Wind-swept all day long, blown by the southeast wind.

Skirting the sunbright uplands stretches a riband of meadow,
Shorn of the laboring grass, bulwarked well from the sea,
Fenced on its seaward border with long clay dikes from the turbid
Surge and flow of the tides vexing the Westmoreland shores.
Yonder, toward the left, lie broad the Westmoreland marshes,—
Miles on miles they extend, level, and grassy, and dim,
Clear from the long red sweep of flats to the sky in the distance,
Save for the outlying heights, green-rampired Cumberland Point;
Miles on miles outrolled, and the river-channels divide them,—
Miles on miles of green, barred by the hurtling gusts.

Miles on miles beyond the tawny bay is Minudie.
There are the low blue hills; villages gleam at their feet.
Nearer a white sail shines across the water, and nearer
Still are the slim, gray masts of fishing boats dry on the flats.
Ah, how well I remember those wide red flats, above tide-mark
Pale with scurf of the salt, seamed and baked in the sun!
Well I remember the piles of blocks and ropes, and the net-reels
Wound with the beaded nets, dripping and dark from the sea!
Now at this season the nets are unwound; they hang from the rafters
Over the fresh-stowed hay in upland barns, and the wind
Blows all day through the chinks, with the streaks of sunlight, and sways them
Softly at will; or they lie heaped in the gloom of a loft.

Now at this season the reels are empty and idle; I see them
Over the lines of the dikes, over the gossiping grass.
Now at this season they swing in the long strong wind, thro' the lonesome
Golden afternoon, shunned by the foraging gulls.
Near about sunset the crane will journey homeward above them;
Round them, under the moon, all the calm night long,

3

Winnowing soft gray wings of marsh-owls wander and wander,
Now to the broad, lit marsh, now to the dusk of the dike.
Soon, thro' their dew-wet frames, in the live keen freshness of morning,
Out of the teeth of the dawn blows back the awakening wind.
Then, as the blue day mounts, and the low-shot shafts of the sunlight
Glance from the tide to the shore, gossamers jewelled with dew
Sparkle and wave, where late sea-spoiling fathoms of drift-net
Myriad-meshed, uploomed sombrely over the land.

Well I remember it all. The salt raw scent of the margin;
While, with men at the windlass, groaned each reel, and the net,
Surging in ponderous lengths, uprose and coiled in its station;
Then each man to his home, — well I remember it all!

Yet, as I sit and watch, this present peace of the landscape,—
Stranded boats, these reels empty and idle, the hush,
One gray hawk slow-wheeling above yon cluster of haystacks,—
More than the old-time stir this stillness welcomes me home.
Ah the old-time stir, how once it stung me with rapture,—
Old-time sweetness, the winds freighted with honey and salt!
Yet will I stay my steps and not go down to the marshland,—
Muse and recall far off, rather remember than see,—
Lest on too close sight I miss the darling illusion,
Spy at their task even here the hands of chance and change.

(1886)[2]

[1] Marshes along the Bay of Fundy coast in New Brunswick, where Roberts
spent his boyhood. Across the bay is the province of Nova Scotia.
[2] The date given for each selection is the date of its first publication in
book form.

THE SOWER

A brown, sad-coloured hillside, where the soil,
    Fresh from the frequent harrow, deep and fine,
    Lies bare; no break in the remote sky-line,
Save where a flock of pigeons streams aloft,
Startled from feed in some low-lying croft,
    Or far-off spires with yellow of sunset shine;
    And here the Sower, unwittingly divine,
Exerts the silent forethought of his toil.

Alone he treads the glebe, his measured stride
      Dumb in the yielding soil; and though small joy
         Dwell in his heavy face, as spreads the blind
Pale grain from his dispensing palm aside,
      This plodding churl grows great in his employ;—
         Godlike, he makes provision for mankind.

(1886)

THE PEA-FIELDS

These are the fields of light, and laughing air,
      And yellow butterflies, and foraging bees,
      And whitish, wayward blossoms winged as these,
And pale green tangles like a seamaid's hair.
Pale, pale the blue, but pure beyond compare,
      And pale the sparkle of the far-off seas,
      A-shimmer like these fluttering slopes of peas,
And pale the open landscape everywhere.

From fence to fence a perfumed breath exhales
      O'er the bright pallor of the well-loved fields,—
My fields of Tantramar in summer-time;
      And, scorning the poor feed their pasture yields,
Up from the bushy lots the cattle climb,
      To gaze with longing through the grey, mossed rails.

(1893)

THE MOWING

This is the voice of high midsummer's heat.
      The rasping vibrant clamour soars and shrills
      O'er all the meadowy range of shadeless hills,
As if a host of giant cicadae beat
The cymbals of their wings with tireless feet,
      Or brazen grasshoppers with triumphing note
      From the long swath proclaimed the fate that smote
The clover and timothy-tops and meadowsweet.

The crying knives glide on; the green swath lies.
  And all noon long the sun, with chemic ray,
  Seals up each cordial essence in its cell,
That in the dusky stalls, some winter's day,
  The spirit of June, here prisoned by his spell,
  May cheer the herds with pasture memories.

(1893)

IN AN OLD BARN

Tons upon tons the brown-green fragrant hay
  O'erbrims the mows beyond the time-warped eaves,
  Up to the rafters where the spider weaves,
Though few flies wander his secluded way.
Through a high chink one lonely golden ray,
  Wherein the dust is dancing, slants unstirred.
  In the dry hush some rustlings light are heard,
Of winter-hidden mice at furtive play.

Far down, the cattle in their shadowed stalls,
  Nose-deep in clover fodder's meadowy scent,
  Forget the snows that whelm their pasture streams,
The frost that bites the world beyond their walls.
  Warm housed, they dream of summer, well content
  In day-long contemplation of their dreams.

(1893)

THE BROOK IN FEBRUARY

A snowy path for squirrel and fox,
  It winds between the wintry firs.
Snow-muffled are its iron rocks,
  And o'er its stillness nothing stirs.

But low, bend low a listening ear!
  Beneath the mask of moveless white
A babbling whisper you shall hear
  Of birds and blossoms, leaves and light.

(1896)

6

ICE

When Winter scourged the meadow and the hill
And in the withered leafage worked his will,
The water shrank, and shuddered, and stood still,—
Then built himself a magic house of glass,
Irised with memories of flowers and grass,
Wherein to sit and watch the fury pass.

(1898)

PHILANDER'S SONG

I sat and read Anacreon.
     Moved by the gay, delicious measure
I mused that lips were made for love,
     And love to charm a poet's leisure.

And as I mused a maid came by
     With something in her look that caught me.
Forgotten was Anacreon's line,
     But not the lesson that he taught me.

(1927)

Bliss Carman
(1861–1929)

Bliss Carman was the most prolific Canadian poet of his generation, and the most famous. A native of Fredericton, New Brunswick, and a graduate of the University of New Brunswick, he spent most of his adult life in the United States but always maintained contact with Canada. His first book, *Low Tide on Grand Pré* (1893), was his best: here he found in the scenery and climate of the Maritime provinces objective correlatives for his characteristic mood of loneliness and sadness. His many later books are often too strident in tone or too emphatic in rhythm, but to the very end of his life he produced occasional lyrics which have a kind of musical magic and a distinctive fragile suggestiveness.

The poems which follow are taken from *The Selected Poems of Bliss Carman*, edited by Lorne Pierce, McClelland and Stewart, Toronto, 1954.

A NORTHERN VIGIL

Here by the gray north sea,
In the wintry heart of the wild,
Comes the old dream of thee,
Guendolen, mistress and child.

The heart of the forest grieves
In the drift against my door;
A voice is under the eaves,
A footfall on the floor.

Threshold, mirror and hall,
Vacant and strangely aware,
Wait for their soul's recall
With the dumb expectant air.

Here when the smouldering west
Burns down into the sea,
I take no heed of rest
And keep the watch for thee.

When day puts out to sea
And night makes in for land,
There is no lock for thee,
Each door awaits thy hand!

When night goes over the hill
And dawn comes down the dale,
It's Oh, for the wild sweet will
That shall no more prevail!

When the zenith moon is round,
And snow-wraiths gather and run,
And there is set no bound
To love beneath the sun,

O wayward will, come near
The old mad wilful way,
The soft mouth at my ear
With words too sweet to say!

Come, for the night is cold,
The ghostly moonlight fills
Hollow and rift and fold
Of the eerie Ardise hills!

The windows of my room
Are dark with bitter frost,
The stillness aches with doom
Of something loved and lost.

Outside, the great blue star
Burns in the ghostland pale,
Where giant Algebar
Holds on the endless trail.

Come, for the years are long,
And silence keeps the door,
Where shapes with the shadows throng
The firelit chamber floor.

Come, for thy kiss was warm,
With the red embers' glare
Across thy folding arm
And dark tumultuous hair!

The curtains seem to part;
A sound is on the stair,
As if at the last . . . I start;
Only the wind is there.

Lo, now far on the hills
The crimson fumes uncurled,
Where the caldron mantles and spills
Another dawn on the world!

(1893)

WINDFLOWER

Between the roadside and the wood,
Between the dawning and the dew,
A tiny flower before the sun,
Ephemeral in time, I grew.

And there upon the trail of spring,
Not death nor love nor any name
Known among men in all their lands
Could blur the wild desire with shame.

But down my dayspan of the year
The feet of straying winds came by;
And all my trembling soul was thrilled
To follow one lost mountain cry.

And then my heart beat once and broke
To hear the sweeping rain forebode
Some ruin in the April world,
Between the woodside and the road.

Tonight can bring no healing now;
The calm of yesternight is gone;
Surely the wind is but the wind,
And I a broken waif thereon.

(1893)

LOW TIDE ON GRAND PRÉ[1]

The sun goes down, and over all
        These barren reaches by the tide
Such unelusive glories fall,
        I almost dream they yet will bide
        Until the coming of the tide.

And yet I know that not for us,
        By any ecstasy of dream,
He lingers to keep luminous
        A little while the grievous stream,
        Which frets, uncomforted of dream—

A grievous stream, that to and fro
        Athrough the fields of Acadie
Goes wandering, as if to know
        Why one beloved face should be
        So long from home and Acadie.

Was it a year or lives ago
        We took the grasses in our hands,
And caught the summer flying low
        Over the waving meadow lands,
        And held it there between our hands?

The while the river at our feet—
    A drowsy inland meadow stream—
At set of sun the after-heat
    Made running gold, and in the gleam
    We freed our birch upon the stream.

There down along the elms at dusk
    We lifted dripping blade to drift,
Through twilight scented fine like musk,
    Where night and gloom awhile uplift,
    Nor sunder soul and soul adrift.

And that we took into our hands
    Spirit of life or subtler thing—
Breathed on us there, and loosed the bands
    Of death, and taught us, whispering,
    The secrets of some wonder-thing.

Then all your face grew light, and seemed
    To hold the shadow of the sun;
The evening faltered, and I deemed
    That time was ripe, and years had done
    Their wheeling underneath the sun.

So all desire and all regret,
    And fear and memory, were naught;
One to remember or forget
    The keen delight our hands had caught;
    Morrow and yesterday were naught.

The night has fallen, and the tide. . .
    Now and again comes drifting home,
Across these aching barrens wide,
    A sigh like driven wind or foam:
    In grief the flood is bursting home.

(1893)

[1] On the Nova Scotia side of the Bay of
Fundy, near Windsor, where Carman spent
several summers with his cousin, Charles
G.D. Roberts. The tidal rivers along the bay
leave wide stretches of mud flats when the
tide is out.

NOONS OF POPPY

Noons of poppy, noons of poppy,
Scarlet leagues along the sea;
Flaxen hair afloat in sunlight,
Love, come down the world to me!

There's a Captain I must ship with,
(Heart, that day be far from now!)
Wears his dark command in silence
With the sea-frost on his brow.

Noons of poppy, noons of poppy,
Purple shadows by the sea;
How should love take thought to wonder
What the destined port may be?

Nay, if love have joy for shipmate
For a night-watch or a year,
Dawn will light o'er Lonely Haven,
Heart to happy heart, as here.

Noons of poppy, noons of poppy,
Scarlet acres by the sea
Burning to the blue above them;
Love, the world is full for me.

(1897)

EYES LIKE SUMMER AFTER SUNDOWN

Eyes like summer after sundown,
Hands like roses after dew,
Lyric as a blown rose garden
The wind wanders through.

Swelling breasts that bud to crimson,
Hair like cobwebs after dawn,
And the rosy mouth wind-rifled
When the wind is gone.

(1904)

ONCE YOU LAY UPON MY BOSOM[1]

Once you lay upon my bosom
While the long blue-silver moonlight
Walked the plain, with that pure passion
    All your own.

Now the moon is gone, the Pleiads
Gone, the dead of night is going;
Slips the hour, and on my bed
    I lie alone.

(1905)

[1] This and the next poem are efforts by
Carman to translate and reconstruct the
songs of Sappho.

I LOVED THEE, ATTHIS, IN THE LONG AGO[1]

I loved thee, Atthis, in the long ago,
When the great oleanders were in flower
In the broad herded meadows full of sun.
And we would often at the fall of dusk
Wander together by the silver stream,
When the soft grass-heads were all wet with dew
And purple-misted in the fading light.
And joy I knew and sorrow at thy voice,
And the superb magnificence of love,—
The loneliness that saddens solitude,
And the sweet speech that makes it durable,—
The bitter longing and the keen desire,
The sweet companionship through quiet days
In the slow ample beauty of the world,
And the unutterable glad release
Within the temple of the holy night.
O Atthis, how I loved thee long ago
In that fair perished summer by the sea!

(1905)

[1] See previous note.

Archibald Lampman
(1861—1899)

Although Lampman did not win the international reputation achieved by Roberts and Carman, he is regarded by most Canadian critics as the most fastidious craftsman and most penetrating thinker among the poets of his generation. Born and brought up in the central province of Ontario, and educated at Trinity College in the University of Toronto, Lampman was preoccupied by the contrasts he saw within nature itself, and between nature and society. Nature he saw as predominantly harmonious, expressive of the eternal movement of life; society, on the other hand, he saw as full of conflict and dissonance. His poetry adds to descriptive accuracy, then, a deeply philosophical and social concern.

   The poems which follow are taken from *Lyrics of Earth*, Musson Book Co., Toronto, 1925.

HEAT

From plains that reel to southward, dim,
    The road runs by me white and bare;
Up the steep hill it seems to swim
    Beyond, and melt into the glare.
Upward half-way, or it may be
    Nearer the summit, slowly steals
A hay-cart, moving dustily
    With idly clacking wheels.

By his cart's side the wagoner
    Is slouching slowly at his ease,
Half-hidden in the windless blur
    Of white dust puffing to his knees.
This wagon on the height above,
    From sky to sky on either hand,
Is the sole thing that seems to move
    In all the heat-held land.

Beyond me in the fields the sun
    Soaks in the grass and hath his will;
I count the marguerites one by one;
    Even the buttercups are still.
On the brook yonder not a breath
    Disturbs the spider or the midge.
The water-bugs draw close beneath
    The cool gloom of the bridge.

Where the far elm-tree shadows flood
    Dark patches in the burning grass,
The cows, each with her peaceful cud,
    Lie waiting for the heat to pass.
From somewhere on the slope near by
    Into the pale depth of the noon
A wandering thrush slides leisurely
    His thin revolving tune.

In intervals of dreams I hear
    The cricket from the droughty ground;
The grasshoppers spin into mine ear
    A small innumerable sound.
I lift mine eyes sometimes to gaze:
    The burning sky-line blinds my sight:
The woods far off are blue with haze:
    The hills are drenched in light.

16

And yet to me not this or that
    Is always sharp or always sweet;
In the sloped shadow of my hat
    I lean at rest, and drain the heat;
Nay more, I think some blessed power
    Hath brought me wandering idly here:
In the full furnace of this hour
    My thoughts grow keen and clear.

(1888)

IN OCTOBER

Along the waste, a great way off, the pines
    Like tall slim priests of storm, stand up and bar
The low long strip of dolorous red that lines
    The under west, where wet winds moan afar.
The cornfields all are brown, and brown the meadows
    With the blown leaves' wind-heaped traceries,
And the brown thistle stems that cast no shadows,
    And bear no bloom for bees.

As slowly earthward leaf by red leaf slips,
    The sad trees rustle in chill misery,
A soft strange inner sound of pain-crazed lips,
    That move and murmur incoherently;
As if all leaves, that yet have breath, were sighing,
    With pale hushed throats, for death is at the door,
So many low soft masses for the dying
    Sweet leaves that live no more.

Here will I sit upon this naked stone,
    Draw my coat closer with my numbèd hands,
And hear the ferns sigh, and the wet woods moan,
    And send my heart out to the ashen lands;
And I will ask myself what golden madness,
    What balmed breaths of dreamland spicery,
What visions of soft laughter and light sadness
    Were sweet last month to me.

The dry dead leaves flit by with thin weird tunes,
    Like failing murmurs of some conquered creed,
Graven in mystic markings with strange runes,
    That none but stars and biting winds may read;
Here I will wait a little; I am weary,
    Not torn with pain of any lurid hue,
But only still and very gray, and dreary,
    Sweet sombre lands, like you.

(1888)

IN NOVEMBER

With loitering step and quiet eye,
Beneath the low November sky,
I wandered in the woods, and found
A clearing, where the broken ground
Was scattered with black stumps and briers,
And the old wreck of forest fires.
It was a bleak and sandy spot,
And, all about, the vacant plot,
Was peopled and inhabited
By scores of mulleins long since dead.
A silent and forsaken brood
In that mute opening of the wood,
So shrivelled and so thin they were,
So gray, so haggard, and austere,
Not plants at all they seemed to me,
But rather some spare company
Of hermit folk, who long ago,
Wandering in bodies to and fro,
Had chanced upon this lonely way,
And rested thus, till death one day
Surprised them at their compline prayer,
And left them standing lifeless there.

There was no sound about the wood
Save the wind's secret stir. I stood
Among the mullein-stalks as still
As if myself had grown to be
One of their sombre company,
A body without wish or will.
And as I stood, quite suddenly,
Down from a furrow in the sky

18

The sun shone out a little space
Across that silent sober place,
Over the sand heaps and brown sod,
The mulleins and dead goldenrod,
And passed beyond the thickets gray,
And lit the fallen leaves that lay,
Level and deep within the wood,
A rustling yellow multitude.

And all around me the thin light,
So sere, so melancholy bright,
Fell like the half-reflected gleam
Or shadow of some former dream;
A moment's golden reverie
Poured out on every plant and tree
A semblance of weird joy, or less,
A sort of spectral happiness;
And I, too, standing idly there,
With muffled hands in the chill air,
Felt the warm glow about my feet,
And shuddering betwixt cold and heat,
Drew my thoughts closer, like a cloak,
While something in my blood awoke,
A nameless and unnatural cheer,
A pleasure secret and austere.

(1895)

SNOWBIRDS

Along the narrow sandy height
      I watch them swiftly come and go,
            Or round the leafless wood,
      Like flurries of wind-driven snow,
Revolving in perpetual flight,
      A changing multitude.

Nearer and nearer still they sway,
      And, scattering in a circled sweep,
            Rush down without a sound;
      And now I see them peer and peep,
Across yon level bleak and gray,
      Searching the frozen ground,—

19

Until a little wind upheaves,
    And makes a sudden rustling there,
        And then they drop their play,
    Flash up into the sunless air,
And like a flight of silver leaves
    Swirl round and sweep away.

(1895)

SNOW

White are the far-off plains, and white
    The fading forests grow;
The wind dies out along the height,
    And denser still the snow,
A gathering weight on roof and tree,
    Falls down scarce audibly.

The road before me smoothes and fills
    Apace, and all about
The fences dwindle, and the hills
    Are blotted slowly out;
The naked trees loom spectrally
    Into the dim white sky.

The meadows and far-sheeted streams
    Lie still without a sound;
Like some soft minister of dreams
    The snow-fall hoods me round;
In wood and water, earth and air,
    A silence everywhere.

Save when at lonely intervals
    Some farmer's sleigh urged on,
With rustling runners and sharp bells,
    Swings by me and is gone;
Or from the empty waste I hear
    A sound remote and clear;

The barking of a dog, or call
    To cattle, sharply pealed,
Borne echoing from some wayside stall
    Or barnyard far afield;
Then all is silent, and the snow
    Falls, settling soft and slow.

The evening deepens, and the gray
     Folds closer earth and sky;
The world seems shrouded far away;
     Its noises sleep, and I,
As secret as yon buried stream,
     Plod dumbly on, and dream.

(1895)

APRIL NIGHT

How deep the April night is in its noon,
The hopeful, solemn, many-murmured night!
The earth lies hushed with expectation; bright
Above the world's dark border burns the moon,
Yellow and large; from forest floorways, strewn
With flowers, and fields that tingle with new birth,
The moist smell of the unimprisoned earth
Comes up, a sigh, a haunting promise. Soon,
Ah, soon, the teeming triumph! At my feet
The river with its stately sweep and wheel
Moves on slow-motioned, luminous, gray like steel.
From fields far off whose watery hollows gleam,
Aye with blown throats that make the long hours sweet,
The sleepless toads are murmuring in their dream.

(1899)

THE CITY OF THE END OF THINGS

Beside the pounding cataracts
Of midnight streams unknown to us
'Tis builded in the leafless tracts
And valleys huge of Tartarus.
Lurid and lofty and vast it seems;
It hath no rounded name that rings,
But I have heard it called in dreams
The City of the End of Things.

Its roofs and iron towers have grown
None knoweth how high within the night,
But in its murky streets far down
A flaming terrible and bright
Shakes all the stalking shadows there,
Across the walls, across the floors,
And shifts upon the upper air
From out a thousand furnace doors;
And all the while an awful sound
Keeps roaring on continually,
And crashes in the ceaseless round
Of a gigantic harmony.
Through its grim depths re-echoing
And all its weary height of walls,
With measured roar and iron ring,
The inhuman music lifts and falls.
Where no thing rests and no man is,
And only fire and night hold sway;
The beat, the thunder, and the hiss
Cease not, and change not, night nor day.
And moving at unheard commands,
The abysses and vast fires between,
Flit figures that with clanking hands
Obey a hideous routine;
They are not flesh, they are not bone,
They see not with the human eye,
And from their iron lips is blown
A dreadful and monotonous cry;
And whoso of our mortal race
Should find that city unaware,
Lean Death would smite him face to face,
And blanch him with its venomed air:
Or caught by the terrific spell,
Each thread of memory snapt and cut,
His soul would shrivel and its shell
Go rattling like an empty nut.

It was not always so, but once,
In days that no man thinks upon,
Fair voices echoed from its stones,
The light above it leaped and shone:
Once there were multitudes of men,
That built that city in their pride,
Until its might was made, and then
They withered age by age and died.
But now of that prodigious race,
Three only in an iron tower,
Set like carved idols face to face,

22

Remain the masters of its power;
And at the city gate a fourth,
Gigantic and with dreadful eyes,
Sits looking toward the lightless north,
Beyond the reach of memories;
Fast rooted to the lurid floor,
A bulk that never moves a jot,
In his pale body dwells no more,
Or mind or soul, — an idiot!
But sometime in the end those three
Shall perish and their hands be still,
And with the master's touch shall flee
Their incommunicable skill.
A stillness absolute as death
Along the slacking wheels shall lie,
And, flagging at a single breath,
The fires shall moulder out and die.
The roar shall vanish at its height,
And over that tremendous town
The silence of eternal night
Shall gather close and settle down.
All its grim grandeur, tower and hall,
Shall be abandoned utterly,
And into rust and dust shall fall
From century to century;
Nor ever living thing shall grow,
Nor trunk of tree, nor blade of grass;
No drop shall fall, no wind shall blow,
Nor sound of any foot shall pass:
Alone of its accursèd state,
One thing the hand of Time shall spare,
For the grim Idiot at the gate
Is deathless and eternal there.

(1899)

*Describing Hell
At one time there wasn't hell
Then there was
Eventually there won't be a hell
nothing will exist except the
remembrances of dead spirit*

23

A SUNSET AT LES EBOULEMENTS[1]

Broad shadows fall. On all the mountain side
The scythe-swept fields are silent. Slowly home
By the long beach the high-piled hay-carts come,
Splashing the pale salt shallows. Over wide
Fawn-colored wastes of mud the slipping tide,
Round the dun rocks and wattled fisheries,
Creeps murmuring in. And now by twos and threes,
O'er the slow spreading pools with clamorous chide,
Belated crows from strip to strip take flight.
Soon will the first star shine; yet ere the night
Reach onward to the pale-green distances,
The sun's last shaft beyond the gray sea-floor
Still dreams upon the Kamouraska[2] shore,
And the long line of golden villages.

(1900)

[1] A village on the north shore of the St. Lawrence
River in Quebec.
[2] A district on the south shore of the St. Lawrence.

Duncan Campbell Scott
(1862—1947)

D.C. Scott, the fourth major poet of the first Canadian generation, resembles the other three in his interest in nature. However, it is the wilder aspects of nature — wilderness settings, and scenes of storm and tumult — that interest him most, in contrast with the more quietly pastoral landscapes of Roberts, Carman and Lampman. Another distinguishing feature of his work — his interest in Indian life — was occasioned by his long career as a civil servant in the Department of Indian Affairs. He was born and died in Ottawa, although he travelled extensively throughout Canada and in Europe. In addition to his poems, he wrote two books of short stories and two biographies.

The poems which follow are taken from *The Poems of Duncan Campbell Scott*, McClelland and Stewart, Toronto, 1926.

THE VOICE AND THE DUSK

The slender moon and one pale star,
    A rose-leaf and a silver bee
From some god's garden blown afar,
    Go down the gold deep tranquilly.

Within the south there rolls and grows
    A mighty town with tower and spire,
From a cloud bastion masked with rose
    The lightning flashes diamond fire.

The purple-martin darts about
    The purlieus of the iris fen;
The king-bird rushes up and out,
    He screams and whirls and screams again.

A thrush is hidden in a maze
    Of cedar buds and tamarac bloom,
He throws his rapid flexile phrase,
    A flash of emeralds in the gloom.

A voice is singing from the hill
    A happy love of long ago;
Ah! tender voice, be still, be still,
    'Tis sometimes better not to know.'

The rapture from the amber height
    Floats tremblingly along the plain,
Where in the reeds with fairy light
    The lingering fireflies gleam again.

Buried in dingles more remote,
    Or drifted from some ferny rise,
The swooning of the golden throat
    Drops in the mellow dusk and dies.

A soft wind passes lightly drawn,
    A wave leaps silverly and stirs
The rustling sedge, and then is gone
    Down the black cavern in the firs.

(1893)

A SUMMER STORM

Last night a storm fell on the world
    From heights of drouth and heat,
The surly clouds for weeks were furled,
    The air could only sway and beat,

The beetles clattered at the blind,
    The hawks fell twanging from the sky,
The west unrolled a feathery wind,
    And the night fell sullenly.

The storm leaped roaring from its lair,
    Like the shadow of doom,
The poignard lightning searched the air,
    The thunder ripped the shattered gloom,

The rain came down with a roar like fire,
    Full-voiced and clamorous and deep,
The weary world had its heart's desire,
    And fell asleep.

And now in the morning early,
    The clouds are sailing by
Clearly, oh! so clearly,
    The distant mountains lie.

The wind is very mild and slow,
    The clouds obey his will,
They part and part and onward go,
    Travelling together still.

'Tis very sweet to be alive,
    On a morning that's so fair,
For nothing seems to stir or strive,
    In the unconscious air.

A tawny thrush is in the wood,
    Ringing so wild and free;
Only one bird has a blither mood,
    The white-throat on the tree.

(1893)

A NIGHT IN JUNE

The world is heated seven times,
    The sky is close above the lawn,
    An oven when the coals are drawn.

There is no stir of air at all,
    Only at times an inward breeze
    Turns back a pale leaf in the trees.

Here the syringa's rich perfume
    Covers the tulip's red retreat,
    A burning pool of scent and heat.

The pallid lightning wavers dim
    Between the trees, then deep and dense
    The darkness settles more intense.

A hawk lies panting in the grass,
    Or plunges upward through the air,
    The lightning shows him whirling there.

A bird calls madly from the eaves,
    Then stops, the silence all at once
    Disturbed, falls dead again and stuns.

A redder lightning flits about,
    But in the north a storm is rolled
    That splits the gloom with vivid gold;

Dead silence, then a little sound,
    The distance chokes the thunder down,
    It shudders faintly in the town.

A fountain plashing in the dark
    Keeps up a mimic dropping strain;
    Ah! God, if it were really rain!

(1893)

THE PIPER OF ARLL

There was in Arll a little cove
Where the salt wind came cool and free:
A foamy beach that one would love,
If he were longing for the sea.

A brook hung sparkling on the hill,
The hill swept far to ring the bay;
The bay was faithful, wild or still,
To the heart of the ocean far away.

There were three pines above the comb
That, when the sun flared and went down,
Grew like three warriors reaving home
The plunder of a burning town.

A piper lived within the grove,
Tending the pasture of his sheep;
His heart was swayed with faithful love
From the springs of God's ocean clear and deep.

And there a ship one evening stood,
Where ship had never stood before,
A pennon bickered red as blood,
An angel glimmered at the prore.

About the coming on of dew,
The sails burned rosy, and the spars
Were gold, and all the tackle grew
Alive with ruby-hearted stars.

The piper heard an outland tongue,
With music in the cadenced fall;
And when the fairy lights were hung,
The sailors gathered one and all,

And leaning on the gunwales dark,
Crusted with shells and dashed with foam,
With all the dreaming hills to hark,
They sang their longing songs of home.

When the sweet airs had fled away,
The piper, with a gentle breath,
Molded a tranquil melody
Of lonely love and longed-for death.

When the fair sound began to lull,
From out the fireflies and the dew,
A silence held the shadowy hull,
Until the eerie tune was through.

Then from the dark and dreamy deck
An alien song began to thrill;
It mingled with the drumming beck,
And stirred the braird upon the hill.

Beneath the stars each sent to each
A message tender, till at last
The piper slept upon the beach,
The sailors slumbered round the mast.

Still as a dream till nearly dawn,
The ship was bosomed on the tide;
The streamlet, murmuring on and on,
Bore the sweet water to her side.

Then shaking out her lawny sails,
Forth on the misty sea she crept;
She left the dawning of the dales,
Yet in his cloak the piper slept.

And when he woke he saw the ship,
Limned black against the crimson sun;
Then from the disc he saw her slip,
A wraith of shadow — she was gone.

He threw his mantle on the beach,
He went apart like one distraught,
His lips were moved — his desperate speech
Stormed his inviolable thought.

He broke his human-throated reed,
And threw it in the idle rill;
But when his passion had its mead,
He found it in the eddy still.

He mended well the patient flue,
Again he tried its varied stops;
The closures answered right and true,
And starting out in piercing drops,

A melody began to drip
That mingled with a ghostly thrill
The vision-spirit of the ship,
The secret of his broken will.

Beneath the pines he piped and swayed,
Master of passion and of power;
He was his soul and what he played,
Immortal for a happy hour.

He, singing into nature's heart,
Guiding his will by the world's will,
With deep, unconscious, childlike art
Had sung his soul out and was still.

And then at evening came the bark
That stirred his dreaming heart's desire;
It burned slow lights along the dark
That died in glooms of crimson fire.

The sailors launched a sombre boat,
And bent with music at the oars;
The rhythm throbbing every throat,
And lapsing round the liquid shores,

Was that true tune the piper sent,
Unto the wave-worn mariners,
When with the beck and ripple blent
He heard that outland song of theirs.

Silent they rowed him, dip and drip,
The oars beat out an exequy,
They laid him down within the ship,
They loosed a rocket to the sky.

It broke in many a crimson sphere
That grew to gold and floated far,
And left the sudden shore-line clear,
With one slow-changing, drifting star.

Then out they shook the magic sails,
That charmed the wind in other seas,
From where the west line pearls and pales,
They waited for a ruffling breeze.

But in the world there was no stir,
The cordage slacked with never a creak,
They heard the flame begin to purr
Within the lantern at the peak.

They could not cry, they could not move,
They felt the lure from the charmed sea;
They could not think of home or love
Or any pleasant land to be.

31

They felt the vessel dip and trim,
And settle down from list to list;
They saw the sea-plain heave and swim
As gently as a rising mist.

And down so slowly, down and down,
Rivet by rivet, plank by plank;
A little flood of ocean flown
Across the deck, she sank and sank.

From knee to breast the water wore,
It crept and crept; ere they were ware
Gone was the angel at the prore,
They felt the water float their hair.

They saw the salt plain spark and shine,
They threw their faces to the sky;
Beneath a deepening film of brine
They saw the star-flash blur and die.

She sank and sank by yard and mast,
Sank down the shimmering gradual dark;
A little drooping pennon last
Showed like the black fin of a shark.

And down she sank till, keeled in sand,
She rested safely balanced true,
With all her upward gazing band,
The piper and the dreaming crew.

And there, unmarked of any chart,
In unrecorded deeps they lie,
Empearled within the purple heart
Of the great sea for aye and aye.

Their eyes are ruby in the green
Long shaft of sun that spreads and rays,
And upward with a wizard sheen
A fan of sea-light leaps and plays.

Tendrils of or and azure creep,
And globes of amber light are rolled,
And in the gloaming of the deep
Their eyes are starry pits of gold.

And sometimes in the liquid night
The hull is changed, a solid gem,
That glows with a soft stony light,
The lost prince of a diadem.

And at the keel a vine is quick,
That spreads its bines and works and weaves
O'er all the timbers veining thick
A plenitude of silver leaves.

(1898)

NIGHT HYMNS ON LAKE NIPIGON[1]

Here in the midnight, where the dark mainland and island
Shadows mingle in shadow deeper, profounder,
Sing we the hymns of the churches, while the dead water
    Whispers before us.

Thunder is travelling slow on the path of the lightning;
One after one the stars and the beaming planets
Look serene in the lake from the edge of the storm-cloud,
    Then have they vanished.

While our canoe, that floats dumb in the bursting thunder,
Gathers her voice in the quiet and thrills and whispers,
Presses her prow in the star-gleam, and all her ripple
    Lapses in blackness.

Sing we the sacred ancient hymns of the churches,
Chanted first in old-world nooks of the desert,
While in the wild, pellucid Nipigon reaches
    Hunted the savage.

Now have the ages met in the Northern midnight,
And on the lonely, loon-haunted Nipigon reaches
Rises the hymn of triumph and courage and comfort,
    Adeste Fideles.

Tones that were fashioned when the faith brooded in darkness,
Joined with sonorous vowels in the noble Latin,
Now are married with the long-drawn Ojibwa,[2]
    Uncouth and mournful.

Soft with the silver drip of the regular paddles
Falling in rhythm, timed with the liquid, plangent
Sounds from the blades where the whirlpools break and are carried
    Down into darkness;

Each long cadence, flying like a dove from her shelter
Deep in the shadow, wheels for a throbbing moment,
Poises in utterance, returning in circles of silver
    To nest in the silence.

All wild nature stirs with the infinite, tender
Plaint of a bygone age whose soul is eternal,
Bound in the lonely phrases that thrill and falter
    Back into quiet.

Back they falter as the deep storm overtakes them,
Whelms them in splendid hollows of booming thunder,
Wraps them in rain, that, sweeping, breaks and onrushes
    Ringing like cymbals.

(1905)

[1] Lake Nipigon lies in northern Ontario and was used by
Indians trading into Hudson Bay.
[2] Ojibwas are a group of Indians belonging to the Algonkian
tribe. They are also known as Chippewas (see next poem).

THE FORSAKEN

Once in the winter
Out on a lake
In the heart of the northland,
Far from the Fort
And far from the hunters,
A Chippewa woman
With her sick baby,
Crouched in the last hours
Of a great storm.
Frozen and hungry,
She fished through the ice
With a line of the twisted
Bark of the cedar,
And a rabbit-bone hook
Polished and barbed;
Fished with the bare hook
All through the wild day,
Fished and caught nothing;
While the young chieftain

Tugged at her breasts,
Or slept in the lacings
Of the warm tikanagan.
All the lake-surface
Streamed with the hissing
Of millions of iceflakes
Hurled by the wind;
Behind her the round
Of a lonely island
Roared like a fire
With the voice of the storm
In the deeps of the cedars.
Valiant, unshaken,
She took of her own flesh,
Baited the fish-hook,
Drew in a gray-trout,
Drew in his fellows,
Heaped them beside her,
Dead in the snow.
Valiant, unshaken,
She faced the long distance,
Wolf-haunted and lonely,
Sure of her goal
And the life of her dear one:
Tramped for two days,
On the third in the morning,
Saw the strong bulk
Of the Fort by the river,
Saw the wood-smoke
Hang soft in the spruces,
Heard the keen yelp
Of the ravenous huskies
Fighting for whitefish:
Then she had rest.

II

Years and years after,
When she was old and withered,
When her son was an old man
And his children filled with vigour,
They came in their northern tour on the verge of winter,
To an island in a lonely lake.
There one night they camped, and on the morrow
Gathered their kettles and birch-bark
Their rabbit-skin robes and their mink-traps,

Launched their canoes and slunk away through the islands,
Left her alone forever,
Without a word of farewell,
Because she was old and useless,
Like a paddle broken and warped,
Or a pole that was splintered.
Then, without a sigh,
Valiant, unshaken,
She smoothed her dark locks under her kerchief,
Composed her shawl in state,
Then folded her hands ridged with sinews and corded with veins,
Folded them across her breasts spent with the nourishing of children,
Gazed at the sky past the tops of the cedars,
Saw two spangled nights arise out of the twilight,
Saw two days go by filled with the tranquil sunshine,
Saw, without pain, or dread, or even a moment of longing:
Then on the third great night there came thronging and thronging
Millions of snowflakes out of a windless cloud;
They covered her close with a beautiful crystal shroud,
Covered her deep and silent.
But in the frost of the dawn,
Up from the life below,
Rose a column of breath
Through a tiny cleft in the snow,
Fragile, delicately drawn,
Wavering with its own weakness,
In the wilderness a sign of the spirit,
Persisting still in the sight of the sun
Till day was done.
Then all light was gathered up by the hand of God and hid in His breast,
Then there was born a silence deeper than silence,
Then she had rest.

(1905)

36

E.J. Pratt
(1883—1964)

E.J. Pratt is generally regarded as the major Canadian poet of this century. Born in Newfoundland, he was educated, and spent most of his life as a professor of English, at the University of Toronto; but he always retained his interest in the sea, in heroic behaviour, and in the contrast and conflict between the primitive and the civilized. He wrote several long narrative poems, such as *The Roosevelt and the Antinoe* (1930), *The Titanic* (1935) and *Brébeuf and His Brethren* (1940), but also many short poems, descriptive, contemplative, almost always richly ironic. A Christian humanist in outlook, he combines in a most interesting way exuberance and subtlety, energy and tenderness, moral seriousness and ironic wit.

The poems which follow are from *The Collected Poems of E.J. Pratt*, edited by Northrop Frye, Macmillan, Toronto, 1958.

THE SHARK

He seemed to know the harbor,
So leisurely he swam;
His fin,
Like a piece of sheet-iron,
Three-cornered,
And with knife-edge,
Stirred not a bubble
As it moved
With its base-line on the water.

His body was tubular
And tapered
And smoke-blue,
And as he passed the wharf
He turned,
And snapped at a flat-fish
That was dead and floating.
And I saw the flash of a white throat,
And a double row of white teeth,
And eyes of metallic gray,
Hard and narrow and slit.

Then out of the harbor,
With that three-cornered fin
Shearing without a bubble the water
Lithely,
Leisurely,
He swam—
That strange fish,
Tubular, tapered, smoke-blue,
Part vulture, part wolf,
Part neither — for his blood was cold.

(1923)

FROM STONE TO STEEL

From stone to bronze, from bronze to steel
Along the road-dust of the sun,
Two revolutions of the wheel
From Java to Geneva run.

The snarl Neanderthal is worn
Close to the smiling Aryan lips,
The civil polish of the horn
Gleams from our praying finger tips.

The evolution of desire
Has but matured a toxic wine,
Drunk long before its heady fire
Reddened Euphrates or the Rhine.

Between the temple and the cave
The boundary lies tissue-thin:
The yearlings still the altars crave
As satisfaction for a sin.

The road goes up, the road goes down—
Let Java or Geneva be—
But whether to the cross or crown,
The path lies through Gethsemane.

(1932)

SILENCES

There is no silence upon the earth or under the earth like the silence under the sea;
No cries announcing birth,
No sounds declaring death.
There is silence when the milt is laid on the spawn in the weeds and fungus of the
        rock-clefts;
And silence in the growth and struggle for life.
The bonitoes pounce upon the mackerel,
And are themselves caught by the barracudas,
The sharks kill the barracudas
And the great molluscs rend the sharks,

39

And all noiselessly—
Though swift be the action and final the conflict,
The drama is silent.

There is no fury upon the earth like the fury under the sea.
For growl and cough and snarl are the tokens of spendthrifts who know not the
    ultimate economy of rage.
Moreover, the pace of the blood is too fast.
But under the waves the blood is sluggard and has the same temperature as that of
    the sea.

There is something pre-reptilian about a silent kill.

Two men may end their hostilities just with their battle-cries.
"The devil take you," says one.
"I'll see you in hell first," says the other.
And these introductory salutes followed by a hail of gutturals and sibilants are
    often the beginning of friendship, for who would not prefer to be lustily
    damned than to be half-heartedly blessed?
No one need fear oaths that are properly enunciated, for they belong to the
    inheritance of just men made perfect, and, for all we know, of such may be
    the Kingdom of Heaven.
But let silent hate be put away for it feeds upon the heart of the hater.
Today I watched two pairs of eyes. One pair was black and the other gray. And
    while the owners thereof, for the space of five seconds, walked past each
    other, the gray snapped at the black and the black riddled the gray.

One looked to say — "The cat,"
And the other — "The cur."
But no words were spoken;
Not so much as a hiss or a murmur came through the perfect enamel of the teeth;
    not so much as a gesture of enmity.
If the right upper lip curled over the canine, it went unnoticed.
The lashes veiled the eyes not for an instant in the passing.
And as between the two in respect to candor of intention or eternity of wish, there
    was no choice, for the stare was mutual and absolute.
A word would have dulled the exquisite edge of the feeling,
An oath would have flawed the crystallization of the hate.
For only such culture could grow in a climate of silence,—
Away back before the emergence of fur or feather, back to the unvocal sea and
    down deep where the darkness spills its wash on the threshold of light, where
    the lids never close upon the eyes, where the inhabitants slay in silence and
    are as silently slain.

(1937)

40

COME AWAY, DEATH

Willy-nilly, he comes or goes, with the clown's logic,
Comic in epitaph, tragic in epithalamium,
And unseduced by any mused rhyme.
However blow the winds over the pollen,
Whatever the course of the garden variables,
He remains the constant,
Ever flowering from the poppy seeds.

There was a time he came in formal dress,
Announced by Silence tapping at the panels
In deep apology.
A touch of chivalry in his approach,
He offered sacramental wine,
And with acanthus leaf
And petals of the hyacinth
He took the fever from the temples
And closed the eyelids,
Then led the way to his cool longitudes
In the dignity of the candles.

His medieval grace is gone—
Gone with the flame of the capitals
And the leisured turn of the thumb
Leafing the manuscripts,
Gone with the marbles
And the Venetian mosaics,
With the bend of the knee
Before the rose-strewn feet of the Virgin.
The paternosters of his priests,
Committing clay to clay,
Have rattled in their throats
Under the gride of his traction tread.

One night we heard his footfall—one September night—
In the outskirts of a village near the sea.
There was a moment when the storm
Delayed its fist, when the surf fell
Like velvet on the rocks—a moment only;
The strangest lull we ever knew!
A sudden truce among the oaks
Released their fratricidal arms;
The poplars straightened to attention
As the winds stopped to listen
To the sound of a motor drone—

41

And then the drone was still.
We heard the tick-tock on the shelf
And the leak of valves in our hearts.
A calm condensed and lidded
As at the core of a cyclone ended breathing.
This was the monologue of Silence
Grave and unequivocal.

What followed was a bolt
Outside the range and target of the thunder,
And human speech curved back upon itself
Through Druid runways and the Piltdown scarps,
Beyond the stammers of the Java caves,
To find its origins in hieroglyphs
On mouths and eyes and cheeks
Etched by a foreign stylus never used
On the outmoded page of the Apocalypse.

(1943)

THE TRUANT

"What have you there?" the great Panjandrum said
To the Master of the Revels who had led
A bucking truant with a stiff backbone
Close to the foot of the Almighty's throne.

"Right Reverend, most adored,
And forcibly acknowledged Lord
By the keen logic of your two-edged sword!
This creature has presumed to classify
Himself—a biped, rational, six feet high
And two feet wide; weighs fourteen stone;
Is guilty of a multitude of sins.
He has abjured his choric origins,
And like an undomesticated slattern,
Walks with tangential step unknown
Within the weave of the atomic pattern.
He has developed concepts, grins
Obscenely at your Royal bulletins,
Possesses what he calls a will
Which challenges your power to kill."

"What is his pedigree?"

42

"The base is guaranteed, your Majesty—
Calcium, carbon, phosphorus, vapor
And other fundamentals spun
From the umbilicus of the sun,
And yet he says he will not caper
Around your throne, nor toe the rules
For the ballet of the fiery molecules."

"His concepts and denials—scrap them, burn them—
To the chemists with them promptly."

                    "Sire,
The stuff is not amenable to fire.
Nothing but their own kind can overturn them.
The chemists have sent back the same old story—
'With our extreme gelatinous apology,
We beg to inform your Imperial Majesty,
Unto whom be dominion and power and glory,
There still remains that strange precipitate
Which has the quality to resist
Our oldest and most trusted catalyst.
It is a substance we cannot cremate
By temperatures known to our Laboratory.' "

And the great Panjandrum's face grew dark—
"I'll put those chemists to their annual purge,
And I myself shall be the thaumaturge
To find the nature of this fellow's spark.
Come, bring him nearer by yon halter rope:
I'll analyse him with the cosmoscope."

Pulled forward with his neck awry,
The little fellow six feet short,
Aware he was about to die,
Committed grave contempt of court
By answering with a flinchless stare
The Awful Presence seated there.

The ALL HIGH swore until his face was black.
He called him a coprophagite,[1]
A genus homo, egomaniac,
Third cousin to the family of worms,
A sporozoan[2] from the ooze of night,
Spawn of a spavined troglodyte:[3]
He swore by all the catalogue of terms
Known since the slang of carboniferous Time.
He said that he would trace him back
To pollywogs and earwigs in the slime.

43

And in his shrillest tenor he began
Reciting his indictment of the man,
Until he closed upon this capital crime—
"You are accused of singing out of key
(A foul unmitigated dissonance),
Of shuffling in the measures of the dance,
Then walking out with that defiant, free
Toss of your head, banging the doors,
Leaving a stench upon the jacinth floors.
You have fallen like a curse
On the mechanics of my Universe.

"Herewith I measure out your penalty—
Hearken while you hear, look while you see:
I send you now upon your homeward route
Where you shall find
Humiliation for your pride of mind.
I shall make deaf the ear, and dim the eye,
Put palsy in your touch, make mute
Your speech, intoxicate your cells and dry
Your blood and marrow, shoot
Arthritic needles through your cartilage,
And having parched you with old age,
I'll pass you wormwise through the mire;
And when your rebel will
Is mouldered, all desire
Shrivelled, all your concepts broken,
Backward in dust I'll blow you till
You join my spiral festival of fire.
Go, Master of the Revels—I have spoken."

And the little genus homo, six feet high,
Standing erect, countered with this reply—
"You dumb insouciant invertebrate,
You rule a lower than a feudal state—
A realm of flunkey decimals that run,
Return; return and run; again return,
Each group around its little sun,
And every sun a satellite.
There they go by day and night,
Nothing to do but run and burn,
Taking turn and turn about,
Light-year in and light-year out,
Dancing, dancing in quadrillions,
Never leaving their pavilions.

44

"Your astronomical conceit
Of bulk and power is anserine.[4] — *goosish*
Your ignorance so thick,
You did not know your own arithmetic.
We flung the graphs about your flying feet;
We measured your diameter—
Merely a line
Of zeros prefaced by an integer.
Before we came
You had no name.
You did not know direction or your pace;
We taught you all you ever knew
Of motion, time, and space.   — *dizziness*
We healed you of your vertigo
And put you in our kindergarten show,
Perambulated you through prisms, drew
Your mileage through the Milky Way,
Lassoed your comets when they ran astray,
Yoked Leo, Taurus, and your team of Bears
To pull your kiddy cars of inverse squares.

"Boast not about your harmony,
Your perfect curves, your rings
Of pure and endless light[5] — 'Twas we
Who pinned upon your Seraphim their wings,
And when your brassy heavens rang
With joy that morning while the planets sang
Their choruses of archangelic lore,   — *stories*
'Twas we who ordered the notes upon their score
Out of our winds and strings.
Yes! all your shapely forms
Are ours—parabolas of silver light,
Those blueprints of your spiral stairs   — *highest*
From nadir depth to zenith height,
Coronas, rainbows after storms,
Auroras on your eastern tapestries
And constellations over western seas.

"And when, one day, grown conscious of your age,
While pondering an eolith,[6]
We turned a human page
And blotted out a cosmic myth
With all its baby symbols to explain
The sunlight in Apollo's eyes,
Our rising pulses and the birth of pain,
Fear, and that fern-and-fungus breath
Stalking our nostrils to our caves of death—
That day we learned how to anatomize
Your body, calibrate your size

45

Subservience *Going against a power* (handwritten annotations)

And set a mirror up before your face
To show you what you really were—a rain
Of dull Lucretian atoms crowding space,
A series of concentric waves which any fool
Might make by dropping stones within a pool,
Or an exploding bomb forever in flight
Bursting like hell through Chaos and Old Night.

"You oldest of the hierarchs   *— where you are in order of things* (handwritten)
Composed of electronic sparks,
We grant you speed,
We grant you power, and fire
That ends in ash, but we concede
To you no pain nor joy nor love nor hate,
No final tableau of desire,
No causes won or lost, no free
Adventure at the outposts—only
The degradation of your energy
When at some late
Slow number of your dance your sergeant-major Fate   *falling over* (handwritten)
Will catch you blind and groping and will send   *— feeling around for something* (handwritten)
You reeling on that long and lonely
Lockstep of your wave-lengths towards your end.

"We who have met
With stubborn calm the dawn's hot fusillades;   *— firing of guns* (handwritten)
Who have seen the forehead sweat
Under the tug of pulleys on the joints,
Under the liquidating tally   *— adding up* (handwritten)
Of the cat-and-truncheon bastinades;
Who have taught our souls to rally
To mountain horns and the sea's rockets
When the needle ran demented through the points;   *crazy* (handwritten)
We who have learned to clench
Our fists and raise our lightless sockets
To morning skies after the midnight raids,
Yet cocked our ears to bugles on the barricades,
And in cathedral rubble found a way to quench
A dying thirst within a Galilean valley—
No! by the Rood, we will not join your ballet."

(1943)

[1] A feeder upon dung
[2] A parasite
[3] A cave man
[4] Goose-like
[5] See "The World" by Henry Vaughan (1622-1695)
   "I saw eternity the other night
   Like a great ring of pure and endless night."
[6] A primitive stone tool

F.R. Scott
(1899—   )

F.R. Scott has been a most influential figure in Canadian literary and social development for almost half a century. In the nineteen-twenties, after graduating from Bishop's University in Quebec, from Oxford, and from McGill's Faculty of Law in Montreal, he helped A.J.M. Smith to establish the *McGill Fortnightly Review* as a medium for literary modernism. Ever since he has been helping to found literary magazines, organizing writers' conferences, and contributing his own verse to the pages of magazines and books. He has also had a distinguished academic career, eventually becoming Dean of the McGill Faculty of Law, and an influential political career, being one of the founders of the Canadian socialist party, the Co-operative Commonwealth Federation (the C.C.F.) which has now become the New Democratic Party (N.D.P.).

Scott's poems are always intense and disciplined, but are otherwise very diverse. Some are crisp, clear natural descriptions in the Imagist manner; others are expressions of political or social idealism; others are metaphysical love poems; the best known are his satirical pieces in which he flays Canadian complacency or pomposity.

The poems which follow are taken from *Selected Poems* by F.R. Scott, Oxford University Press, Toronto, 1966, and *The Dance is One*, McClelland and Stewart, 1973.

NORTH STREAM

Ice mothers me
My bed is rock
Over sand I move silently.

I am crystal clear
To a sunbeam.
No grasses grow in me
My banks are clean.

Foam runs from the rapid
To rest on my dark pools.

(1936)

THE CANADIAN AUTHORS MEET

Expansive puppets percolate self-unction
Beneath a portrait of the Prince of Wales.
Miss Crotchet's muse has somehow failed to function,
Yet she's a poetess. Beaming, she sails

From group to chattering group, with such a dear
Victorian saintliness, as is her fashion,
Greeting the other unknowns with a cheer—
Virgins of sixty who still write of passion.

The air is heavy with "Canadian" topics,
And Carman, Lampman, Roberts, Campbell, Scott,
Are measured for their faith and philanthropics,
Their zeal for God and King, their earnest thought.

The cakes are sweet, but sweeter is the feeling
That one is mixing with the literati;
It warms the old, and melts the most congealing.
Really, it is a most delightful party.

Shall we go round the mulberry bush, or shall
We gather at the river, or shall we
Appoint a poet laureate this Fall,
Or shall we have another cup of tea?

48

O Canada, O Canada, Oh can
A day go by without new authors springing
To paint the native maple, and to plan
More ways to set the selfsame welkin ringing?

(1936)　　　　　　　　　　heaers

LAURENTIAN SHIELD

Hidden in wonder and snow, or sudden with summer,
This land stares at the sun in a huge silence
Endlessly repeating something we cannot hear.
Inarticulate, arctic,
Not written on by history, empty as paper,
It leans away from the world with songs in its lakes
Older than love, and lost in the miles.

This waiting is wanting.
It will choose its language
When it has chosen its technic,
A tongue to shape the vowels of its productivity.

A language of flesh and of roses.

Now there are pre-words,
Cabin syllables,
Nouns of settlement
Slowly forming, with steel syntax,
The long sentence of its exploitation.

The first cry was the hunter, hungry for fur,
And the digger for gold, nomad, no-man, a particle;
Then the bold commands of monopoly, big with machines,
Carving its kingdoms out of the public wealth;
And now the drone of the plane, scouting the ice,
Fills all the emptiness with neighbourhood
And links our future over the vanished pole.

But a deeper note is sounding, heard in the mines,
The scattered camps and the mills, a language of life,
And what will be written in the full culture of occupation
Will come, presently, tomorrow,
From millions whose hands can turn this rock into children.

(1954)

LAKESHORE

The lake is sharp along the shore
Trimming the bevelled edge of land
To level curves; the fretted sands
Go slanting down through liquid air
Till stones below shift here and there
Floating upon their broken sky
All netted by the prism wave
And rippled where the currents are.

I stare through windows at this cave
Where fish, like planes, slow-motioned, fly.
Poised in a still of gravity
The narrow minnow, flicking fin,
Hangs in a paler, ochre sun,
His doorways open everywhere.

And I am a tall frond that waves
Its head below its rooted feet
Seeking the light that draws it down
To forest floors beyond its reach
Vivid with gloom and eerie dreams.

The water's deepest colonnades
Contract the blood, and to this home
That stirs the dark amphibian
With me the naked swimmers come
Drawn to their prehistoric womb.

They too are liquid as they fall
Like tumbled water loosed above
Until they lie, diagonal,
Within the cool and sheltered grove
Stroked by the fingertips of love.

Silent, our sport is drowned in fact
Too virginal for speech or sound
And each is personal and laned
Along his private aqueduct.

Too soon the tether of the lungs
Is taut and straining, and we rise
Upon our undeveloped wings
Toward the prison of our ground
A secret anguish in our thighs
And mermaids in our memories.

This is our talent, to have grown
Upright in posture, false-erect,
A landed gentry, circumspect,
Tied to a horizontal soil
The floor and ceiling of the soul;
Striving, with cold and fishy care
To make an ocean of the air.

Sometimes, upon a crowded street,
I feel the sudden rain come down
And in the old, magnetic sound
I hear the opening of a gate
That loosens all the seven seas.
Watching the whole creation drown
I muse, alone, on Ararat.

(1954)

WILL TO WIN

Your tall French legs, my V for victory,
My sign and symphony, Eroica,
Uphold me in these days of my occupation
And stir my underground resistance.

Crushed by the insidious infiltration of routine
I was wholly overrun and quite cut off.
The secret agents of my daily detail
Had my capital city under their rule and thumb.

Only a handful of me escaped to the hillside,
Your side, my sweet and holy inside,
And cowering there for a moment I drew breath,
Grew solid as trees, took root in a fertile soil.

Here, by my hidden fires, drop your supplies—
Love, insight, sensibility, and myth—
Thousands of fragments rally to my cause.
I ride like Joan to conquer my whole man.

(1954)

BONNE ENTENTE

The advantages of living with two cultures
Strike one at every turn,
Especially when one finds a notice in an office building:
'This elevator will not run on Ascension Day;'
Or reads in the *Montreal Star:*
'Tomorrow being the feast of the Immaculate Conception,
There will be no collection of garbage in the city';
Or sees on the restaurant menu the bilingual dish:

DEEP APPLE PIE
TARTE AUX POMMES PROFONDES

(1957)

THIS IS A LAW

Who says Go
When the Green says Go
And who says No
When the Red says No?
Asked I.

I, said the Law,
I say Go
When the Green says Go
And don't you Go
When the Red says No,
Said the Law.

Who are you
To tell me so
To tell me Go
When the Green says Go
And tell me No
When the Red says No?
Asked I.

I am you
Said the Law.

Are you me
As I want to be?
I don't even know
Who you are.

I speak for you
Said the Law.

You speak for me?
Who told you you should?
Who told you you could?
How can this thing be
When I'm not the same as before?

I was made for you
I am made by you
I am human too
So change me if you will
Change the Green to Red
Shoot the ruling class
Stand me on my head
I will not be dead
I'll be telling you Go
I'll be telling you No
For this is a Law
Said the Law.

(1973)

DANCING

Long ago
when I first danced
I danced
holding her
back and arm
making her move
as I moved

she was best
when she was
least herself
lost herself

Now I dance
seeing her
dance away from
me   she
looks at me
dancing   we
are closer
held in the movement of the dance
I no longer dance
with myself
we are two
not one
the dance
is one

(1973)

A.J.M. Smith
(1902 —   )

Arthur James Marshall Smith, like his friend F.R. Scott, has been a most influential figure in Canadian poetry for almost half a century. A graduate of McGill and Edinburgh universities, he has spent most of his life as Professor of English at Michigan State University in the U.S.A., but has spent periods of the year in Canada and has taken a continuous interest in Canadian literary development. He has, for example, edited several anthologies of Canadian poetry and prose, and has written a number of critical articles upholding high standards of poetic craftsmanship.

His own poems are relatively few in number but high in quality. An exigent craftsman, he writes poems which are intense in feeling and complex in attitude. Upon a romantic sensibility, obsessed with pain and suffering, he imposes a classical economy and harmony of form, and often weaves in also a strain of metaphysical wit.

The poems which follow are from *Collected Poems*, Oxford University Press, Toronto, 1962.

THE LONELY LAND

Cedar and jagged fir
uplift sharp barbs
against the gray
and cloud-piled sky;
and in the bay
blown spume and windrift
and thin, bitter spray
snap
at the whirling sky;
and the pine trees
lean one way.

A wild duck calls
to her mate,
and the ragged
and passionate tones
stagger and fall,
and recover,
and stagger and fall,
on these stones—
are lost
in the lapping of water
on smooth, flat stones.

This is a beauty
of dissonance,
this resonance
of stony strand,
this smoky cry
curled over a black pine
and wind-battered branch
when the wind
bends the tops of the pines
and curdles the sky
from the north.

This is the beauty
of strength
broken by strength
and still strong.

(1936)

56

LIKE AN OLD PROUD KING IN A PARABLE

A bitter king in anger to be gone
From fawning courtier and doting queen
Flung hollow sceptre and gilt crown away,
And breaking bound of all his counties green
He made a meadow in the northern stone
And breathed a palace of inviolable air
To cage a heart that carolled like a swan,
And slept alone, immaculate and gay,
With only his pride for a paramour.

O who is that bitter king? It is not I.

Let me, I beseech thee, Father, die
From this fat royal life, and lie
As naked as a bridegroom by his bride,
And let that girl be the cold goddess Pride.

And I will sing to the barren rock
Your difficult, lonely music, heart,
Like an old proud king in a parable.

(1936)

NEWS OF THE PHOENIX

They say the Phoenix is dying, some say dead.
Dead without issue is what one message said,
But that has been suppressed, officially denied.

I think, myself, the man who sent it lied.
In any case, I'm told, he has been shot,
As a precautionary measure, whether he did or not.

(1936)

A HYACINTH FOR EDITH[1]

Now that the ashen rain of gummy April
Clacks like a weedy and stain'd mill,

So that all the tall purple trees
Are pied porpoises in swishing seas,

And the yellow horses and milch cows
Come out of their long frosty house

To gape at the straining flags
The brown pompous hill wags,

I'll seek within the wood's black plinth
A candy-sweet sleek wooden hyacinth—

And in its creaking naked glaze,
And in the varnish of its blaze,

The bird of ecstasy shall sing again,
The bearded sun shall spring again—

A new ripe fruit upon the sky's high tree,
A flowery island in the sky's wide sea—

And childish cold ballades, long dead, long mute,
Shall mingle with the gayety of bird and fruit,

And fall like cool and soothing rain
On all the ardour, all the pain

Lurking within this tinsel paradise
Of trams and cinemas and manufactured ice,

Till I am grown again my own lost ghost
Of joy, long lost, long given up for lost,

And walk again the wild and sweet wildwood
Of our lost innocence, our ghostly childhood.

(1936)

[1]   The Edith referred to is probably Edith
      Sitwell, who influenced this poem.

THE PLOT AGAINST PROTEUS

This is a theme for muted coronets
To dangle from debilitated heads
Of navigation, kings, or riverbeds
That rot or rise what time the seamew sets
Her course by stars among the smoky tides
Entangled. Old saltencrusted Proteus treads
Once more the watery shore that water weds
While rocking fathom bell rings round and rides.

Now when the blind king of the water thinks
The sharp hail of the salt out of his eyes
To abdicate, run thou, O Prince, and fall
Upon him. This cracked walrus skin that stinks
Of the rank sweat of a mermaid's thighs
Cast off, and nab him; when you have him, call.

(1943)

FOR HEALING

Spread your long arms
To the salt stinging wave:
Let its breathless enveloping
Cleanliness lave
Arms, breast, and shoulders,
Sinews and thighs
From the yellow of love,
Her immoderate eyes,
The ache of her fingers,
The whips of her hair,
And the bruise where her mouth
Moved here and there.

(1943)

THE ARCHER

Bend back thy bow, O Archer, till the string
Is level with thine ear, thy body taut,
Its nature art, thyself thy statue wrought
Of marble blood, thy weapon the poised wing
Of coiled and acquiline Fate. Then, loosening, fling
The hissing arrow like a burning thought
Into the empty sky that smokes as the hot
Shaft plunges to the bullseye's quenching ring.

So for a moment, motionless, serene,
Fixed between time and time, I aim and wait;
Nothing remains for breath now but to waive
His prior claim and let the barb fly clean
Into the heart of what I know and hate—
That central black, the ringed and targeted grave.

(1943)

CHINOISERIE
After Théophile Gautier

It is not you, no, madam, whom I love,
Nor you either, Juliet, nor you,
Ophelia, nor Beatrice, nor that dove,
Fair-haired Laura with the big eyes; No.

She is in China whom I love just now;
She lives at home and cares for her old parents;
From a tower of porcelain she leans her brow,
By the Yellow River, where haunt the cormorants.

She has upward-slanting eyes, a foot to hold
In your hand—that small; the colour shed
By lamps is less clear than her coppery gold;
And her long nails are stained with carmine red.

From her trellis she leans out so far
That the dipping swallows are within her reach,
And like a poet, to the evening star
She sings the willow and the flowering peach.

(1954)

Earle Birney
(1904—   )

Earle Birney was born in Calgary, Alberta, and obtained his B.A. from the University of British Columbia and his M.A. and Ph.D. from the University of Toronto. Much of his life has been spent as a university teacher of English at Toronto and U.B.C., and his scholarly knowledge of Anglo-Saxon and Middle English poetry has had a marked influence on his own poetry. In addition to his university work, Birney saw service with the Canadian Army overseas during World War II and with the Canadian Broadcasting Corporation in the years immediately following that war. He has travelled extensively as a kind of unofficial cultural ambassador for Canada, and has written two novels and many critical articles as well as several volumes of verse.

A very versatile poet, Birney has written narratives, lyrics, satires and verse dramas, in all of which he shows his compassion for human suffering and his social idealism, and in many of them his wit.

The poems which follow are from *Selected Poems*, McClelland and Stewart, Toronto, 1966.

VANCOUVER LIGHTS

About me the night   moonless   wimples the mountains
wraps ocean   land   air   and mounting
sucks at the stars   The city   throbbing below
webs the sable peninsula   Streaming   the golden
strands overleap the seajet   by bridge and buoy
vault the shears of the inlet   climb the woods
toward me   falter   and halt   Across to the firefly
haze of a ship on the gulf's erased horizon
roll the lambent spokes of a restless lighthouse

Through the feckless years we have come to the time
when to look on this quilt of lamps is a troubling delight
Welling from Europe's bog   through Africa flowing
and Asia   drowning the lonely lumes on the oceans
tiding up over Halifax   now to this winking
outpost comes flooding the primal ink

On this mountain's brutish forehead with terror of space
I stir   of the changeless night and the stark ranges
of nothing   pulsing down from beyond and between
the fragile planets   We are a spark beleaguered
by darkness   this twinkle we make in a corner of emptiness
how shall we utter our fear that the black Experimentress
will never in the range of her microscope find it?   Our Phoebus
himself is a bubble that dries on Her slide   while the Nubian
wears for an evening's whim a necklace of nebulae

(1942)

SLUG IN WOODS

For eyes he waves greentipped
taut horns of slime   They dipped
hours back   across a reef
a salmonberry leaf
then strained to grope past fin
of spruce   Now eyes suck in
as through the hemlock butts
of his day's ledge there cuts
a vixen chipmunk   Stilled
is he — green mucus chilled

or blotched and soapy stone
pinguid in moss   alone
Hours on   he will resume
his silver scrawl   illume
his palimpsest   emboss
his diver's line across
that waving green illim-
itable seafloor   Slim
young jay his sudden shark
The wrecks he skirts are dark
and fungussed firlogs   whom
spirea sprays emplume
encoral   Dew his shell
while mounting boles foretell
of isles in dappled air
fathoms above his care
Azygous muted life
himself his viscid wife
foodward he noses cold beneath his sea
So spends a summer's jasper century

(1942)

ANGLOSAXON STREET

Dawndrizzle ended,   dampness steams from
blotching brick and   blank plasterwaste.
Faded housepatterns,   hoary and finicky,
unfold stuttering,   stick like a phonograph.
Over the eaves and   over dank roofs
peep giraffetowers,   pasted planless
against graysky,   great dronecliffs
like cutouts for kids,   clipped in two dimensions.

Here is a ghetto   gotten for goyim,
O with care denuded   of nigger and kike.
No coonsmell rankles,   reeks only cellarrot,
attar of carexhaust,   catcorpse and cookinggrease.
Imperial hearts   heave in this haven.
Cracks across windows   are welded with slogans:
There'll Always Be An England   enhances geraniums,
and V's for a Victory   vanquish the housefly.

Ho! with climbing sun,   heading from cocoons,
go bleached beldames,   garnished in bargainbasements,
festooned with shoppingbags,   farded, flatarched,
bigthewed Saxonwives,   stepping over buttrivers,
waddling back to suckle   smallfry, wienerladen.

Hoy! with sunslope,   shrieking over hydrants,
flood from learninghall   the lean fingerlings,
Nordic, nobblecheeked,   not all clean of nose,
leaping Commando-wise   into leprous lanes.

What! after whistleblow,   spewed from wheelboat,
after daylong doughtiness,   dire handplay
in sewertrench or sandpit,   come Saxonthegns,
Junebrown Jutekings,   jawslack for meat.

Sit after supper   on smeared doorsteps,
not humbly swearing   hatedeeds on Huns,
profiteers, politicians,   pacifists, Jews.

Then by twobit magic   to muse in movie,
unlock picturehoard,   or lope to alehall,
soaking bleakly   in beer, skittleless.

Home again to hot box   and humid husbandhood,
in slumbertrough adding   sleepily to Anglekin.
Alongside in lanenooks   carling and leman
caterwaul and clip,   careless of Saxonry,
with moonglow and haste   and a higher heartbeat.

Slumbers now slumtrack,   unstinks, cooling,
waiting brief for milkhind,   mornstar and worldrise.

(1942)

TIME BOMB

In this friend's face I know
        the grizzly still   and in the mirror
lay my ear to the radio's conch
        and hear the atom's terror

Within the politician's ribs
        within my own   the time-bombs tick
O men be swift to be mankind
        or let the grizzly take

(1945)

CANADA: CASE HISTORY

This is the case of a high-school land,
deadset in adolescence,
loud treble laughs and sudden fists,
bright cheeks, and gangling presence.
This boy is wonderful at sports
and physically quite healthy;
he's taken to church on Sunday still ——
and keeps his prurience stealthy.
He doesn't like books except about bears,
collects new coins and model planes,
and never refuses a dare.
His Uncle spoils him with candy, of course,
yet shouts him down when he talks at table.
You will note he's got some of his French mother's looks,
though he's not so witty and no more stable.
He's really much more like his father and yet
if you say so he'll pull a great face.
He wants to be different from everyone else
and daydreams of winning the global race.
Parents unmarried and living abroad,
relatives keen to bag the estate,
schizophrenia not excluded,
will he learn to grow up before it's too late?

(1948)

BUSHED

He invented a rainbow but lightning struck it
shattered it into the lake-lap of a mountain
so big his mind slowed when he looked at it

Yet he built a shack on the shore
learned to roast porcupine belly and
wore the quills on his hatband

At first he was out with the dawn
whether it yellowed bright as wood-columbine
or was only a fuzzed moth in a flannel of storm
But he found the mountain was clearly alive
sent messages whizzing down every hot morning
boomed proclamations at noon and spread out
a white guard of goat
before falling asleep on its feet at sundown

When he tried his eyes on the lake   ospreys
would fall like valkyries
choosing the cut-throat
He took then to waiting
till the night smoke rose from the boil of the sunset

But the moon carved unknown totems
out of the lakeshore
owls in the beardusky woods derided him
moosehorned cedars circled his swamps and tossed
their antlers up to the stars
Then he knew   though the mountain slept   the winds
were shaping its peak to an arrowhead
poised

And now he could only
bar himself in and wait
for the great flint to come singing into his heart

(1952)

THE BEAR ON THE DELHI ROAD

Unreal   tall as a myth
by the road the Himalayan bear
is beating the brilliant air
with his crooked arms
About him two men   bare
spindly as locusts   leap

One pulls on a ring
in the great soft nose   His mate
flicks   flicks with a stick
up at the rolling eyes

They have not led him here
down from the fabulous hills
to this bald alien plain
and the clamorous world   to kill
but simply to teach him to dance

They are peaceful both   these spare
men of Kashmir   and the bear
alive is their living   too
If   far on the Delhi way
around him galvanic they dance
it is merely to wear   wear
from his shaggy body the tranced
wish forever to stay
only an ambling bear
four-footed in berries

It is no more joyous for them
in this hot dust to prance
out of reach of the praying claws
sharpened to paw for ants
in the shadows of deodars
It is not easy to free
myth from reality
or rear this fellow up
to lurch   lurch with them
in the tranced dancing of men

(1962)

A.M. Klein
(1909—1972)

A.M. Klein was born in Montreal and educated at McGill University and, in law, at the University of Montreal. He was an expert in Hebrew literature and history, and played a prominent part in the Zionist movement and in other Jewish causes in Montreal.

Klein's poetry began to appear when he was a student at McGill, and was influenced by his Jewish erudition and background and by the modernist impulses received from his association with such other Montreal poets as A.J.M. Smith and F.R. Scott. His sympathy with the French-speaking inhabitants of Quebec was symbolized by his decision to seek his legal education at the University of Montreal, and frequently found expression in his poetry, especially in the volume *The Rocking Chair and Other Poems* (1948).

In addition to his poetry, Klein wrote a novel, *The Second Scroll* (1951), critical essays on James Joyce, and many articles on Jewish themes.

The poems which follow are from *Hath Not a Jew . . .* (1940) and *The Rocking Chair,* Ryerson Press, Toronto, 1948.

HEIRLOOM

My father bequeathed me no wide estates;
No keys and ledgers were my heritage;
Only some holy books with *yahrzeit* dates
Writ mournfully upon a blank front page—

Books of the Baal Shem Tov, and of his wonders;
Pamphlets anent the devil and his crew;
Prayers against road demons, witches, thunders;
And sundry other tomes for a good Jew.

Beautiful: though no pictures on them, save
The Scorpion crawling on a printed track;
The Virgin floating on a scriptural wave,
Square letters twinkling in the Zodiac.

The snuff left on this page, now brown and old,
The tallow stains of midnight liturgy—
These are my coat of arms, and these unfold
My noble lineage, my proud ancestry!

And my tears, too, have stained this heirloomed ground,
When reading in these treatises some weird
Miracle, I turned a leaf and found
A white hair fallen from my father's beard.

(1940)

BESTIARY

God breathe a blessing on
His small bones, every one!
The little boy, who stalks
The Bible's plains and rocks
To hunt in grammar'd woods
Strange litters and wild broods;
The little boy who seeks
Beast-muzzles and bird-beaks
In cave and den and crypt,
In copse of holy script;
The little boy who looks
For quarry in holy books.

Before his eyes is born
The elusive unicorn;
There, scampering, arrive
The golden mice, the five;
Also in antic shape,
Gay peacock and glum ape.

He hears a snort of wrath:
The fiery behemoth!
And then on biblic breeze
The crocodile's sneeze.—
He sees the lion eat
Green stalks.— At tigress-teat,
As if of the same ilk,
The young lamb sucking milk.

Hard by, as fleet as wind,
They pass, the roe and hind.
Bravely, and with no risk,
He halts the basilisk,
Pygarg and cockatrice.
And there, most forest-wise
Among the bestiaries,
The little hunter eyes
Him crawling at his leisure:
The beast Nebuchadnezzar.

(1940)

FOR THE SISTERS OF THE HOTEL DIEU

In pairs,
as if to illustrate their sisterhood,
the sisters pace the hospital garden walks.
In their robes black and white immaculate hoods
they are like birds,
the safe domestic fowl of the House of God.

O biblic birds,
who fluttered to me in my childhood illnesses
—me little, afraid, ill, not of your race,—
the cool wing for my fever, the hovering solace,
the sense of angels—
be thanked, O plumage of paradise, be praised.

(1948)

LONE BATHER

Upon the ecstatic diving board the diver,
poised for parabolas, lets go
lets go his manshape to become a bird.
Is bird, and topsy-turvy
the pool floats overhead, and the white tiles snow
their crazy hexagons. Is dolphin. Then
is plant with lilies bursting from his heels.

Himself, suddenly mysterious and marine,
bobs up a merman leaning on his hills.
Splashes and plays alone the deserted pool;
as those, is free, who think themselves unseen.
He rolls in his heap of fruit,
he slides his belly over
the melonrinds of water, curved and smooth and green.
Feels good: and trains, like little acrobats
his echoes dropping from the galleries;
circules himself over a rung of water;
swims fancy and gay; taking a notion, hides
under the satins of his great big bed,—
and then comes up to float until he thinks
the ceiling at his brow, and nowhere any sides.

His thighs are a shoal of fishes: scattered: he
turns with many gloves of greeting
towards the sunnier water and the tiles.

Upon the tiles he dangles from his toes
lazily the eight reins of his ponies.

An afternoon, far from the world
a street sound throws like a stone, with paper, through the glass.
Up, he is chipped enamel, grained with hair.
The gloss of his footsteps follows him to the showers,
the showers, and the male room, and the towel
which rubs the bird, the plant, the dolphin back again
personable plain.

(1948)

71

THE ROCKING CHAIR

It seconds the crickets of the province. Heard
in the clean lamplit farmhouses of Quebec,—
wooden, — it is no less a national bird;
and rivals, in its cage, the mere stuttering clock.
To its time, the evenings are rolled away;
and in its peace the pensive mother knits
contentment to be worn by her family,
grown-up, but still cradled by the chair in which she sits.

It is also the old man's pet, pair to his pipe,
the two aids of his arithmetic and plans,
plans rocking and puffing into market-shape;
and it is the toddler's game and dangerous dance.
Moved to the verandah, on summer Sundays, it is,
among the hanging plants, the girls, the boy-friends,
sabbatical and clumsy, like the white haloes
dangling above the blue serge suits of the young men.

It has a personality of its own;
is a character (like that old drunk Lacoste,
exhaling amber, and toppling on his pins);
it is alive; individual; and no less
an identity than those about it. And
it is tradition. Centuries have been flicked
from its arcs, alternately flicked and pinned.
It rolls with the gait of St. Malo. It is act

and symbol, symbol of this static folk
which moves in segments, and returns to base,—
a sunken pendulum: *invoke, revoke;*
loosed yon, leashed hither, motion on no space.
O, like some Anjou ballad, all refrain,
which turns about its longing, and seems to move
to make a pleasure out of repeated pain,
its music moves, as if always back to a first love.

(1948)

GRAIN ELEVATOR

Up from the low-roofed dockyard warehouses
it rises blind and babylonian
like something out of legend. Something seen
in a children's coloured book. Leviathan
swamped on our shore? The cliffs of some other river?
The blind ark lost and petrified? A cave
built to look innocent, by pirates? Or
some eastern tomb a travelled patron here makes local?

But even when known, it's more than what it is:
for here, as in a Josephdream, bow down
the sheaves, the grains, the scruples of the sun
garnered for darkness; and Saskatchewan
is rolled like a rug of a thick and golden thread.
O prison of prairies, ship in whose galleys roll
sunshines like so many shaven heads,
waiting the bushel-burst out of the beached bastille!

Sometimes, it makes me think Arabian,
the grain picked up, like tic-tacs out of time:
first one; an other; singly; one by one;—
to save life. Sometimes, some other races claim
the twinship of my thought, — as the river stirs
restless in a white Caucasian sleep,
or, as in the steerage of the elevators,
the grains, Mongolian and crowded, dream.

A box: cement, hugeness, and rightangles—
merely the sight of it leaning in my eyes
mixes up continents and makes a montage
of inconsequent time and uncontiguous space.
It's because it's bread. It's because
bread is its theme, an absolute. Because
always this great box flowers over us
with all the coloured faces of mankind. . .

(1948)

MONTREAL[1]

I

O city metropole, isle riverain!
Your ancient pavages and sainted routes
Traverse my spirit's conjured avenues!
Splendor erablic of your promenades
Foliates there, and there your maisonry
Of pendent balcon and escalier'd march,
Unique midst English habitat,
Is vivid Normandy!

II

You populate the pupils of my eyes:
Thus, does the Indian, plumed, furtivate
Still through your painted autumns, Ville-Marie!
Though palisades have passed, though calumet
With tabac of your peace enfumes the air,
Still do I spy the phantom, aquiline,
Genuflect, moccasin'd, behind
His statue in the square!

III

Thus, costumed images before me pass,
Haunting your archives architectural:
Coureur de bois, in posts where pelts were portaged;
Seigneur within his candled manoir; Scot
Ambulant through his bank, pillar'd and vast.
Within your chapels, voyaged mariners
Still pray, and personage departed,
All present from your past!

IV

Grand port of navigations, multiple
The lexicons uncargo'd at your quays,
Sonnant though strange to me; but chiefest, I,
Auditor of your music, cherish the
Joined double-melodied vocabulaire
Where English vocable and roll Ecossic,
Mollified by the parle of French
Bilinguefact your air!

74

V

Such your suaver voice, hushed Hochelaga!
But for me also sound your potencies,
Fortissimos of sirens fluvial,
Bruit of manufactory, and thunder
From foundry issuant, all puissant tone
Implenishing your hebdomad; and then
Sanct silence, and your argent belfries
Clamant in orison!

VI

You are a part of me, O all your quartiers—
And of dire pauvrete and of richesse—
To finished time my homage loyal claim;
You are locale of infancy, milieu
Vital of institutes that formed my fate;
And you above the city, scintillant,
Mount Royal, are my spirit's mother,
Almative, poitrinate!

VII

Never do I sojourn in alien place
But I do languish for your scenes and sounds,
City of reverie, nostalgic isle,
Pendant most brilliant on Laurentian cord!
The coigns of your boulevards — my signiory—
Your suburbs are my exile's verdure fresh,
Your parks, your fountain'd parks—
Pasture of memory!

VIII

City, O city, you are vision'd as
A parchemin roll of saecular exploit
Inked with the script of eterne souvenir!
You are in sound, chanson and instrument!
Mental, you rest forever edified
With tower and dome; and in these beating valves,
Here in these beating valves, you will
For all my mortal time reside!

(1948)

¹ As befits a bilingual city, this is an attempt to
write a bilingual poem, making use of both
French and English words.

THE SNOWSHOERS

The jolly icicles ringing in their throats,
their mouths meerschaums of vapor,
from the saints' parishes they come, like snowmen
spangled, with spectrum color
patching the scarf green, sash red, sky-blue the coat—
come to the crystal course. Their airy hooves
unslung from their backs are ready
to stamp their goodlucks on the solid foam.
Till then, the saints all heralded,
they snowball their banter below the angular eaves.

O gala garb, bright with assomption, flags
on limb and torso curled—
furling of white, blue zigzags, rondures red!
A candy-colored world!
And moods as primary as their tuques and togs,—
of tingling cold, and the air rubbed down with snow
and winter well-being!
Like a slapdash backdrop, the street moves with colors,
the zones and rhomboids moving
toward the enhancing whiteness of the snow.

And now, clomping the packed-down snow of the street
they walk on sinews
gingerly, as if their feet were really swollen,
eager for release
from the blinders of buildings; suddenly they cut
a corner, and — the water they will walk!
Surf of the sun!
World of white wealth! Wind's tilth! Waves
of dazzling dominion
on which their colored sails will billow and rock!

(1948)

MONSIEUR GASTON

You remember the big Gaston, for whom everyone
    predicted
a bad end?—
Gaston, the neighbour's gossip and his mother's cross?
You remember him *vaurien*[1], always out of a job,
with just enough clinking coinage
for pool, bright neckties, and blondes,—
the scented Gaston in the poolroom lolling
in meadows of green baize?
In clover now. Through politics. *Monsieur* Gaston.

They say the Minister of a certain department does
    not move
without him; and they say, to make it innocent,—
chauffeur.
But everyone understands. Why, wherever our
    Gaston smiles
a nightclub rises and the neons flash.
To his slightest whisper
the bottled rye, like a fawning pet-dog, gurgles.
The burlesque queen will not undress
unless Monsieur Gaston says yes.
And the Madame will shake her head behind the
    curtain-rods
unless he nods.

A changed man, Gaston; almost a civil servant,
keeps records, appointments, women; speaks tough
    English;
is very much respected.
You should hear with what greetings his distinguished
    approach is greeted;
you should see the gifts he gets,
with compliments for his season.

(1948)

[1] A good-for-nothing

Dorothy Livesay
(1909—   )

Born in Winnipeg, Dorothy Livesay spent her girlhood in Ontario and was educated at the University of Toronto and the Sorbonne. In Paris she wrote a dissertation on the influence of French symbolism on modern English poetry, and became interested in the cause of social reform under the inspiration of Henri Barbusse and his League of Revolutionary Writers. Her middle years were spent as a social worker, mainly in Vancouver, but in recent years she has been a lecturer in English at the Universities of British Columbia, New Brunswick, Alberta and Victoria, in that order.

Dorothy Livesay's early poems were written in the Imagist manner, under the influence of such American women poets as Emily Dickinson, Elinor Wylie, and H.D. (Hilda Doolittle). In the 1930s, however, her own interest in social reform and the influence of such left-wing English poets as Cecil Day-Lewis and Stephen Spender led her to write poetry of social protest or social idealism. In the last two decades, while retaining her interest in reform, she has written a more personal and humanistic type of verse.

The poems which follow are from her *Collected Poems*, McGraw-Hill Ryerson, 1972.

SUCH SILENCE

Some silence that is with beauty swept
With beauty swept all clean:
Some silence that is by summer kept,
By summer kept all green. . . .

Give me such silence in a little wood
Where grass and quiet sun
Shall make no sound where I have run
Nor where my feet have stood.

(1928)

FIRE AND REASON

I cannot shut out the night—
Nor its sharp clarity.

The many blinds we draw,
You and I,
The many fires we light
Can never quite obliterate
The irony of stars,
The deliberate moon,
The last, unsolved finality
Of night.

(1928)

AT ENGLISH BAY: DECEMBER, 1937

By the winter-stripped willows in the Park I walked
Gold-washed fountains in the sudden sun;
Brisk the air, white-capped the mountains,
Close at my feet the rim of the land's end—
Everything held in a silent axis, carved in sunlight
Except for the ocean pounding below me, relentless reminder:
Thoughts in my mind clear as heaven's azure
Till the heave, the roar of encroaching armies
Broke on my heart's shore.

Water that has washed the coasts of China,
Shanghai's city, yellow Yangtse;
Water that has cleansed the bloodied hands
And healed the wounds
Signed the death-warrant on too tell-tale lips
Sent to oblivion the iron ships;
Water forever restless, forever in struggle

As a man feels in himself his fevered spirit
Rising and falling, urging and being spent
Into new deeps and further continents—
Until he begins to move with others
Seizing the willows as banners—
Gold-washed fountains in the sudden sun!

(1937)

THE LIZARD: OCTOBER, 1939

No one has come from the fronts we knew—
Shanghai and Yenan — for a long session:
Silent now the Madrid broadcasts. So was Vienna once
Blotted out. We remember her voices fading.
No one has come. Letters unanswered. The stricken
Refugees smothered then, after
Years of ditch stumbling?
The battling, thin tunics gored to death
In the country of the bull, in the country of the dragon?

In the sheltered rocks of our homeland, the Pacific waters
Hills shrouded with evergreen and the valleys yellow
With corn and apples; within the walls of our houses
Splashed with a vivid wallpaper,
Radios blare the censored version of our living:
Wrestlers rage, baseball bouncers rant,
The words of a recipe tinkle on the ear—
Lord Halifax speaks sprightly from London
Where the people run about gladly
Attending to air-raid precautions.

In the sheltered rocks, stealthily, a lizard
Slips hesitant into sunlight; tunes himself
To the wind's message. We slip out in pairs, as lovers
Strip ourselves, longing
To see bodies bare and flesh uncloseted,
To hear real voices again, to uphold the song
Of one coming from Madrid, Shanghai or Yenan
Bearers of good news
From the fronts we knew.

(1939)

THE THREE EMILY'S[1]

These women crying in my head
Walk alone, uncomforted:
The Emily's, these three
Cry to be set free—
And others whom I will not name
Each different, each the same.

Yet they had liberty!
Their kingdom was the sky:
They batted clouds with easy hand,
Found a mountain for their stand;
From wandering lonely they could catch
The inner magic of a heath—
A lake their palette, any tree
Their brush could be.

And still they cry to me
As in reproach—
I, born to hear their inner storm
Of separate man in woman's form,
I yet possess another kingdom, barred
To them, these three, this Emily.
I move as mother in a frame,
My arteries
Flow the immemorial way
Towards the child, the man;
And only for brief span
Am I an Emily on mountain snows
And one of these.

And so the whole that I possess
Is still much less—
They move triumphant through my head:
I am the one
Uncomforted.

(1948)

1 Emily Bronte, Emily Dickinson and Emily
Carr.

LAMENT
for J.F.B.L.[1]

What moved me, was the way your hand
Lay in my hand, not withering,
But warm, like a hand cooled in a stream
And purling still; or a bird caught in a snare
Wings folded stiff, eyes in a stare,
But still alive with the fear,
Heart hoarse with hope—
So your hand, your dead hand, my dear.

And the veins, still mounting as blue rivers,
Mounting towards the tentative finger-tips,
The delta where four seas come in—
Your fingers promontories into colourless air
Were rosy still — not chalk (like cliffs
You knew in boyhood, Isle of Wight):
But blushed with colour from the sun you sought
And muscular from garden toil;
Stained with the purple of an iris bloom,
Violas grown for a certain room;
Hands seeking faïence, filagree,
Chinese lacquer and ivory—
Brussels lace; and a walnut piece
Carved by a hand now phosphorus.

What moved me, was the way your hand
Held life, although the pulse was gone.
The hand that carpentered a children's chair,
Carved out a stair
Held leash upon a dog in strain
Gripped wheel, swung sail,
Flicked horse's rein
And then again

82

Moved kings and queens meticulous on a board,
Slashed out the cards, cut bread, and poured
A purring cup of tea;

The hand so neat and nimble
Could make a tennis partner tremble,
Write a resounding round
Of sonorous verbs and nouns—
Hand that would not strike a child, and yet
Could ring a bell and send a man to doom.

And now unmoving in this Spartan room
The hand still speaks:
After the brain was fogged
And the tight lips tighter shut,
After the shy appraising eyes
Relinquished fire for the sea's green gaze—
The hand still breathes, fastens its hold on life;
Demands the whole, establishes the strife.

What moved me, was the way your hand
Lay cool in mine, not withering;
As bird still breathes, and stream runs clear—
So your hand; your dead hand, my dear.

(1957)

[1] J.F.B. Livesay, the poet's father, a distinguished
journalist.

BARTOK AND THE GERANIUM

She lifts her green umbrellas
Towards the pane
Seeking her fill of sunlight
Or of rain;
Whatever falls
She has no commentary
Accepts, extends,
Blows out her furbelows,
Her bustling boughs;

And all the while he whirls
Explodes in space,
Never content with this small room:
Not even can he be
Confined to sky
But must speed high and higher still

83

From galaxy to galaxy,
Wrench from the stars their momentary notes
Steal music from the moon.

She's daylight
He is dark
She's heaven-held breath
He storms and crackles
Spits with hell's own spark.

Yet in this room, this moment now
These together breathe and be:
She, essence of serenity,
He in a mad intensity
Soars beyond sight
Then hurls, lost Lucifer,
From heaven's height.

And when he's done, he's out:
She leans a lip against the glass
And preens herself in light.

(1957)

THE TAMING

Be woman. You did say me, be
woman.   I did not know
the measure of the words

     until a black man
     as I prepared him chicken
     made me listen:
     —No, dammit.
     Not so much salt.
     Do what I say, woman:
     just that
     and nothing more.

Be woman. I did not know
the measure of the words
until that night
when you denied me darkness,
even the right
to turn in my own light.

Do as I say, I heard you faintly
over me fainting:
be woman.

(1967)

THE UNQUIET BED

The woman I am
is not what you see
I'm not just bones
and crockery

the woman I am
knew love and hate
hating the chains
that parents make

longing that love
might set men free
yet hold them fast
in loyalty

the woman I am
is not what you see
move over love
make room for me

(1967)

THE UNINVITED

Always a third one's there
where any two are walking out
along a river-bank   so mirror-still
sheathed in sheets
of sky   pillows of cloud—
their footprints crunch the hardening earth
their eyes delight in trees   stripped clean
winter-prepared
with only the rose-hips red
and the plump fingers of sumach

And always between the two
(scuffing the leaves, laughing
and fingers locked)
goes a third lover   his or hers
who walked this way with one or other   once
flung back the head   snapped branches of dark pine
in armfuls   before snowfall

     I walk beside you
     trace
     a shadow's shade
     skating on silver
     hear
     another voice
     singing under ice

(1968)

Irving Layton
(1912—   )

Irving Layton, the most prolific and in some ways the most influential Canadian poet of this century, was born in Rumania but was brought to Montreal as a small boy by his parents. He was educated at Macdonald College and at McGill University, and has been a teacher for most of his adult life, mainly at Sir George Williams University in Montreal and, more recently, at York University in Toronto.

Layton, together with Louis Dudek, Raymond Souster, P.K. Page and others, was one of a group of poets who, during and after World War II, sought to bring a new element of social realism and political radicalism into Canadian poetry. He has published about twenty volumes of verse and a number of short stories, and has become a well-known public figure by means of his controversial appearances on television and often angry letters to newspaper editors.

His development has been marked by a steady ascent towards mastery of craftsmanship and maturity of outlook. Sometimes dismissed as angry and bombastic, he actually has a very wide range of effects: he can be tender and gentle as well as bitter and scornful, and he can praise life as eloquently as he can damn the enemies of life.

The following poems are from his *Collected Poems* (1965) and *Lovers and Lesser Men,* McClelland and Stewart, Toronto, 1973. An enlarged *Collected Poems* appeared in 1971.

FIRST SNOW: LAKE ACHIGAN

No noise of rowlocks, no ecstasy of hands,
No sound of crickets in the inextricable air:
But a Roman silence for a lone drummer's call.

Now noiseless as a transaction, a brown hare
Breaks from the cold fields, bounds ahead;
Now slowly slowly the season unwinters
On its spool of white thread.

Lonely and fleshed with hates, who here
Would be God's angry man, a thundering Paul
When December, a toga'd Cato, slow to anger,
At last speaks the word that condemns us all.

(1954)

THE BIRTH OF TRAGEDY

And me happiest when I compose poems.
        Love, power, the huzza of battle
        are something, are much;
yet a poem includes them like a pool
        water and reflection.
In me, nature's divided things—
        tree, mold on tree—
        have their fruition;
I am their core. Let them swap,
bandy, like a flame swerve
I am their mouth; as a mouth I serve.

And I observe how the sensual moths
        big with odor and sunshine
        dart into the perilous shrubbery;
or drop their visiting shadows
        upon the garden I one year made
of flowering stone to be a footstool
        for the perfect gods:
        who, friends to the ascending orders,
sustain all passionate meditations
and call down pardons
for the insurgent blood.

88

A quiet madman, never far from tears,
  I lie like a slain thing
  under the green air the trees
inhabit, or rest upon a chair
   towards which the inflammable air
tumbles on many robins' wings;
  noting how seasonably
  leaf and blossom uncurl
and living things arrange their death,
while someone from afar off
blows birthday candles for the world.

(1954)

COMPOSITION IN LATE SPRING

When Love ensnares my mind unbidden
  I am lost in the usual way
On a crowded street or avenue
Where I am lord of all the marquees,
And the traffic cop moving his lips
  Like a poet composing
Whistles a discovery of sparrows
About my head.

My mind, full of goats and pirates
  And simpler than a boy's,
I walk through a forest of white arms
That embrace me like window-shoppers;
Friends praise me like a Turkish delight
  Or a new kind of suspender
And children love me
Like a story.

Conscience more flat than cardboard
  Over the gap in a sole,
I avoid the fanatic whose subway
Collapsed in his brain;
There's a sinking, but the madonna
  Who clings to my hairlock
Is saved: on shore the damned ones
Applaud with the vigour of bees.

The sparrows' golden plummeting
    From fearful rooftop
Shows the flesh dying into sunshine.
Fled to the green suburbs, Death
Lies scared to death under a heap of bones.
    Beauty buds from mire
And I, a singer in season, observe
Death is a name for beauty not in use.

No one is more happy, none can do more tricks.
    The sun melts like butter
Over my sweetcorn thoughts;
And, at last, both famous and good
I'm a Doge, a dog
    At the end of a terrace
Where poems like angels like flakes of powder
Quaver above my prickling skin.

(1954)

SONG FOR NAOMI

Who is that in the tall grasses singing
By herself, near the water?
I can not see her
But can it be her
Than whom the grasses so tall
Are taller,
My daughter,
My lovely daughter?

Who is that in the tall grasses running
Beside her, near the water?
She can not see there
Time that pursued her
In the deep grasses so fast
And faster
And caught her,
My foolish daughter.

What is the wind in the fair grass saying
Like a verse, near the water?
Saviours that over
All things have power
Make Time himself grow kind

And kinder
That sought her,
My little daughter.

Who is that at the close of the summer
Near the deep lake? Who wrought her
Comely and slender?
Time but attends and befriends her
Than whom the grasses though tall
Are not taller,
My daughter,
My gentle daughter.

(1955)

THE BULL CALF

The thing could barely stand. Yet taken
from his mother and the barn smells
he still impressed with his pride,
with the promise of sovereignty in the way
his head moved to take us in.
The fierce sunlight tugging the maize from the ground
licked at his shapely flanks.
He was too young for all that pride.
I thought of the deposed Richard II.

"No money in bull calves," Freeman had said.
The visiting clergyman rubbed the nostrils
now snuffing pathetically at the windless day.
"A pity," he sighed.
My gaze slipped off his hat toward the empty sky
that circled over the black knot of men,
over us and the calf waiting for the first blow.

Struck,
the bull calf drew in his thin forelegs
as if gathering strength for a mad rush . . .
tottered . . . raised his darkening eyes to us,
and I saw we were at the far end
of his frightened look, growing smaller and smaller
till we were only the ponderous mallet
that flicked his bleeding ear
and pushed him over on his side, stiffly,
like a block of wood.

Below the hill's crest
the river snuffled on the improvised beach.
We dug a deep pit and threw the dead calf into it.
It made a wet sound, a sepulchral gurgle,
as the warm sides bulged and flattened.
Settled, the bull calf lay as if asleep,
one foreleg over the other,
bereft of pride and so beautiful now,
without movement, perfectly still in the cool pit,
I turned away and wept.

(1956)

ON SEEING THE STATUETTES
OF EZEKIEL AND JEREMIAH
IN THE CHURCH OF NOTRE-DAME [1]

They have given you French names
        and made you captive, my rugged
troublesome compatriots;
        your splendid beards, here, are epicene,
plaster white
                and your angers
unclothed with Palestinian hills quite lost
in this immense and ugly edifice.

You are bored — I see it — sultry prophets
        with priests and nuns
(What coarse jokes must pass between you!)
        and with those morbidly religious
i.e. my prize brother-in-law
                    ex-Lawrencian
pawing his rosary, and his wife
sick with many guilts.

Believe me I would gladly take you
        from this spidery church
its bad melodrama, its musty smell of candle
        and set you both free again
in no make-believe world
                of sin and penitence
but the sunlit square opposite
alive at noon with arrogant men.

92

Yet cheer up Ezekiel and you Jeremiah
        who were once cast into a pit;
I shall not leave you here incensed, uneasy
        among alien Catholic saints
but shall bring you from time to time
                my hot Hebrew heart
as passionate as your own, and stand
with you here awhile in aching confraternity.

(1956)

¹ In Montreal

BERRY PICKING

Silently my wife walks on the still wet furze
Now darkgreen the leaves are full of metaphors
Now lit up is each tiny lamp of blueberry.
The white nails of rain have dropped and the sun is free.

And whether she bends or straightens to each bush
To find the children's laughter among the leaves
Her quiet hands seem to make the quiet summer hush—
Berries or children, patient she is with these.

I only vex and perplex her; madness, rage
Are endearing perhaps put down upon the page;
Even silence daylong and sullen can then
Enamour as restraint or classic discipline.

So I envy the berries she puts in her mouth,
The red and succulent juice that stains her lips;
I shall never taste that good to her, nor will they
Displease her with a thousand barbarous jests.

How they lie easily for her hand to take,
Part of the unoffending world that is hers;
Here beyond complexity she stands and stares
And leans her marvellous head as if for answers.

No more the easy soul my childish craft deceives
Nor the simpler one for whom yes is always yes;
No, now her voice comes to me from a far way off
Though her lips are redder than the raspberries.

(1958)

STELLA

All afternoon she sits in the doorway, a tourist attraction
    to be stared at by Greeks or the foreigners
Who know her story. Old and ill and her feet swollen
    to rhinoceros size
Once, long ago, she was a wild creature so fair and disdainful
    she made the sober merchants dream at their tills
And fishermen haul in lascivious sea-nymphs all night long.
Their wives, even the comeliest of virgins, cursed her beauty
    praying their merciful God
To strike her with plague or leprosy. One day He lifted a petitioner's
    taper from its tiny brass socket
And turned it into a man handsome and clever with words, poet
    and talked-about novelist from another island.
She saw him and fell, his curious fire loosening her limbs;
In the crumbling Genoese castle, surrounded by ears, they made love.
The furious villagers rejoiced. At last the contemptuous beauty
    had been roiled in the mire
Her scented petticoats pulled over her head, her besmutted buttocks
    for all to see.
O the fetid dreams of men! How they besmeared the white breasts
    that had made them groan in their sleep
How they reviled what for so long they had longed for in vain
While the women and girls so lit up the church with grateful candles
    you'd think for weeks God's face was shining there.
He lifted yet another taper and blew out its flame: the teller of tales
    made off for Athens to compose
A moving novel about their tragic love and never saw her again
But overnight she became the ruined unhappy heroine of a thousand
    lustful dreams
Such that aesthetes and bored rich women dream and wandered from place
    to place to return at last comfortless and impenitent
To her village and the filthy leers of men, the compassionate jeers
    of wives and virgins
To live solitary and infamous in the house where you see her now.
All that was long ago. Day by remorseless day her famed and troubling
    beauty crumbled into commemorative moles,
    wrinkles and yellowing parchment skin

And the heartbreak of an old woman's toothless grin.
Now there isn't a villager, old or young, who doesn't run up to embrace
    this hairy misshapen crone
    with the wild gone look in her eyes
And the sour excremental smell that fills up her doorway.
Not one who does not feel glad and right having someone whom daily
    he can forgive and pity
Or whose heart is not made proud to fix her hoary and humbled at the end
    of his benevolent stare;
Especially since the government itself is rumoured to allow her
    a small stipend to sit in the doorway
    to be gawked at, an Aeschylean lesson for all Greeks,
Her fabled loveliness caught forever in a work of imperishing art
    while her dying decrepit self,
A tourist attraction in the village, puts still more drachmas
    in the merchants' tills.

Molibos, Greece
July 21, 1972

(1973)

P.K. Page
(1916—   )

Patricia K. Page was born in England but came to Canada as a small child. During World War II she lived in Montreal and, later, in Ottawa, and was closely associated with the group of poets and prose writers who produced the magazines *Preview* and *Northern Review,* both of which began with the ambition to unite modernist form with social relevance. After the war she married Arthur Irwin, and with her husband, who became a member of the Canadian diplomatic service, lived for some years in Mexico and Australia. Miss Page is an accomplished graphic artist as well as a poet, and has written one novel.

P.K. Page's poetry is marked above all by her gift of empathy, of entering imaginatively into the lives of other human beings and indeed, on occasion, into the lives of plants, animals, and inanimate matter. Prolific in imagery, she keeps her imaginative exuberance under strict intellectual control.

The poems which follow are from *Cry Ararat, Poems New and Selected,* McClelland and Stewart, Toronto, 1967.

THE BANDS AND THE BEAUTIFUL CHILDREN

Band makes a tunnel of the open street
at first, hearing it;
seeing it band becomes
high: brasses ascending on the strings of sun
build their own auditorium of light,
windows from cornets
and a dome of drums.

And always attendant on bands, the beautiful children
white with running and innocence;
and the arthritic old
who, patient behind their windows
are no longer split by the quick yellow of imagination
or carried beyond their angular limits of distance.

But the children move
in the trembling building of sound,
sure as a choir
until band breaks and scatters,
crumbles about them and is made of men
tired and grumbling
on the straggling grass.

And the children, lost, lost,
in an open space,
remember the certainty of the anchored home
and cry on the unknown edge of their own city
their lips stiff from an imaginary trumpet.

(1946)

STORIES OF SNOW

Those in the vegetable rain retain
an area behind their sprouting eyes
held soft and rounded with the dream of snow
precious and reminiscent as those globes—
souvenir of some never nether land—
which hold their snow storms circular, complete,
high in a tall and teakwood cabinet.

In countries where the leaves are large as hands
where flowers protrude their fleshy chins
and call their colours
an imaginary snow storm sometimes falls
among the lilies.
And in the early morning one will waken
to think the glowing linen of his pillow
a northern drift, will find himself mistaken
and lie back weeping.

And there the story shifts from head to head,
of how, in Holland, from their feather beds
hunters arise and part the flakes and go
forth to the frozen lakes in search of swans—
the snow light falling white along their guns,
their breath in plumes.
While tethered in the wind like sleeping gulls
ice boats wait the raising of their wings
to skim the electric ice at such a speed
they leap the jet strips of the naked water,
and how these flying, sailing hunters feel
air in their mouths as terrible as ether.
And on the story runs that even drinks
in that white landscape dare to be no colour;
how, flasked and water clear, the liquor slips
silver against the hunters' moving hips.

And of the swan in death these dreamers tell
of its last flight and how it falls, a plummet,
pierced by the freezing bullet
and how three feathers, loosened by the shot,
descend like snow upon it.
While hunters plunge their fingers in its down
deep as a drift, and dive their hands
up to the neck of the wrist
in that warm metamorphosis of snow
as gentle as the sort that woodsmen know
who, lost in the white circle, fall at last
and dream their way to death.

And stories of this kind are often told
in countries where great flowers bar the roads
with reds and blues which seal the route to snow—
as if, in telling, raconteurs unlock
the colour with its complement and go
through to the area behind the eyes
where silent, unrefractive whiteness lies.

(1946)

THE STENOGRAPHERS

After the brief bivouac of Sunday,
their eyes, in the forced march of Monday to Saturday,
hoist the white flag, flutter in the snow storm of paper,
haul it down and crack in the midsun of temper.

In the pause between the first draft and the carbon
they glimpse the smooth hours when they were children—
the ride on the ice-cart, the ice-man's name,
the end of the route and the long walk home;

remember the sea where floats at high tide
were sea marrows growing on the scatter-green vine
or spools of gray toffee, or wasps' nests on water;
remember the sand and the leaves of the country.

Bell rings and they go and the voice draws their pencil
like a sled across snow; when its runners are frozen
rope snaps and the voice then is pulling no burden
but runs like a dog on the winter of paper.

Their climates are winter and summer—no wind
for the kites of their hearts—no wind for a flight;
a breeze at the most, to tumble them over
and leave them like rubbish—the boy-friends of blood.

In the inch of the noon as they move they are stagnant.
The terrible calm of the noon is their anguish;
the lip of the counter, the shapes of the straws
like icicles breaking their tongues are invaders.

Their beds are their oceans — salt water of weeping;
the waves that they know—the tide before sleep;
and fighting to drown they assemble their sheep
in columns and watch them leap desks for their fences
and stare at them with their own mirror-worn faces.

In the felt of the morning the calico minded,
sufficiently starched, insert papers, hit keys,
efficient and sure as their adding machines;
yet they weep in the vault, they are taut as net curtains
stretched upon frames. In their eyes I have seen
the pin men of madness in marathon trim
race round the track of the stadium pupil.

(1946)

LANDLADY

Through sepia air the boarders come and go,
impersonal as trains. Pass silently
the craving silence swallowing her speech;
click doors like shutters on her camera eye.

Because of her their lives become exact:
their entrances and exits are designed;
phone calls are cryptic. Oh, her ticklish ears
advance and fall back stunned.

Nothing is unprepared. They hold the walls
about them when they weep or laugh. Each face
is dialled to zero publicly. She peers
stippled with curious flesh;

pads on the patient landing like a pulse,
unlocks their keyholes with the wire of sight,
searches their rooms for clues when they are out,
pricks when they come home late.

Wonders when they are quiet, jumps when they move,
dreams that they dope or drink, trembles to know
the traffic of their brains, jaywalks their street
in clumsy shoes.

Yet knows them better than their closest friends:
their cupboards and the secrets of their drawers,
their books, their private mail, their photographs
are theirs and hers.

Knows when they wash, how frequently their clothes
go to the cleaners, what they like to eat,
their curvature of health, but even so
is not content.

For, like a lover, must know all, all, all.
Prays she may catch them unprepared at last
and palm the dreadful riddle of their skulls—
hoping the worst.

(1946)

100

THE MOLE

The mole goes down the slow dark personal passage—
a haberdasher's sample of wet velvet moving
on fine feet through an earth that only
the gardener and the excavator know.

The mole is a specialist and truly
opens his own doors; digs as he needs them
his tubular alleyways; and all his hills
are mountains left behind him.

(1946)

YOUNG GIRLS

Nothing, not even fear of punishment
can stop the giggle in a girl.
Oh mothers' trim
shapes on the chesterfield cannot dispel
their lolloping fatness.
Adolescence tumbles about in them
on the cinder schoolyard or behind the expensive gates.

See them in class like porpoises
with smiles and tears
loosed from the same subterranean faucet; some
find individual adventure in
the obtuse angle, some in a phrase
that leaps like a smaller fish from a sea of words.
But most, deep in their daze, dawdle and roll;
their little breasts like wounds beneath their clothes.

A shoal of them in a room makes it a pool.
How can one teacher keep the water out,
or, being adult, find the springs and taps
of their tempers and tortures?
Who, on a field filled with their female cries
can reel them in on a line of words
or land them neatly in a net?
On the dry ground they goggle, flounder, flap.

Too much weeping in them and unfamiliar blood
has set them perilously afloat.
Not divers these — but as if the water rose up in a flood
making them partially amphibious
and always drowning a little and hearing bells;
until the day the shore line wavers less,
and caught and swung on the bright hooks of their sex, earth becomes
        home — their natural element.

(1954)

ANOTHER SPACE

Those people in a circle on the sand
are dark against its gold
turn like a wheel
revolving in a horizontal plane
whose axis — do I dream it?—
vertical
invisible
immeasurably tall
rotates a starry spool.

Yet *if* I dream
why in the name of heaven are fixed parts
within me set in motion
like a poem?

Those people in a circle reel me in.
Down the whole length of golden beach I come
willingly pulled by their rotation
slow
as a moon pulls waters
on a string
their turning circle winds around its rim.

I see them there in three dimensions yet
their height implies another space
their clothes'
surprising chiaroscuro postulates
a different spectrum.

What kaleidoscope
does air construct
that all their movements make a compass rose
surging and altering?
I speculate
on some dimension I can barely guess.

Nearer I see them dark-skinned.
They are dark. And beautiful.
Great human sunflowers spinning in a ring
cosmic as any bumble-top
the vast
procession of the planets in their dance.
And nearer still, I see them— 'a Chagall'—
each fiddling on an instrument—its strings
of some black woollen fibre
and its bow—feathered—
an arrow almost.

      Arrow *is*.

For now the headman—one step forward—shoots
(or does he bow or does he lift a kite
up and over the bright pale dunes of air?)
to strike the absolute centre of my skull
my absolute centre somehow
with such skill
such staggering lightness
that the blow is love.

And something in me melts.
It is as if a glass partition melts—
or something I had always thought was glass—
some pane that halved my heart
is proved, in its melting, ice.

And to-fro all the atoms pass
in bright osmosis
hitherto
in stasis locked
where now a new
direction opens like an eye.

(1974)

LEVIATHAN IN A POOL

I

Black and white plastic
inflatable
a child's giant toy
teeth perfectly conical
tongue pink
eyes where ears are
blowhole (fontanelle
a rip in a wet inner tube
Third Eye)
out of which speech
breath
and beautiful fountains flower

So much for linear description
phrases in place of whale

This creature fills that pool
as an eye its socket
Moves   laughs like an eye
shines like an eye   eyebright
eyeshaped   mandorla
of meeting worlds
forked tail attached
and fin like a funny sail

It is rotund and yet
flexible as a whip
lighter than air going up
and heavy as a truckload of bricks
It leaps sky-high   it flies
and comes down *whack*
on its freshly painted side
and the spectators get wet
drenched
soaked to the hide

Tongue lolling like a dog's
after a fast run
pleased with itself   and you
it seems to want to be petted
rears its great head up
hangs it   its tiny eyes gleam
Herring   minute as whitebait

slip down its throat
Dear whale   we say as if to a child
We beam

And it disappears   Utterly
With so dark a thrust
of its muscle
through silver tines
of water
only streamers of brine
tiny tinsels of brine
remain

II

Swim round the pool vocalizing   the boy says
and *Toot*   they call through their blowholes
Toot toot   Toot
At sea they will sometimes sing for thirty minutes
cadences   recognizable series of notes   songs which carry
hundreds of miles   Sing together   Sing singly
Here in a small pool they vocalize on command
joyous short toots   calls

Why am I crying?

III

Haida and Nootka respond to whistle signals
Each whistle has its own pitch
and each whale knows which is which

Haida and Nootka respond to hand signals
Fresh from the wild Pacific
they answer to hand signals

(The words are for us
who have not yet learned
that two blasts
mean

Give your trainer a big kiss
or a flick of the wrist
means   *Vocalize*)

Chimo   white as Moby
albino   and still a baby
is deaf
and has poor vision
like white cats

(white men and women?)

so Chimo
cannot respond to hand or whistle

Yet this high-spirited
'lissome'
girl of a whale
unexpectedly pale
as if caught undressed
performs
She leaps like Nootka
flaps like Haida
vocalizes

What are her cues and signals?
In what realm
do her lightning actions rise?

I lean upon the pool's wet rail
Through eyes'
sightless sideways glances
seem to see
a red line on the air
as bright as blood
that threads them on one string
trainer and whales

(1974)

Miriam Waddington
(1917—   )

Miriam Waddington (née Dworkin) was born in Winnipeg, and educated at the Universities of Toronto and Pennsylvania, specializing at the latter place in sociology. She has worked as a social worker, and more recently as a professor of English at York University. *Green World* (1945), her first volume of poetry, was followed by *Second Silence* (1955), *The Season's Lovers* (1958), *The Glass Trumpet* (1966), *Call Them Canadians* (1968), *Say Yes* (1969) and *Driving Home* (1972).

Mrs. Waddington writes on a wide range of subjects in a variety of verse forms, and explores with a deep sense of social awareness the several meanings of love, nature, patriotism and reality in a language which draws on the resources of myth, Jewish folklore, symbolism and the relation between sound and sense. Her greatest strengths are her capacity to enter sympathetically into the lives of the less fortunate members of society and to express her own moods and experiences in a rich language to which all can respond.

The poems which follow are taken from *Driving Home*, Oxford University Press, Toronto, 1972.

THE SEASON'S LOVERS

In the daisied lap of summer
the lovers lay, they dozed
and lay in sun unending
they lay in light they slept
and only stirred
each one to find the other's lips.
At times they sighed
or spoke a word
that wavered on uneven breath,
he had no name and she forgot
the ransomed kingdom of her death.

When at last the sun went down
and chilly evening stained the fields
the lovers rose and rubbed their eyes:
they saw the pale wash of grass
heighten to metallic green
and spindly tongues of granite mauve
lick up the milk of afternoon
they gathered all the scattered light
of daisies to one place of white
and ghostly poets lent their speech
to the stillness of the air
the lovers listened, each to each.

Into the solid wall of night
the lovers looked, their clearer sight
went through that dark intensity
to the other side of light.
The lovers stood, it seemed to them
they hung upon the world's rim—
he clung to self, and she to him;
he rocked her with his body's hymn
and murmured to her shuddering cry
you are all states, all princes I,[1]
and sang against her trembling limbs
nothing else is, he sang, *but I.*

They lifted the transparent lid
from world false and world true
and in the space of both they flew.
He found a name, she lost her death
and summer lulled them in its lap
with a leafy lullaby.

There they sleep unending sleep
the lovers lie
he with a name, she free of death
in a country hard to find
unless you read love's double mind
or invent its polar map.

(1958)

¹ See Donne's poem "The Sun Rising".

THE THIEF

Armand Perrault, petty thief
what do I know of your belief?
I have seen the brown-robed monks in spring
with sandalled feet go clattering
down the hill on Côte des Neiges
your church with golden roof a cage
for wandering birds and captive saints.

I have watched your little sisters go
solemn to their first Communion
with veils askew and hair ablow—
stiff paper bouquets in their hands
and flimsy crosses on their necks,
then seen them hide by the stone cliff
of some poor church in Maisonneuve.

From the same parish, aunts in hats
green and painted loud as parrots
have issued forth to board the buses;
between their words, small cries, and fusses
I've heard their false teeth click and clamour
and answered with my English stammer.

However I try to imagine you
Armand Perrault, you don't come through.
At nine years old on a clinic bench
in shorts cut down from your father's pants
with braces too wide for your narrow
        shoulders
or leaning against your mother in church,
you heard the priest at his masses and
        mutters;

109

Or I see you beside the kitchen stove
nursing a toothache with camphor and clove.

Let's try the path your memory takes,
follow the thread until it breaks:
it was hot, from the oak buffet you took
your mother's purse though fingers shook;
you longed for money, the weighty coins
that fell in the pool of your future years
with widening circles; thread breaks here—
the first time you stole, however clear
you figured the reason in later years.

Reasons have not much place with us;
I listen astonished to what you say
about honour and friends and the clever way
there is to stealing and then you ask
disregarding this room, this desk—
if I wouldn't do the same as you
if you were me and I were you?

This is the point we spin around
and this is the answer I haven't found
what have I learned from talking to you
apart from the tricks every pickpocket knew
before he left the public school?
Apart from the pride that is the rule
among the friends you tell me of,
your story is familiar enough.

I haven't heard much that was new to me
or brought any word that was new to you;
it seems our separate selves must curve
wide from the central pulsing nerve
which ought to unite us, you and me;
and only our social selves can meet,
like foreign sympathies, touch and greet,

And out of this force, this difference, build
a small safe area; a bridge; a shield.

(1958)

THE CITY'S LIFE

She is a woman possessed by cities
in love with imperfect faltering man,
her time is taken with analysis
of eyes screened off by glasses, thinning hair
blood out of season, limbs that scan
with perfect measure to the count of death:
these elements freeze into the air
or melt against the salt of road beneath,
and bring her to a strange inverted bliss.

She has no face to fit such ancient pities;
she knows of old the loose-limbed syphilitic
who shuffles beneath the city's towered clocks;
the unshipped seaman who has no union card
is as familiar as her own sharp headache—
the thief, impelled by frequent search for mother
reads life as she does, mean and hard;
lonely; no sister swallow, no bird-brother
listens to their songs or inner talks.

She does not own the burglar's forcing tools
or have his abstract grasp of puzzling parts;
all she has are her own human channels
eyes that observe, a pulse that beats
a heart that moves to other troubled hearts;
somewhere she keeps her mind's prepared collation—
projects, theories, and some orphan facts;
but she is impatient and values them much less
than all the discontinuous evidence
which haunts her every step and holds her powerless
against the city's life, its crowded annals.

(1958; revised 1972)

THE LAND
WHERE HE DWELLS IN

I wake to think about
your lost and broken beauty
and my speechless love.
Of our embraces I remember

only my own whisperings
and your silence,
and the dead centres
when I arrived at those quiet
terrifying balances where
you never spoke my name.

I ask myself, what
was my hope of us and
what was my intention?
I would have liked simply
to hang by my teeth
from your teeth
on those high wires
that criss-cross the striped
circus of the world.

Or to have swum with you
under the water
among the coloured fish
silent and narrow
where hands and fins
brush under darkness
and where medals of light
decorate champion swimmers.

My sleep in your arms
did never awaken you,
my staring at the noble
mask of your face
did never make it live,
and I thought to myself:
what magnificence,
carved and ancient.

This and the shape
of your ear is what
stays in my mind, pictures
that tremble and change,
like what is left over
after a visit to a
breathtaking exhibition
in the museum of a foreign country.

(1966)

ICONS

Suddenly
in middle age
instead of withering
into blindness
and burying myself
underground
I grow delicate
and fragile
superstitious;
I carry icons
I have begun
to worship
images.

I take them out
and prop them up
on bureau tops
in hotel rooms
in Spain
I study them
in locked libraries
in Leningrad
I untie them
from tourist packages
in Italy
they warm me
in the heatless winters
of London in the
hurry-up buses
of Picadilly.

My icons are not
angels or holy
babies they have
nothing to do
with saints or
madonnas, they
are mostly of
seashores summer
and love which I no
longer believe in
but I still believe
in the images,
I still preserve
the icons:

a Spanish factory
worker talks to me
in a street behind
the cathedral he
offers me *un poco
amor,* the scars on
his hand, his wounded
country and the black-
jacketed police; he
touches me on the
arm and other places,
and the alcoholic
in the blazing square
drinks brandy, confides
that fortunes can still
be made in Birmingham
but he has a bad
lung is hard of
hearing and owns
an apartment in Palma.

In Montreal a man
in a white shirt
with his sleeves
rolled up is reading
a book and waiting
for me in a room
with the door ajar,
the light falls
through the open
door the book
falls from his
open hand and he
stands up and
looks at me with
open eyes.

Of course I know
these are only
icons; there is
no such thing
as love left in
the world but
there is still
the image of it
which doesn't let
me wither into
blindness which

doesn't let me
bury myself
underground which
doesn't let me
say yes to the
black leather police
or the empty libraries
or the lonely rooms
or the foggy windows
of cold London buses.

The world is getting
dark but I carry
icons, I remember
the summer
I will never forget
the light.

(1969)

SAD WINTER IN
THE LAND OF CAN. LIT.

I tell myself
I am sad because
it is winter:
but Nelly Sachs[1]
lived through
many such winters
and poured biblical
summer through the
blackest chimneys.

Madame Nathalie[2]
lived through them
too; she comes from
Moscow like my
grandmother and now
she will visit
Toronto and speak
to us in English.
Will I learn
anything from her?

There are many
things I must learn
in order to write
better in Canada.
I must learn to
write & for *and*
and *wll* for *will:*
to put *:* at the
beginning of a line
instead of at the end;
to spell everything
my own swt way just
to prve my indep
endens of all thr
shtty authrty.

I must learn to
write about dead
horses with myths
in my mouth, dead
birds and frogs
that I shot with
tears in my eyes
but compassion in
my heart just
because I'm human
and was born to
original sin.

I must learn to
sing the joy of
penises and all
their frequencies;
the gloriousness
of blow jobs and
how avant garde
is everything in
London Ontario;
they will then
maybe mistake me
for a 26-year-old
white-protestant-
anglo-saxon-or-
duddy-kravitz-ok-
type-jew—a man—or
someone who at least
reads comic books
and was once a cree

indian or a wistful
eskimo.

Dear Nelly Sachs,
dear Nathalie Sarraute,
isn't there anything
you can teach me
about how to write
better in Canada?

(1972)

¹ Nelly Sachs (1891-1971), a German-born Jewish
   poet and dramatist who shared the Nobel Prize
   for literature in 1966.
² Nathalie Sarraute (b. 1900), a French novelist.

EAVESDROPPING

I live in the drawer
of an empty bureau
in one of the rooms
in my house in Toronto,
when the telephone rings
I spy on myself, I wonder
who is telephoning me
when I'm not even here,
when I've gone to
London (except that
I've really stayed
here folded away
in this empty drawer).

Maybe someone is calling
to say: your last book
was a runaway bestseller
you're famous and you're
going to get 15% net
in royalties and a Governor
General's medal and
you can retire on the
movie rights and

You can be a full
professor at last, maybe
a resident poet, take it
easy, go on exchange
to a college in California
eat breakfast on the
terrace in January and get
two years tax exemption.

You can be in
Who's Who this year
next year and last
year and have students
writing you respectful
letters: dear Professor
Waddington what is your
frank opinion of other
Canadian poets?

Or maybe it's that man
from Chicago telephoning
at last to ask me to
dinner to say how he
can't live without me
another minute and
can we please be
happily ever after?

But the telephone
keeps on ringing and
I know if I answer it
it will only be the
insurance adjuster
saying: your car is
a total wreck madam
but not a complete
write-off so what
do you want us to do
about it?

(1972)

TRANSFORMATIONS

The blood of my ancestors
has died in me
I have forsaken the steppes
of Russia for the prairies
of Winnipeg, I have turned
my back on Minneapolis
and the Detroit lakes
I love only St. Boniface
its grey wooden churches
I want to spend my life
in Gimli listening to the
roar of emptiness in the
wild snow, scanning the lake
for the music of rainbow-
skinned fishes, I will compose
my songs to gold-eye tunes
send them across the land
in smoke-spaces, ice-signals
and concentrate all winter
on Henry Hudson adrift
in a boat, when he comes home
I will come home too and
the blood of my ancestors
will flower on Mennonite bushes

(1972)

Louis Dudek
(1918—   )

Louis Dudek is a native of Montreal and a professor of English at McGill University. He has distinguished himself as both a creative writer and critic. One of the new young poets who, in the nineteen-forties, brought a new vitality and a sense of social urgency into Canadian poetry, he has continued to write poetry steadily over the years and has established himself as one of our most conscientious craftsmen. He has also been a most influential literary figure, editing the magazine *Delta* in Montreal, publishing a number of books of verse by young writers, and writing critical and historical essays on Canadian poetic development.

Although Dudek's poetry often is concerned with ideas, his best poems are usually simple lyrics in which he records his delight in the beauty of nature or his compassion for suffering humanity. In all his poems he seeks to avoid stereotyped verse patterns in favour of organic form.

The poems which follow are from *East of the City* (1946) and *The Transparent Sea* (1956), both published by the Ryerson Press, Toronto. His *Collected Poetry* appeared in 1971.

TREE IN A STREET

Why will not that tree adapt itself to our tempo?
We have lopped off several branches,
cut her skin to the white bone,
run wires through her body and her loins,
yet she will not change.
Ignorant of traffic, of dynamos and steel,
as uncontemporary
as bloomers and bustles
she stands there like a green cliché.

(1946)

NOON

Along the piers and by the dockyards,
Like a weird cloud, or a ghost in a cathedral,
Floating, I go towards the freight-cars
And the railings, feeling the brittle sun:
But I become a shrill cloud seen at noontime
Under the sharp silk shot from the sun.

I had imagined that maggots had eaten me
And abandoned my bones to the cheerless air,
I had thought that death had made me a stone
Dull to the sun, and to the life it sprinkles . . .

But now the sun wields his ax from a scabbard
And splits the sidewalk like a slab of steel;
The glass of the buildings that he has shattered
Falls ringing on the square, on the heads of people.

(1946)

BASEMENT WORKERS

Let me give you reminders to keep the image clear,
of roofs too near overhead,
of air sharp with particles, like gravel in sand,
boxes, and tables with torn fringe of metal,
blocked doors, stacks
of coffined cribs ready for crouching mummies,
paper to wrap around our pale corpses:
so, these dispersed, hang in the air between floor and
    ceiling,
where we, darker than miners between the hours
filter the dust in our collapsing lungs—
and think how noon light up there is rocking buildings,
and winds fling skirts about, cooling ankles.

(1946)

BE YOUNG WITH ME

Be young with me, have no pity for the poor,
For the crippled son and the girls already whoring
About the streets, father limping home with a gashed
    head
In drunken joy, his eye forecasting Sunday's pain.

Be young. Have no pity for these poor,
For men unloading spittle, and women clutching
Bags of cotton, garlic puff, and putrid pork.
Have no pity. These are the architecture of the age.

Sympathy like cords trips up the legs of youth
When he lifts the drunk from the sewage cover,
It ravages like measles the upright young daughter
Who fries her own face in the tenth drain of mazola.

But let not your brain sleep among the architectures.
Heap them on the mound of yourself, and let social
    anger
Make ruins in you like an Aztec temple. Be young—
But carry an ax of stone to this murderous civilization.

(1946)

THE DIVER

When your body dives into the lake,
        among the bubbles, some
cling longer to the drum of your skin
than the rest, and when you lie in the sun
        tight spheres of water
hang on to your brown shoulder, before the air takes them
away in vapour—then you run
        and the air chases you
not wanting to leave you, and grass
        catches gladly at your feet.
How is it possible then
        that once you are near me and pass me
my thoughts should not follow you
        also, like a train of servants?

(1956)

TO AN UNKNOWN IN A RESTAURANT

Thank you for sitting,
though the picture I have made of you
        will not be an action
but a meditation, like frost on a window.
You have been very obliging, and patient,
not only to me, but to everyone, the world;
        therefore I will not think of you
with a gun to your temple, nor crying out
like Philoctetes[1], but make you the lonely figure
        in a meditative portrait,
almost lost in your background—not the sufferer
who wakes up to find he has been crucified, but like those
caged animals, born in captivity, who do not know
        why they are unhappy.

(1956)

[1] The legendary Greek hero who killed Paris with a
   poisoned arrow in the Trojan War — also the sub-
   ject of a play by Sophocles.

123

Alfred W. Purdy
(1918—   )

Alfred Purdy was born in Wooler, Ontario; he has travelled extensively in Canada and in Cuba, but has always returned to the rural Ontario countryside which he knows best. He has written about a dozen books of verse and edited an anthology of Canadians' views of the United States, *The New Romans*.

Purdy's verse has developed consistently towards a marked individuality of style and content. His early work was traditional and romantic, but increasingly he has experimented with free forms and with a personal vision which combines exhilaration and gusto, on the one hand, with disillusionment and scepticism on the other. He has always been fascinated with the old, the neglected, the ruined and the unfashionable, and he can see beauty in the most unlikely persons and places.

The poems which follow are selected from *Emu, Remember,* Fiddlehead Books, Fredericton, 1956; *The Cariboo Horses,* McClelland and Stewart, Toronto, 1965; and *Wild Grape Wine,* McClelland and Stewart, 1968. His *Selected Poems* appeared in 1972.

124

ELEGY FOR A GRANDFATHER

Well, he died I guess. They said he did.
His wide whalebone hips will make a prehistoric barrow
men of the future may find and perhaps may not:
where this man's relatives ducked their heads
in real and pretended sorrow
for the dearly beloved gone thank Christ to God,
after a bad century: a tough big-bellied Pharaoh,
with a deck of cards in his pocket and a Presbyterian grin —

Maybe he did die, but the boy didn't understand it,
the man knows now and the scandal never grows old
of a happy lumberjack who lived on rotten whiskey,
and died of sin and Quaker oats age 90 or so.
But all he was was too much for any man to be,
a life so full he couldn't include one more thing,
nor tell the same story twice if he'd wanted to,
and didn't and didn't —

Just the same he's dead. A sticky religious voice
folded his century sideways to get it out of sight,
and lowered him into the ground like someone still alive
who made other people uncomfortable:
barn raiser and backwoods farmer,
become an old man in a one-room apartment
over a drygoods store —
And earth takes him as it takes more beautiful things:
populations of whole countries,
museums and works of art,
and women with such a glow
it makes their background vanish
        they vanish too,
and Lesbia's singer in her sunny islands
stopped when the sun went down —

No, my grandfather was decidedly unbeautiful,
250 pounds of scarred slag.
And I've somehow become his memory,
taking on flesh and blood again
the way he imagined me,
floating among the pictures in his mind
where his dead body is,
laid deep in the earth —
and such a relayed picture perhaps
outlives any work of art,
survives among its alternatives.

(1956; revised 1968)

SNOW AT ROBLIN LAKE

The exactitude of snow is such
that even the Eskimo
achieved mere mention of the stuff
with his 20 names for snow:

the woodpile slowly disappears
all colours blur to white
the shoremiles fade to infinite
distance in the white night —

In fifteen minutes more the house
itself is buried deep
in half an hour the world is lost
on a lazy nebular dead end street —

My little lake is not a lake
but endless ocean where I'll fish
some cosmic Tonga Trench and take
Leviathan on a bent pin —

(1965)

AMELIASBURG¹ STEW

In the bad days
no job and no money
living in this rural paradise
among the friendly cannibals
eating rabbits
when a neighbour killed one
with his car
eating rabbit stew
week after week sometimes
and life was not
just a bowl of cherries

        In the moonlight
on snowy fields
they dance and sing together
celebrating amnesty with dogs
running on their hind legs

like furry people
with cold pink noses
One of them points to this house
near the county road
and mutters to a friend
"That's the guy that eats us
he lives there"
They shudder together
the pink noses turn white
a cloud hides the moon
and there's no one left
in the snowy fields

Now I can't eat rabbit
and a bloody patch on the road
makes me remember
the bad days and think
this patch of smeared red jam
on the highway
will dance no more

(1968)

¹   A village in Ontario where Purdy lives

WILDERNESS GOTHIC

Across Roblin Lake, two shores away,
they are sheathing the church spire
with new metal. Someone hangs in the sky
over there from a piece of rope,
hammering and fitting God's belly-scratcher,
working his way up along the spire
until there's nothing left to nail on —
Perhaps the workman's faith reaches beyond:
touches intangibles, wrestles with Jacob,
replacing rotten timber with pine thews,
pounds hard in the blue cave of the sky,
contends heroically with difficult problems
of gravity, sky navigation and mythopeia,
his volunteer time and labour donated to God,
minus sick benefits of course on a non-union job —

Fields around are yellowing into harvest,
nestling and fingerling are sky and water borne,

death is yodelling quiet in green woodlots,
and bodies of three young birds have disappeared
in the sub-surface of the new county highway —

That picture is incomplete; part left out
that might alter the whole Dürer landscape:
gothic ancestors peer from medieval sky,
dour faces trapped in photograph albums escaping
to clop down iron roads with matched greys:
work-sodden wives groping inside their flesh
for what keeps moving and changing and flashing
beyond and past the long frozen Victorian day.
A sign of fire and brimstone? A two-headed calf
born in the barn last night? A sharp female agony?
An age and a faith moving into transition,
the dinner cold and new-baked bread a failure,
deep woods shiver and water drops hang pendant,
double yolked eggs and the house creaks a little —
Something is about to happen. Leaves are still.
Two shores away, a man hammering in the sky.
Perhaps he will fall.

(1968)

SKELETON BY AN OLD CEDAR

Now the bird's bones are little wires
that thrummed the air and
ants and other insects
negotiate the girders
and small wingbones
that slipped between raindrops
and hemispheres
are wrestled to earth
by nothing
but death
which had no form and shape
in the bird's mind
but came just as the wingtips
circled round this cedar
to meet from another direction
the black speck of his mate
(flightwind opening grey
down on her throat
like a silver pulse)

128

Circling the ragged cedar here
he came
        but never meeting her
four farms away
down by the county road instead
encountering some violence
that left no trace here
encountering a concept
beyond animal understanding
over the darkening pasturelands
that stops all meetings
and halts all travellers
        halfway home

(1968)

LAST YEAR'S CABBAGES
(In a field near Stouffville, Ont.)

Grey heads protruding
at spaced intervals
for 10 acres
of April earth
From a distance
they acquire human features
a mouth and eyes
with a patient expression
But stepped on
they give a rotten squelch
like dead men buried to their necks
a defeated army
tortured by their enemies
and left there
awaiting marching orders
that never come
But fantasy aside
I hate so much waste
my own or another's
and keep thinking about it
on the road home
resolving then and there
when I die
to donate my body to science
all the way to Toronto

(1968)

Raymond Souster
(1921—   )

Raymond Souster was born and educated in Toronto and, except for a period during World War II when he served with the Royal Canadian Air Force in various parts of Canada and England, has spent most of his life in that city. He is a bank clerk by occupation.

Souster was one of a group of young poets—others were Louis Dudek, Irving Layton, and Miriam Waddington—who during World War II began to substitute for the intellectual, witty kind of modern verse established in Canada by A.J.M. Smith, F.R. Scott and the other members of the Montreal Group of the 1920s, a more direct, simple and colloquial style and a more consciously proletarian content. Souster has been a most prolific poet, and since 1944 has published over a dozen volumes of verse. In all his work similar qualities appear: a deceptively simple style, direct observation of his immediate environment, pity for the poor and neglected, and occasional gleams of fun and fantasy.

The poems which follow are taken from *The Colour of the Times*, The Collected Poems of Raymond Souster, Ryerson Press, Toronto, 1964.

THE ENEMIES

What do they care for your books, will they ever read a chapter through or
    a verse without yawning,
Do you ever think they will stand before your painting and enjoy it
Without something lewd to suggest to the mind, or something they do not
    understand to be laughed at,
What do they care how you eat your heart out, how you kill yourself slowly
    or quickly, how you go mad.

You are not of their world, you are strangers, you are enemies, the hated,
Because you laugh at their money, their women, the cheapness of their lives,

Because they cannot laugh off, cannot pay off, the epitaph you have written.

(1944)

SEARCH

Not another bite, not another cigarette,
Nor a final coffee from the shining coffee-urn before you
    leave
The warmth steaming at the windows of the hamburger-joint
    where the Wurlitzer
Booms all night without a stop, where the onions are thick
    between the buns.
Wrap yourself well in that cheap coat that holds back the
    wind like a sieve,
You have a long way to go, and the streets are dark, you may
    have to walk all night before you find
Another heart as lonely, so nearly mad with boredom, so
    filled with such strength, such tenderness of love.

(1944)

THE PENNY FLUTE

On the side street as we came along it in the darkness
an old man, hat beside him on the pavement, was playing
    a penny flute.
The sound was small and sweet, a whisper beside the machinery
of the cloth factory across the street (almost as if he wasn't playing
for an audience, only for himself).
                                 I wondered
who he was, how long he'd been standing there
piping that thin string of music.
                            But we were late
    for where we were going
and young and impatient: we didn't have time for old men
    and thin lonely tunes,
especially tunes played on a penny flute.

(1946)

THE HUNTER

I carry the ground-hog along by the tail
all the way back to the farm, with the blood
dripping from his mouth a couple of drops at a time,
leaving a perfect trail for anyone to follow.

The half-wit hired-man is blasting imaginary rabbits
somewhere on our left. We walk through fields steaming after rain,
jumping the mud: and watching the swing of your girl's hips
ahead of me, the proud way your hand holds the gun,
and remembering how you held it
up to the hog caught in the trap and blew his head in

wonder what fate you have in store for me.

(1947)

MAN DYING

I read it in his eyes: *This is my last summer,*
as he sits day-long through the hours
cap on his head, eyes looking straight ahead
except to turn to follow with a bird
its sudden darting arrow across the grass.

Nothing the doctors know can save him now.
He sits and feels the power in his muscles
slowly diminishing (a struggle to light his pipe).
But when he looks at me there's no fear
in those eyes; death's look is there already.

So Jew fights Jew and Russia's sabre rattles
angrily over Europe. A jet-plane with roar of hell
goes over the house-tops leaving the air tingling.
He sits in his chair and it is nothing to him,
all of it nothing. He's done with us now forever.

(1951)

OLD MAN LEANING ON A FENCE

I'd hate to be that fence
under the old man.

Holding up not just
the withered, shrivelled-up
ready-for-death body,

but the weight of all
the wasted bitter years,
multiplied, grown immense,
bending the shoulders over.

No fence should be expected
to hold up under that load.

(1954)

DOWNTOWN CORNER NEWS STAND

It will need all of death to take you from this corner.
It has become your world, and you its unshaved
bleary-eyed, foot-stamping king. In winter
you curse the cold, huddled in your coat from the wind,
you fry in summer like an egg hopping on a griddle;
and always the whining voice, the nervous-flinging arms,
the red face, shifting eyes watching, waiting
under the grimy cap for God knows what
to happen. (But nothing ever does, downtown Toronto
goes to sleep and wakes the next morning
always the same, except a little dirtier.)
And you stand with your armful of Stars and Telys,[1]
the peak of your cap well down against the sun,
and all the city's restless seething river
surges beside you, but not once do you plunge
into its flood, are carried or tossed away:
but reappear always, beard longer than ever, nose running,
to catch the noon editions at King and Bay.[2]

(1954, 1964)

[1] The Toronto daily newspapers were the *Star* and the *Telegram*.
[2] King and Bay are two of Toronto's main streets, which inter-
sect in the centre of town.

FLIGHT OF THE ROLLER-COASTER[1]

Once more around should do it, the man confided . . .

and sure enough, when the roller-coaster reached the peak
of the giant curve above me, screech of its wheels
almost drowned out by the shriller cries of the riders,

instead of the dip and plunge with its landslide of screams,
it rose in the air like a movieland magic carpet,
    some wonderful bird,

and without fuss or fanfare swooped slowly across
    the amusement-park,
over Spook's Castle, ice-cream booths, shooting-gallery.
    And losing no height

134

made the last yards above the beach, where the cucumber-cool
brakeman in the last seat saluted
a lady about to change from her bathing-suit.

Then, as many witnesses reported, headed leisurely
        out over the water,
disappearing all too soon behind a low-flying flight of clouds.

(1955)

[1] The setting of this poem is obviously Sunnyside, an amusement
park in Toronto on the shore of Lake Ontario.

THIS WIND

This wind comes charging at the house
like a creature unchained, puts its fists
through cracks around windows and gives
curtains enormous breasts, takes a bird
downwind and turns him every way, bruises
tree branches past endurance and leaves them wailing
after each onslaught, then goes careening
over the roof-tops, powdering the air
with snow-sugar.
        O but this wind
of December is the same wind we'll later feel
soft as a girl's touch on our face, warmer
than her embrace, and coming with the scent
of just-opened lilacs sweeter than all
but her most mysterious, never-dreamt-of
long-past-midnight places!

(1964)

THE WILD WOLVES OF WINTER

The wild wolves of winter
swept through the streets last night. Hate glared
in their eyes like unexploded neon
the wind of their howling a thousand moon-curdling moans
the teeth of their hunger endless fields of aching snow.

The wild wolves of winter
welcome nowhere, scratched at doors and windows,
ripped at roofs, tore at chimneys, kept us wide awake,
nervous in our warm, sleep-calling beds.
The wind moan. The crazy clawing. The shaken doors.
    Then as suddenly
were gone, all was quiet. We turned a last time
in our beds and slept.

(1964)

Eli Mandel
(1922—   )

Eli Mandel was born in Saskatchewan, served in the Canadian Army Medical Corps during World War II, completed his doctorate in English at the University of Toronto, and has since been a professor of English at Collège Militaire Royale, the University of Alberta, and York University in Toronto. In addition to writing several books of verse, Mandel has edited anthologies of Canadian verse, written literary criticism, and appeared as a lecturer on the Canadian Broadcasting Corporation networks.

Like James Reaney, Mandel was a student of the mythopoeic critic, Northrop Frye, at the University of Toronto, and his own poetry has strong roots in mythology. His poetry combines violence and tenderness: he sees man as at once predator and prey, the trapper and the trapped.

The poems which follow are selected from *Black and Secret Man*, Ryerson Press, Toronto, 1964, and *An Idiot Joy*, Hurtig, Edmonton, 1967.

THIEF HANGING IN BAPTIST HALLS
After a Sculpture by George Wallace

Amid the congratulations of summer,
polite vegetation, deans, a presbyterian sun,
brick minds quaintly shaped in gothic and glass,
here where the poise and thrust of speech
gleams like polished teak
I did not expect to see myself.

But there he hangs
shrugging on his hung lines,
soft as a pulped fruit or bird
in his welded soft suit of steel.

I wish he would not shrug
and smile weakly at me
as if ashamed that he is hanging there,
his dean's suit fallen off, his leg cocked
as if to run
or (too weak, too tired, too undone)
to do what can be done
about his nakedness.

Why should he hang there,
my insulting self, my deanship, all undone?

He dangles while the city bursts in green and steel,
black flower in the mouth of my speech:
the proud halls reel,
gothic and steel melt in the spinning sun.

(1964)

YONGE STREET MINSTREL
For Raymond Souster

seeing your head weave
        your cheeks twitch
        your shoulders jump
I wonder who hit you
        whom do you hate
        for those early slaps

and seeing you, greyer now,
     but edgy
        all growl
I ask myself what bell rings
in the clamorous arena of your mind

and who will you take on next,
     at forty, the punch
     hard as before, reflexes
     quick, your eyes clear

don't you know they will get you
     in the ring or in some alley
     that they will break your mouth
that even the best go blind
     hear unevident birds

or do you care, thinking of brutes
     buckled and crushed
     the great roar
and the white centre blind with light?

(1964)

THE GARDEN AND THE GARDENER ARE ONE

The mower bucks and roars.
Three passing motorists
bug-eyed as their cars
bulge with Sunday fruit.

In attitude of prayer
her bottom skyward bends
the bulging housewife
as she bows to weed.

Oh God, how tired you must be
of howls and asses.
Weren't these the sounds you heard,
the sights you saw,
when Eve bowed down her apple-cheeks
and Adam roared?

(1964)

HIPPOLYTUS[1]

In the unknowable space between this room
and the running mane of the horizon
where dimmer than thunder the clouds
shudder and toss under the wind's whip
I have been dreaming of horses

I have known mothers larger than boxcars
carrying the freight of years and wars
toward some stockyard of their minds
where they can count the slaughtered time

I too know something of punishment
there have been drownings even here
beside the dry reeds of the lakeless fields
hands have been held out to me
I dare not touch beside that unseen water
and once a beaten animal stumbled by
looking like someone's brother

easier then to praise passion
the strong in one another's arms
testing the machinery of love
the freight that moves the world's
horizons
        everyone knows the rules
what to ignore, when and how to whip
the beaten and to bruise the animals

at the edge of these dark waters
hearing the drums of the world movers
again begins the sound of hoofs
and I see the wet heaving horses of a last rain.

(1964)

[1] Hipploytus, the son of Theseus and
   Hippolyta, was unjustly accused of ravishing
   his stepmother, Phaedra, and was trampled
   to death by horses.

COLD PASTORAL

I thought someone said cathedral
     stature of gold
     artificial bird
and eyes through shining hair.

I thought someone said drowning
     gather of weed
     swirling word
and shining eyes through water.

No one ever said ice ice ice
     globed blood
     wordless wind
and glacial eyes in the cadaver.

(1964)

THREE RAVENS ON A TREE

In a dark world where a black sun rises
I have known three crows like judges
Brooding on a tree: one is in my heart
Which beats thickly a dark tide of blood
Whelming in my throat where the second croaks
Malicious words toward the third who draws
With, ah, bent wings across my eyes his claws.

Do not think I ask for pity, Dove,
Whose warm eggs hatch merciful birds.

(1967)

STREETLIGHTS

they're not sunflowers
yet they burn on their stems
like the golden eyes of those other plants

and they bend
in such an iron complaint
toward the street's inverted sky

I'd like to think
they know as much of final things
as any living creature who endures the dark.

(1967)

SIGNATURES

I have seen the need for the occult
in the eyes of lovers and mothers.
Gardens recently frighten me, grunts
from earth, deep growing things.
I think of Schweitzer dead at last,
his organs mutilated by those roots.
As for the tumult in the streets,
there are knives in water, in taps,
and once I took up from the tracks
beside the water-tower in my town
a huge beet, hairy and huge, that lay
in my hands like an under-water thing.

Thugs rampage. Marines draw down the head,
ancient and tight, her hair in ecstasy,
some Viet-Nam woman who had loved deeply
or who'd wept over her gunman son,
draw down into a pool that head
I've seen in paintings where there was no blood.

What scream issuing from the page
darkens my difficult, philosophic mind?
The room is alien: threats uttered
where only the print and I engage
our locked dialogue.
        Out of the blind
years, remotely, as in earth stirred
by slugs or worms, heaves a memory
of beets and roots; things unuttered
and unutterable, echoing out of print,
out of streams, a signature of rage.

And carnal knives dipped in the water rise.

(1967)

142

Elizabeth Brewster
(1922—   )

Elizabeth Brewster was born in Chipman, N.B., and her first poem to be published appeared in the Saint John *Telegraph* when she was twelve. In the early forties she attended the University of New Brunswick and came under the influence of the group which, in 1945, founded *The Fiddlehead* magazine, in which several of Miss Brewster's early poems appeared. After graduation from U.N.B., she spent a year at Radcliffe College in Cambridge, Mass., and was a Beaverbrook Overseas Scholar at the University of London. She qualified as a librarian from the University of Toronto, and received her Ph.D. in English from the University of Indiana. She has worked as a librarian and teacher; presently she is an Assistant Professor of English at the University of Saskatchewan in Saskatoon.

Her poetry is remarkable for the deliberate cultivation of a "plain" style, for its control over intense feelings, and for its honesty of recollection and insight. Her early poems appeared in the Ryerson Poetry Chapbook series *(East Coast; Lillooet; Roads)*. *Passage of Summer*, the first substantial collection, was published in 1969, and it was followed in 1972 by *Sunrise North*.

The poems which follow are taken from *Passage of Summer*, Ryerson Press, Toronto, 1969, and *Sunrise North*, Clarke, Irwin and Company Limited, Toronto, 1972.

THE LONELINESS THAT WRAPPED HER ROUND

The loneliness that wrapped her round
Was thick as drifted snow,
So thick it seemed to make a sound
Like birds that come and go,
Like startled birds that flap their wings,
And rise, and flutter low.

So thick the air lay on her breast,
As still as vanished mirth;
"Suppose," she thought in that still night,
"Suppose this air were earth."

(1951)

PASSAGE OF SUMMER

It was a long summer, watching my father die,
A cold summer, though, with wind and rain.
　　"I remember," once he told me,
"The time my father died. I was nine years old.
They couldn't tear me away, I remember.
And I remember playing in the caves
By the sea shore, gathering shells.
I remember your grandmother, after she died, came to me
In a dream and said, 'Come, Johnnie, come.' "

He woke and slept and slept and woke again,
And said "Is it day or night? Why are you going to bed
When it's noon outside? But it's such a dark day now."

"There was a joke I used to tell," he said.
"Maybe it was about Pat and Mike or maybe it was about Sandy and Mac,
But now I can't remember. Did I ever tell you that joke?
You would have laughed. I think it was a good one."

"This morning," he said, "I was telling your mother about you.
I thought you had never met before, and I must explain
Just who you were, but then she said she knew you."

"I wish," he said, "I could start all over again,
Have the same time over again, but different.
Only eighty years. I wish I could be young."

144

And then, "I am so tired, so tired, so tired.
I wish it were over."
        Then, "Do you suppose, maybe
A cigarette, or maybe a pill for the pain?"

(1969)

THE MOON IS A MIGHTY MAGNET

The moon is a mighty magnet. It draws
With all its force
The foaming tides
Up the long reaches
Of the shore.
Also it raises the tides of blood and life
In menstruous women
Twisting their bowels and bellies.

It draws desire,
Although it has falsely been called
Diana's bow, the bow of chastity.
Lunatics, it is said,
Are made restless by its changes —
Not just Elizabethan lunatics
But our own less beautifully named
"Mentally ill," in their inspected institutions.

I know a little boy
Who loves magnets,
Keeps them in his pocket,
Makes houses and worlds with them.
I think what he would most like for a birthday present
Is the moon in his pocket. For why?
Because the moon is a mighty magnet.

The moon draws so many things:
Now it is drawing men.
They are drawn up
Like nails or needles
In their metal space capsules.
Soon they will reach the moon,
Explore its hollows and crevices,
Mountains, craters.

145

And will those feet
Plonk-plonk along
The silent silver pastures
Of the moon?

(1969)

GREAT-AUNT REBECCA

I remember my mother's Aunt Rebecca
Who remembered very well Confederation
And what a time of mourning it was.
She remembered the days before the railway,
And how when the first train came through
Everybody got on and visited it,
Scraping off their shoes first
So as not to dirty the carriage.
She remembered the remoteness, the long walks between
        neighbours.
Her own mother had died young, in childbirth,
But she had lived till her eighties,
Had borne eleven children,
Managed to raise nine of them,
In spite of scarlet fever.
She had clothed them with the work of her own fingers,
Wool from her own sheep, spun at home,
Woven at home, sewed at home
Without benefit of machine.
She had fed them with pancakes and salt pork
And cakes sweetened with maple sugar.
She had taught them one by one to memorize
"The chief end of man is to know God,"
And she had also taught them to make porridge
And the right way of lighting a wood fire,
Had told the boys to be kind and courageous
And the girls never to raise their voices
Or argue with their husbands.

I remember her as an old woman,
Rheumatic, with folded hands,
In a rocking chair in a corner of the living room,
Bullied (for her own good) by one of her daughters.
She marveled a little, gently and politely,
At radios, cars, telephones;

146

But really they were not as present to her
As the world of her prime, the farmhouse
In the midst of woods, the hayfields
Where her husband and the boys swung their scythes
Through the burning afternoon, until she called for supper.

For me also, the visiting child, she made that world more
        real
Than the present could be. I too
Wished to be a pioneer,
To walk on snowshoes through remote pastures,
To live away from settlements an independent life
With a few loved people only; to be like Aunt Rebecca,
Soft as silk and tough as that thin wire
They use for snaring rabbits.

(1969)

AFTERNOON AT CURRIE'S MOUNTAIN

The April afternoon
Is still and sweet.
Limp and winter-white,
We lie in the moist heat,

And feel the searching sun
Counting our bones
With cold-hot touch.
We might be sticks or stones,

Or last year's leaves,
Or needles fallen down
From pines that stir above,
Remote and green.

How good to be like ferns
Or roots of trees
Whose branches grow entwined
In forest silences,

Not separated by
The cold dividing mind,
Conscience, or cowardice,
Or the tongue's wound,

147

But leaning close, without
Word, or sigh, or moan,
Sentient but motionless,
In the renewing sun.

(1969)

ON AWAKENING AT NIGHT

I awake at night
from restless dreams
and yearn for the comfort
of flesh on warm flesh
for your hands on my breasts
for your mouth
for your body on mine;

and I long for you
as I might long
for the flow of sunshine
or for water fountains bursting
in my hot mouth.

(1972)

NOVEMBER SUNDAY

I awoke tired
having dreamed of you,
but I cannot remember the dream.

Beyond my window
beyond the city
there are fields
and the fields roll eastward.
I see in my mind
cars driving
the wide flat highways
towards home.

I wonder again, as always,
if I truly love you
or if only my breasts love you,
wanting your hand.

Can I analyse longing
or weigh desire,
dispel an illusion
by reducing it to so much chemistry,
an attraction of atoms for atoms?

I admit I do not understand you.

Nor do you understand me.
My mind has caves
secret and deep
and darkly shaded.
If you came in
you might be lost there
forever.
I also might be lost
exploring you,
might forget the boundaries
of my own selfhood.

To understand
and to be understood
and yet to be beloved
in spite of understanding
or because of it
is, I suppose,
what we all want.

Yet another person
is an island world
alien, dangerous.
All around the shores
are piercing rocks
and on the branches of the flowering trees
are thorns that thirst for blood.

(1972)

BLUEFLAG

So that I would not pick the blueflag
in the midst of the pond
(and get my clothes wet)
my mother told me that it was poison.

I watched this beautiful, frightening flower
growing up from the water
from its green reeds,
washed blue, sunveined,
and wanted it more
than all the flowers I was allowed to pick,
wild roses, pink and smooth as soap,
or the milk-thin daisies
with butterblob centres.

I noticed that the midges
that covered the surface of the water
were not poisoned by the blueflag,
but I thought they must have
a different kind of life from mine.

Even now, if I pick one,
fear comes over me, a trembling.
I half expect to be struck dead
by the flower's magic

a potency seeping
from its dangerous blue skin
its veined centre.

(1972)

James Reaney
(1926—   )

James Reaney was born near Stratford, Ontario, educated at the University of Toronto, and has been a university teacher of English in Winnipeg, Manitoba and in London, Ontario. He has published two books of verse and several verse pamphlets, several plays and dramatic sketches, and has edited the literary magazine *Alphabet*.

Reaney's first book of verse, *The Red Heart*, created something of a sensation in Canada when it appeared in 1949, while he was still a student. Its lightness of touch, its element of fantasy and its delightful combination of childish innocence and adult experience, marked an abrupt break with the then prevalent tradition of earnest social realism. His later work, though more sophisticated and at least equally clever, has never quite recaptured the fresh *insouciance* of that first book.

The poems which follow are selected from *The Red Heart*, McClelland & Stewart, Toronto, 1949 and from *Twelve Letters to a Small Town*, Ryerson Press, Toronto, 1962.

THE RED HEART

The only leaf upon its tree of blood,
My red heart hangs heavily
And will never fall loose,
But grow so heavy
After only a certain number of seasons
(Sixty winters, and fifty-nine falls,
Fifty-eight summers, and fifty-seven springs)
That it will bring bough
Tree and the fences of my bones
Down to a grave in the forest
Of my still upright fellows.

So does the sun hang now
From a branch of Time
In this wild fall sunset.
Who shall pick the sun
From the tree of Eternity?
Who shall thresh the ripe sun?
What midwife shall deliver
The Sun's great heir?
It seems that no one can,
And so the sun shall drag
Gods, goddesses and parliament buildings,
Time, Fate, gramophones and Man
To a gray grave
Where all shall be trampled
Beneath the dancing feet of crowds
Of other still-living suns and stars.

(1949)

THE SCHOOL GLOBE

Sometimes when I hold
Our faded old globe
That we used at school
To see where oceans were
And the five continents,
The lines of latitude and longitude,
The North Pole, the Equator and the South
        Pole —

152

Sometimes when I hold this
Wrecked blue cardboard pumpkin
I think: here in my hands
Rest the fair fields and lands
Of my childhood
Where still lie or still wander
Old games, tops and pets;
A house where I was little
And afraid to swear
Because God might hear and
Send a bear
To eat me up;
Rooms where I was as old
As I was high;
Where I loved the pink clenches,
The white, red and pink fists
Of roses; where I watched the rain
That Heaven's clouds threw down
In puddles and rutfuls
And irregular mirrors
Of soft brown glass upon the ground.
This school globe is a parcel of my past,
A basket of pluperfect things.
And here I stand with it
Sometime in the summertime
All alone in an empty schoolroom
Where about me hang
Old maps, an abacus, pictures,
Blackboards, empty desks.
If I raise my hand
No tall teacher will demand
What I want.
But if someone in authority
Were here, I'd say
Give me this old world back
Whose husk I clasp
And I'll give you in exchange
The great sad real one
That's filled
Not with a child's remembered and pleasant
        skies,
But with blood, pus, horror, death, step-
        mothers, and lies.

(1949)

CLOUDS

These clouds are soft fat horses
That draw Weather in his wagon
Who bears in his old hands
Streaked whips and strokes of lightning.
The hooves of his cattle are made
Of limp water, that stamp
Upon the roof during a storm
And fall from dripping eaves;
Yet these hooves have worn away mountains
In their trotting over Earth.
And for manes these clouds
Have the soft and various winds
That still can push
A ship into the sea
And for neighs, the sable thunder.

(1949)

THE PLUM TREE

The plums are like blue pendulums
That thrum the gold-wired winds of summer.
In the opium-still noon they hang or fall,
The plump, ripe plums.
I suppose my little sister died
Dreaming of looking up at them,
Of lying beneath that crooked plum tree,
That green heaven with blue stars pied.
In this lonely haunted farmhouse
All things are voiceless save the sound
Of some plums falling through the summer air
Straight to the ground.
And there is no listener, no hearer
For the small thunders of their falling
(Falling as dead stars rush to a winter sea)
Save a child who, lolling
Among the trunks and old featherticks
That fill the room where he was born,
Hears them in his silent dreaming
On a dark engraving to a fairy-tale forlorn.
Only he hears their intermittent soft tattoo
Upon the dry, brown summer ground
At the edge of the old orchard.
Only he hears, and farther away,
Some happy animal's slow, listless moo.

(1949)

WINNIPEG SEEN AS A BODY OF TIME AND SPACE

Winnipeg, what once were you? You were,
Your hair was grass by the river ten feet tall,
Your arms were burr oaks and ash leaf maples,
Your backbone was a crooked silver muddy river,
Your thoughts were ravens in flocks, your bones were snow,
Your legs were trails and your blood was a people
      Who did what the stars did and the sun.

Then what were you? You were cracked enamel like
Into parishes and strips that come down to the river.
Convents were built, the river lined with nuns
Praying and windmills turning and your people
Had a blood that did what a star did and a Son.

Then on top of you fell
A Boneyard wrecked auto gent, his hair
Made of rusted car door handles, his fingernails
Of red Snowflake Pastry signs, his belly
Of buildings downtown; his arms of sewers,
His nerves electric wires, his mouth a telephone,
His backbone — a cracked cement street. His heart
An orange pendulum bus crawling with the human fleas
Of a so-so civilization — half gadget, half flesh —
        I don't know what I would have instead —
    And they did what they did more or less.

SPEAKER:

In the past it was decided. While the English beat
the French at Waterloo the French Métis beat the
English at the Battle of Seven Oaks[1] but then in the
end, dear listener, Waterloo counted for more than
Seven Oaks.

(1962)

[1] This battle took place near Winnipeg on June 19, 1816.
French Métis (French-Indian half-breeds) and a few
Indians killed Robert Semple, the governor of Assiniboia,
and twenty of his men, and drove out the Scottish settlers.

THE BICYCLE

Halfway between childhood & manhood,
    More than a hoop but never a car,
The bicycle talks gravel and rain pavement
    On the highway where the dead frogs are.

Like sharkfish the cars blur by,
    Filled with the two-backed beast
One dreams of, yet knows not the word for,
    The accumulating sexual yeast.

Past the house where the bees winter,
    I climb on the stairs of my pedals
To school murmuring irregular verbs
    Past the lion with legs like a table's.

Autumn blows the windfalls down
    With a twilight horn of dead leaves.
I pick them up in the fence of November
    And burrs on my sweater sleeves.

Where a secret robin is wintering
    By the lake in the fir grove dark
Through the fresh new snow we stumble
    That Winter has whistled sharp.

The March wind blows me ruts over,
    Puddles past, under red maple buds,
Over culvert of streamling, under
    White clouds and beside bluebirds.

Fireflies tell their blinking player
    Piano hesitant tales
Down at the bridge through the swamp
    Where the ogre clips his rusty nails.

Between the highschool & the farmhouse
    In the country and the town
It was a world of love and of feeling
    Continually floating down.

On a soul whose only knowledge
    Was that everything was something,
This was like that, that was like this —
    In short, everything was
The bicycle of which I sing.

(1962)

Alden A. Nowlan
(1933—)

Alden Nowlan was born in Windsor, Nova Scotia, dropped out of school in Grade 5, and worked at a variety of manual occupations as a youth. Since 1952 he has lived in New Brunswick, first as editor of a small town newspaper, then as news editor of the Saint John *Telegraph-Journal*, and since 1968 as writer-in-residence at the University of New Brunswick.

Nowlan published his first book of verse in 1958, and has since published seven other books of verse, a volume of short stories and a novel. His poetry and fiction exhibit regionalism at its best: they deal realistically, often ironically but always compassionately, with the ordinary lives of the people of Nova Scotia and New Brunswick, but they do so in such an honest and penetrating way that they break through into universality.

The poems which follow are selected from *Under the Ice*, Ryerson, Toronto, 1961, *The Things Which Are*, Contact Press, Toronto, 1962, *Bread, Wine and Salt*, Clarke Irwin, Toronto, 1967, and *The Mysterious Naked Man*, Clarke Irwin, 1969.

SATURDAY NIGHT

Every five minutes they turn,
with their tires like sirens,
tusking the dirt up on the creek road,
and drive back through town —

      slowing down on Main Street, manoeuvring
      between the farmers' cars, hooting
      at girls on the pavement who reply
      with little hen movements, laughing, waiting.

The boys sport leather jackets and levis,
but that's their underwear,
the car is their real clothing:
at Taylor's Corner they turn again,
their Hollywood mufflers
making sounds furious, derisive, vulgar —
like a bear growling and breaking wind,

      and roar through Main Street again.

(1961)

LOOKING FOR NANCY

Looking for Nancy
      everywhere, I've stopped
girls in trenchcoats
and blue dresses,
      said
Nancy I've looked
    all over
      hell for you,
Nancy I've been afraid
that I'd die
before I found you.

      But there's always
      been some mistake:

a broken streetlight,
too much rum or merely
my wanting too much
for it to be her.

(1961)

THE BULL MOOSE

Down from the purple mist of trees on the mountain,
lurching through forests of white spruce and cedar,
stumbling through tamarack swamps,
came the bull moose
to be stopped at last by a pole-fenced pasture.

Too tired to turn or, perhaps, aware
there was no place left to go, he stood with the cattle.
They, scenting the musk of death, seeing his great head
like the ritual mask of a blood god, moved to the other end
of the field, and waited.

The neighbours heard of it, and by afternoon
cars lined the road. The children teased him
with alder switches and he gazed at them
like an old, tolerant collie. The women asked
if he could have escaped from a Fair.

The oldest man in the parish remembered seeing
a gelded moose yoked with an ox for plowing.
The young men snickered and tried to pour beer
down his throat, while their girl friends took their pictures.

And the bull moose let them stroke his tick-ravaged flanks,
let them pry open his jaws with bottles, let a giggling girl
plant a little purple cap
of thistles on his head.

When the wardens came, everyone agreed it was a shame
to shoot anything so shaggy and cuddlesome.
He looked liked the kind of pet
women put to bed with their sons.

So they held their fire. But just as the sun dropped in the river
the bull moose gathered his strength
like a scaffolded king, straightened and lifted his horns
so that even the wardens backed away as they raised their rifles.
When he roared, people ran to their cars. All the young men
leaned on their automobile horns as he toppled.

(1962)

THE EXECUTION

On the night of the execution
a man at the door
mistook me for the coroner.
"Press", I said.

But he didn't understand. He led me
into the wrong room
where the sheriff greeted me:
"You're late, Padre".

"You're wrong", I told him. "I'm Press".
"Yes, of course, Reverend Press".
We went down a stairway.

"Ah, Mr. Ellis", said the Deputy.
"Press!" I shouted. But he shoved me
through a black curtain.
The lights were so bright
I couldn't see the faces
of the men sitting
opposite. But, thank God, I thought
they can see me!

"Look!", I cried. "Look at my face!
Doesn't anybody know me?"

Then a hood covered my head.
"Don't make it harder for us", the hangman whispered.

(1962)

I, ICARUS

There was a time when I could fly. I swear it.
Perhaps, if I think hard for a moment, I can even tell you the year.
My room was on the ground floor at the rear of the house.
My bed faced a window.
Night after night I lay on my bed and willed myself to fly.
It was hard work, I can tell you.
Sometimes I lay perfectly still for an hour before I felt
      my body rising from the bed.

I rose slowly, slowly until I floated three or four feet
      above the floor.
Then, with a kind of swimming motion, I propelled myself
      toward the window.
Outside, I rose higher and higher, above the pasture fence,
      above the clothesline, above the dark, haunted trees
      beyond the pasture.
And, all the time, I heard the music of flutes.
It seemed the wind made this music.
And sometimes there were voices singing.

(1967)

ESCAPE FROM EDEN

When I was near death,
these little nurses
stripped me naked
and bathed me.
When it appeared
I would live,
they covered
my loins
with a sheet.
When I learned to sit up
and drink consomme
through a straw,
they somehow managed
to wash my back
without removing
my pajama jacket.
Now that I can walk
to the sink and back
without falling,
they knock loudly,
pause,
before slowly opening
the door
of my room.

(1967)

THE MYSTERIOUS NAKED MAN

A mysterious naked man has been reported
on Cranston Avenue. The police are performing
the usual ceremonies with coloured lights and sirens.
Almost everyone is outdoors and strangers are conversing
        excitedly
as they do during disasters when their involvement is
        peripheral.
"What did he look like?" the lieutenant is asking.
"I don't know," says the witness. "He was naked."
There is talk of dogs — this is no ordinary case
of indecent exposure, the man has been seen
a dozen times since the milkman spotted him and now
the sky is turning purple and voices
carry a long way and the children
have gone a little crazy as they often do at dusk
and cars are arriving
from other sections of the city.
And the mysterious naked man
is kneeling behind a garbage can or lying on his belly
in somebody's garden
or maybe even hiding in the branches of a tree,
where the wind from the harbour
whips at his naked body,
and by now he's probably done
whatever it was he wanted to do
and wishes he could go to sleep
or die
or take to the air like Superman.

(1969)

ON THE NATURE OF HUMAN COMPASSION

I said to a herring gull with a broken wing:
Bird, I am sad for you.
If I could make you trust me
I'd take you up in my hands,
carry you back to the city
and hire a veterinarian to heal you.
Or if my stomach were stronger
I'd use a stone or a club of driftwood
to shorten your death.
　　　And the herring gull answered:
Man, you are not sad for me,
but for yourself, so great an egotist
you can put on the body of a bird
or play Mephistopheles to a housefly,
what you call your compassion the conceit
that all living things are Alden Nowlan in disguise.

(1969)

Leonard Cohen
(1934 —   )

Leonard Cohen is well-known as a folk-singer, poet, and novelist. Born and educated in Montreal, at McGill University, Cohen published his first book of verse, *Let
Us Compare Mythologies*, while he was still a student. He has since published six
other books of verse, and two novels, *The Favourite Game* (1963) and *Beautiful
Losers* (1966). He has also travelled extensively in North America and Europe as a
folk-singer.

Like Irving Layton, who influenced his early work, Cohen has a broad range of
interests and attitudes. His poetry is sometimes deeply tender and compassionate,
sometimes light and cynically gay, sometimes bitter and contemptuous. Through all
that he writes runs a strong current of religious feeling, a desire to find personal
salvation and a sense of communion through ecstasy.

The poems which follow are from *Selected Poems, 1956-1968*, Viking Press, New
York, 1968.

PRAYER FOR MESSIAH

His blood on my arm is warm as a bird
his heart in my hand is heavy as lead
his eyes through my eyes shine brighter than love
O send out the raven ahead of the dove

His life in my mouth is less than a man
his death on my breast is harder than stone
his eyes through my eyes shine brighter than love
O send out the raven ahead of the dove

O send out the raven ahead of the dove
O sing from your chains where you're chained in a cave
your eyes through my eyes shine brighter than love
your blood in my ballad collapses the grave

O sing from your chains where you're chained in a cave
your eyes through my eyes shine brighter than love
your heart in my hand is heavy as lead
your blood on my arm is warm as a bird

O break from your branches a green branch of love
after the raven has died for the dove

(1956)

SUMMER NIGHT

The moon dangling wet like a half-plucked eye
was bright for my friends bred in close avenues
of stone, and let us see too much.
The vast treeless field and huge wounded sky,
opposing each other like continents,
made us and our smoking fire quite irrelevant
between their eternal attitudes.
We knew we were intruders. Worse. Intruders
unnoticed and undespised.
        Through orchards of black weeds
with a sigh the river urged its silver flesh.

165

From their damp nests bull-frogs croaked
warnings, but to each other.
And occasional birds, in a private grudge,
flew noiselessly at the moon.
What could we do? We ran naked into the river,
but our flesh insulted the thick slow water.
We tried to sit naked on the stones,
but they were cold and we soon dressed.
One squeezed a little human music from his box:
mostly it was lost in the grass
where one struggled in an ignorant embrace.
One argued with the slight old hills
and the goose-fleshed naked girls, I will not be old.
One, for his protest, registered a sexual groan.
And the girl in my arms
broke suddenly away, and shouted for us all,
Help! Help! I am alone. But then all subtlety was gone
and it was stupid to be obvious before the field and sky,
experts in simplicity. So we fled on the highways,
in our armoured cars, back to air-conditioned homes.

(1956)

YOU HAVE THE LOVERS

You have the lovers,
they are nameless, their histories only for each other,
and you have the room, the bed and the windows.
Pretend it is a ritual.
Unfurl the bed, bury the lovers, blacken the windows,
let them live in that house for a generation or two.
No one dares disturb them.
Visitors in the corridor tip-toe past the long closed door,
they listen for sounds, for a moan, for a song:
nothing is heard, not even breathing.
You know they are not dead,
you can feel the presence of their intense love.
Your children grow up, they leave you,
they have become soldiers and riders.
Your mate dies after a life of service.
Who knows you? Who remembers you?

But in your house a ritual is in progress:
it is not finished: it needs more people.
One day the door is opened to the lover's chamber.
The room has become a dense garden,
full of colours, smells, sounds you have never known.
The bed is smooth as a wafer of sunlight,
in the midst of the garden it stands alone.
In the bed the lovers, slowly and deliberately and silently,
perform the act of love.
Their eyes are closed,
as tightly as if heavy coins of flesh lay on them.
Their lips are bruised with new and old bruises.
Her hair and his beard are hopelessly tangled.
When he puts his mouth against her shoulder
she is uncertain whether her shoulder
has given or received the kiss.

All her flesh is like a mouth.
He carries his fingers along her waist
and feels his own waist caressed.
She holds him closer and his own arms tighten around her.
She kisses the hand beside her mouth.
It is his hand or her hand, it hardly matters,
there are so many more kisses.
You stand beside the bed, weeping with happiness,
you carefully peel away the sheets
from the slow-moving bodies.
Your eyes are filled with tears, you barely make out the
        lovers.
As you undress you sing out, and your voice is magnificent
because now you believe it is the first human voice
heard in that room.
The garments you let fall grow into vines.
You climb into bed and recover the flesh.
You close your eyes and allow them to be sewn shut.
You create an embrace and fall into it.
There is only one moment of pain or doubt
as you wonder how many multitudes are lying beside your
        body,
but a mouth kisses and a hand soothes the moment away.

(1961)

AS THE MIST LEAVES NO SCAR

As the mist leaves no scar
On the dark green hill,
So my body leaves no scar
On you, nor ever will.

When wind and hawk encounter,
What remains to keep?
So you and I encounter,
Then turn, then fall to sleep.

As many nights endure
Without a moon or star,
So will we endure
When one is gone and far.

(1961)

FOR MARIANNE

It's so simple
to wake up beside your ears
and count the pearls
with my two heads

It takes me back to blackboards
and I'm running with Jane[1]
and seeing the dog run

It makes it so easy
to govern this country
I've already thought up the laws
I'll work hard all day
in Parliament

Then let's go to bed
right after supper
Let's sleep and wake up
all night

(1964)

SUZANNE TAKES YOU DOWN

Suzanne takes you down
to her place near the river,
you can hear the boats go by
you can stay the night beside her.
And you know that she's half crazy
but that's why you want to be there
and she feeds you tea and oranges
that come all the way from China.
Just when you mean to tell her
that you have no gifts to give her,
she gets you on her wave-length
and she lets the river answer
that you've always been her lover.
        And you want to travel with her,
        you want to travel blind
        and you know that she can trust you
        because you've touched her perfect body
        with your mind.

Jesus was a sailor
when he walked upon the water
and he spent a long time watching
from a lonely wooden tower
and when he knew for certain
only drowning men could see him
he said All men will be sailors then
until the sea shall free them,

but he himself was broken
long before the sky would open,
forsaken, almost human,
he sank beneath your wisdom like a stone.
>   And you want to travel with him,
>   you want to travel blind
>   and you think maybe you'll trust him
>   because he touched your perfect body
>   with his mind.

Suzanne takes your hand
and she leads you to the river,
she is wearing rags and feathers
from Salvation Army counters.
The sun pours down like honey
on our lady of the harbour
as she shows you where to look
among the garbage and the flowers,
there are heroes in the seaweed
there are children in the morning,
they are leaning out for love
they will lean that way forever
while Suzanne she holds the mirror.
>   And you want to travel with her
>   and you want to travel blind
>   and you're sure that she can find you
>   because she's touched her perfect body
>   with her mind.

(1966)

SHORT STORIES
and SKETCHES

Stephen Leacock
(1869—1944)

Canada's most famous humourist was born in England but emigrated to an Ontario farm with his family as a small boy. He was educated at Upper Canada College and the Universities of Toronto (B.A. 1891) and Chicago (Ph.D. 1903). After graduating from Toronto he spent ten years as a master at Upper Canada College; after obtaining his doctorate from Chicago he became a professor of economics and political science at McGill University in Montreal. He retired from his professorship at McGill in 1936.

Leacock wrote some dozen books on history, economics and political science, but it was his many books of humour, beginning with *Literary Lapses* in 1910, that made him world famous. Perhaps his best single book of humour was *Sunshine Sketches of a Little Town* (1912), which mingles satire, farce, pathos and good humour into a most piquant mélange.

The sketch which follows is from *Literary Lapses*, 1910.

MY FINANCIAL CAREER

When I go into a bank I get rattled. The clerks rattle me; the wickets rattle me; the sight of the money rattles me; everything rattles me.

The moment I cross the threshold of a bank and attempt to transact business there, I become an irresponsible idiot.

I knew this beforehand, but my salary had been raised to fifty dollars a month and I felt that the bank was the only place for it.

So I shambled in and looked timidly round at the clerks. I had an idea that a person about to open an account must needs consult the manager.

I went up to a wicket marked "Accountant." The accountant was a tall, cool devil. The very sight of him rattled me. My voice was sepulchral.

"Can I see the manager?" I said, and added solemnly, "alone." I don't know why I said "alone."

"Certainly," said the accountant, and fetched him.

The manager was a grave, calm man. I held my fifty-six dollars clutched in a crumpled ball in my pocket.

"Are you the manager?" I said. God knows I didn't doubt it.

"Yes," he said.

"Can I see you," I asked, "alone?" I didn't want to say "alone" again, but without it the thing seemed self-evident.

The manager looked at me in some alarm. He felt that I had an awful secret to reveal.

"Come in here," he said, and led the way to a private room. He turned the key in the lock.

"We are safe from interruption here," he said; "sit down."

We both sat down and looked at each other. I found no voice to speak.

"You are one of Pinkerton's men, I presume," he said.

He had gathered from my mysterious manner that I was a detective. I knew what he was thinking, and it made me worse.

"No, not from Pinkerton's," I said, seeming to imply that I came from a rival agency.

"To tell the truth," I went on, as if I had been prompted to lie about it, "I am not a detective at all. I have come to open an account. I intend to keep all my money in this bank."

The manager looked relieved but still serious; he concluded now that I was a son of Baron Rothschild or a young Gould.

"A large account, I suppose," he said.

"Fairly large," I whispered, "I propose to deposit fifty-six dollars now and fifty dollars a month regularly."

The manager got up and opened the door. He called to the accountant.

"Mr. Montgomery," he said unkindly loud, "this gentleman is opening an account; he will deposit fifty-six dollars. Good morning."

I rose.

A big iron door stood open at the side of the room.

"Good morning," I said, and stepped into the safe.

"Come out," said the manager coldly, and showed me the other way.

I went up to the accountant's wicket and poked the ball of money at him with a quick convulsive movement as if I were doing a conjuring trick.

My face was ghastly pale.

"Here," I said, "deposit it." The tone of the words seemed to mean, "Let us do this painful thing while the fit is on us."

He took the money and gave it to another clerk.

He made me write the sum on a slip and sign my name in a book. I no longer knew what I was doing. The bank swam before my eyes.

"Is it deposited?" I asked in a hollow, vibrating voice.

"It is," said the accountant.

"Then I want to draw a cheque."

My idea was to draw out six dollars of it for present use. Someone gave me a cheque book through a wicket and someone else began telling me how to write it out. The people in the bank had the impression that I was an invalid millionaire. I wrote something on the cheque and thrust it in at the clerk. He looked at it.

"What! are you drawing it all out again?" he asked in surprise. Then I realized that I had written fifty-six instead of six. I was too far gone to reason now. I had a feeling that it was impossible to explain the thing. All the clerks had stopped writing to look at me.

Reckless with misery, I made a plunge.

"Yes, the whole thing."

"You withdraw your money from the bank?"

"Every cent of it."

"Are you not going to deposit any more?" said the clerk, astonished.

"Never."

An idiot hope struck me that they might think something had insulted me while I was writing the cheque and that I had changed my mind. I made a wretched attempt to look like a man with a fearfully quick temper.

The clerk prepared to pay the money.

"How will you have it?" he said.

"What?"

"How will you have it?"

"Oh" — I caught his meaning and answered without even trying to think — "in fifties."

He gave me a fifty-dollar bill.

"And the six?" he asked dryly.

"In sixes," I said.

He gave it to me and I rushed out.

As the big door swung behind me I caught the echo of a roar of laughter that went up to the ceiling of the bank. Since then I bank no more. I keep my money in cash in my trousers' pocket and my savings in silver dollars in a sock.

(1910)

Frederick Philip Grove
(1871(?)—1948)

Grove settled in Manitoba in 1912 and became a teacher in various small towns of that province. In 1929 he moved east to Ontario and, after a brief sojourn in Ottawa, bought a farm near Simcoe where he lived until his death. The facts of this Canadian phase of his life are well documented; his life prior to 1912 remains a mystery. In his autobiography, *In Search of Myself* (1946), Grove claims to have been the son of a wealthy Anglo-Swedish family, been brought up in a castle on the southwestern coast of Sweden, and been educated at Gymnasia in Berlin and Hamburg and at the Universities of Paris, Munich and Rome. He asserts that in Paris he was an intimate of the best young writers of the day, and infers a close friendship with André Gide. He claims to have emigrated to America in 1892, and to have spent the next twenty years mainly as a hobo or itinerant farm worker. Current research indicates that the story of his early life is correct in its main outlines, but that his real name was Felix Paul Greve, that he was born in 1879, and that he first came to Canada about 1909.

Grove is usually considered the most powerful Canadian novelist yet to emerge. He was the author of three books of essays, eight novels, the "autobiography" already alluded to, and some seventy short stories. Most of his best work present a grim but accurate picture of life on the prairies in the early decades of this century.

The story which follows first appeared in *The Winnipeg Tribune Magazine* under the title "Lost" in 1926; in the form and under the title printed below it appeared first in *Queen's Quarterly* in 1932. It also has appeared in a number of anthologies of Canadian short stories. A collection of Grove's short stories, entitled *Tales from the Margin* and edited by Desmond Pacey, was published by McGraw-Hill Ryerson, Toronto, in 1971.

SNOW

Towards morning the blizzard had died down, though it was still far from daylight. Stars without number blazed in the dark-blue sky which presented that brilliant and uncompromising appearance always characterizing, on the northern plains of America, those nights in the dead of winter when the thermometer dips to its lowest levels.

In the west, Orion was sinking to the horizon. It was between five and six o'clock.

In the bush-fringe of the Big Marsh, sheltered by thick but bare bluffs of aspens, stood a large house, built of logs, white-washed, solid — such as a settler who is still single would put up only when he thinks of getting married. It, too, looked ice-cold, frozen in the night. Not a breath stirred where it stood; a thin thread of whitish smoke, reaching up to the level of the tree-tops, seemed to be suspended into the chimney rather than to issue from it.

Through the deep snow of the yard, newly packed, a man was fighting his way to the door. Arrived there, he knocked and knocked, first tapping with his knuckles, then hammering with his fists.

Two, three minutes passed. Then a sound awoke in the house, as of somebody stirring, getting out of bed.

The figure on the door-slab — a medium-sized, slim man in sheepskin and high rubber boots into which his trousers were tucked, with the earflaps of his cap pulled down — stood and waited, bent over, hands thrust into the pockets of the short coat, as if he wished to shrink into the smallest possible surface to the attack of the cold. In order to get rid of the dry, powdery snow which filled every crease of his foot-gear and trousers, he stamped his feet. His chin was drawn deep into the turned-up collar on whose points his breath had settled in the form of a thick layer of hoarfrost.

At last a bolt was withdrawn inside.

The face of a man peered out, just discernible in the starlight.

Then the door was opened; in ominous silence the figure from the outside entered, still stamping its feet.

Not a word was spoken till the door had been closed. Then a voice sounded through the cold and dreary darkness of the room.

"Redcliff hasn't come home. He went to town about noon and expected to get back by midnight. We're afraid he's lost."

The other man, quite invisible in the dark, had listened, his teeth chattering with the cold. "Are you sure he started out from town?"

"Well," the newcomer answered hesitatingly, "one of the horses came to the yard."

"One of his horses?"

"Yes. One of those he drove. The woman worked her way to my place to get help."

The owner of the house did not speak again. He went, in the dark, to the door in the rear and opened it. There, he groped about for matches and, finding them, lighted a lamp. In the room stood a big stove, a coal-stove of the self-feeder type; but the fuel used was wood. He opened the drafts and shook the grate clear of ashes; there were two big blocks of spruce in the fire-box smouldering away for the night. In less than a minute they blazed up.

The newcomer entered, blinking in the light of the lamp, and looked on. Before many minutes the heat from the stove began to tell.

"I'll call Bill," the owner of the house said. He was himself of medium height or only slightly above it, but of enormous breadth of shoulder: a figure built for lifting loads. By his side the other man looked small, weakly, dwarfed.

He left the room and, returning through the cold, bare hall in front, went upstairs.

A few minutes later a tall, slender, well-built youth bolted into the room where the newcomer was waiting. Bill, Carroll's hired man, was in his underwear and carried his clothes, thrown in a heap over his arm. Without loss of time, but jumping, stamping, swinging his arms, he began at once to dress.

He greeted the visitor. "Hello, Mike! What's that Abe tells me? Redcliff got lost?"

"Seems that way," said Mike listlessly.

"By gringo," Bill went on, "I shouldn't wonder. In that storm! I'd have waited in town! Wouldn't catch me going out in that kind of weather!"

"Didn't start till late in the afternoon," Mike Sobotski said in his shivering way.

"No. And didn't last long, either," Bill agreed while he shouldered into his overalls. "But while she lasted . . . ."

At this moment Abe Carroll, the owner of the farm, reentered, with sheepskin, fur cap, and long woollen scarf on his arm. His deeply lined, striking, square face bore a settled frown while he held the inside of his sheepskin to the stove, to warm it up. Then, without saying a word, he got deliberately into it.

Mike Sobotski still stood bent over, shivering, though he had opened his coat and, on his side of the stove, was catching all the heat it afforded.

Abe, with the least motion needed to complete dressing, made for the door. In passing Bill, he flung out an elbow which touched the young man's arm. "Come on," he said; and to the other, pointing to the stove, "Close the drafts."

A few minutes later a noise as of rearing and snorting horses in front of the house . . . .

Mike, buttoning up his coat and pulling his mitts over his hands, went out.

They mounted three unsaddled horses. Abe leading, they dashed through the new drifts in the yard and out through the gate to the road. Here, where the shelter of the bluffs screening the house was no longer effective, a light but freshening breeze from the northwest made itself felt as if fine little knives were cutting into the flesh of their faces.

Abe dug his heels into the flank of his rearing mount. The horse was unwilling to obey his guidance, for Abe wanted to leave the road and to cut across wild land to the southwest.

The darkness was still inky black, though here and there, where the slope of the drifts slanted in the right direction, starlight was dimly reflected from the snow. The drifts were six, eight, in places ten feet high; and the snow was once more crawling up their flanks, it was so light and fine. It would fill the tracks in half an hour. As the horses plunged through, the crystals dusted up in clouds, flying aloft over horses and riders.

In less than half an hour they came to a group of two little buildings, of logs, that seemed to squat on their haunches in the snow. Having entered the yard through a gate, they passed one of the buildings and made for the other, a little stable; their horses snorting, they stopped in its lee.

Mike dismounted, throwing the halter-shank of his horse to Bill. He went to the house, which stood a hundred feet or so away. The shack was even smaller than the stable, twelve by fifteen feet perhaps. From its flue-pipe a thick, white plume of smoke blew to the southeast.

Mike returned with a lantern; the other two sprang to the ground; and they opened the door to examine the horse which the woman had allowed to enter.

The horse was there, still excited, snorting at the leaping light and shadows from the lantern, its eyes wild, its nostrils dilated. It was covered with white frost and fully harnessed, though its traces were tied up to the back-band.

"He let him go," said Mike, taking in these signs. "Must have stopped and un-hitched him."

"Must have been stuck in a drift," Bill said, assenting.

"And tried to walk it," Abe added.

For a minute or so they stood silent, each following his own gloomy thoughts. Weird, luminous little clouds issued fitfully from the nostrils of the horse inside.

"I'll get the cutter," Abe said at last.

"I'll get it," Bill volunteered. "I'll take the drivers along. We'll leave the filly here in the stable."

"All right."

Bill remounted, leading Abe's horse. He disappeared into the night.

Abe and Mike, having tied the filly and the other horse in their stalls, went out, closed the door, and turned to the house.

There, by the light of a little coal-oil lamp, they saw the woman sitting at the stove, pale, shivering, her teeth achatter, trying to warm her hands, which were cold with fever, and looking with lack-lustre eyes at the men as they entered.

The children were sleeping; the oldest, a girl, on the floor, wrapped in a blanket and curled up like a dog; four others in one narrow bed, with hay for a mattress, two at the head, two at the foot; the baby on, rather than in, a sort of cradle made of a wide board slung by thin ropes to the pole-roof of the shack.

The other bed was empty and unmade. The air was stifling from a night of exhalations.

"We're going to hunt for him," Mike said quietly. "We've sent for a cutter. He must have tried to walk."

The woman did not answer. She sat and shivered.

"We'll take some blankets," Mike went on. "And some whisky if you've got any in the house."

He and Abe were standing by the stove, opposite the woman, and warming their hands, their mitts held under their armpits.

The woman pointed with a look to a home-made little cupboard nailed to the wall and apathetically turned back to the stove. Mike went, opened the door of the cupboard, took a bottle from it, and slipped it into the pocket of his sheepskin. Then he raised the blankets from the empty bed, rolled them roughly into a bundle, dropped it, and returned to the stove where, with stiff fingers, he fell to rolling a cigarette.

Thus they stood for an hour or so.

Abe's eye was fastened on the woman. He would have liked to say a word of comfort, of hope. What was there to be said?

She was the daughter of a German settler in the bush, some six or seven miles northeast of Abe's place. Her father, an oldish, unctuous, bearded man, had, some ten years ago, got tired of the hard life in the bush where work meant clearing, picking stones, and digging stumps. He had sold his homestead and bought a prairie farm, half a section, on crop-payments, giving notes for the equipment which he needed to handle the place. He had not been able to make it a "go." His bush farm had fallen back on his hands; he had lost his all and returned to the place. He had been counting on the help of his two boys — big, strapping young fellows — who were to clear much land and to raise crops which would lift the debt. But the boys had refused to go back to the bush; they could get easy work in town. Ready money would help. But the ready money had melted away in their hands. Redcliff, the old people's son-in-law, had been their last hope. They were on the point of losing even their bush farm. Here they might perhaps still have found a refuge for their old age — though Redcliff's homestead lay on the sandflats bordering on the marsh where the soil was thin, dreadfully thin; it drifted when the scrub-brush was cleared off. Still, with Redcliff living, this place had been a hope. What were they to do if he was gone? And this woman, hardly more than a girl, in spite of her six children!

The two tiny, square windows of the shack began to turn grey.

At last Abe, thinking he heard a sound, went to the door and stepped out. Bill was there; the horses were shaking the snow out of their pelts; one of them was pawing the ground.

Once more Abe opened the door and gave Mike a look for a signal. Mike gathered the bundle of blankets into his arms, pulled on his mitts, and came out.

Abe reached for the lines, but Bill objected.

"No. Let me drive. I found something."

And as soon as the older men had climbed in, squeezing into the scant space on the seat, he clicked his tongue.

"Get up there!" he shouted, hitting the horses' backs with his lines. And with a leap they darted away.

Bill turned, heading back to the Carroll farm. The horses plunged, reared, snorted, and then, throwing their heads, shot along in a gallop, scattering snow-slabs right and left and throwing wing-waves of the fresh, powdery snow, especially on the lee side. Repeatedly they tried to turn into the wind, which they were cutting at right angles. But Bill plied the whip and guided them expertly.

Nothing was visible anywhere; nothing but the snow in the first grey of dawn. Then, like enormous ghosts, or like evanescent apparitions, the trees of the bluff were adumbrated behind the lingering veils of the night.

Bill turned to the south, along the straight trail which bordered Abe Carroll's farm. He kept looking sharply to right and left. But after awhile he drew his galloping horses in.

"Whoa!" he shouted, tearing at the lines in seesaw fashion. And when the rearing horses came to a stop, excited and breathless, he added, "I've missed it." He turned.

"What is it?" Abe asked.

"The other horse," Bill answered. "It must have had the scent of our yard. It's dead . . . frozen stiff."

A few minutes later he pointed to a huge white mound on top of a drift to the

179

left. "That's it," he said, turned the horses into the wind, and stopped.

To the right, the bluffs of the farm slowly outlined themselves in the morning greyness.

The two older men alighted and, with their hands, shovelled the snow away. There lay the horse, stiff and cold, frozen into a rock-like mass.

"Must have been here a long while," Abe said.

Mike nodded. "Five, six hours." Then he added, "Couldn't have had the smell of the yard. Unless the wind has turned."

"It has," Abe answered and pointed to a fold in the flank of the snowdrift which indicated that the present drift had been superimposed on a lower one whose longitudinal axis ran to the northeast.

For a moment longer they stood and pondered.

Then Abe went back to the cutter and reached for the lines. "I'll drive," he said. Mike climbed in.

Abe took his bearings, looking for landmarks. They were only two or three hundred feet from his fence. That enabled him to estimate the exact direction of the breeze. He clicked his tongue. "Get up!"

And the horses, catching the infection of a dull excitement, shot away. They went straight into the desert of drifts to the west, plunging ahead without any trail, without any landmark in front to guide them.

They went for half an hour, an hour, and longer.

None of the three men said a word. Abe knew the sandflats better than any other; Abe reasoned better than they. If anyone could find the missing man, it was Abe.

Abe's thought ran thus. The horse had gone against the wind. It would never have done so without good reason; that reason could have been no other than a scent to follow. If that was so, however, it would have gone in as straight a line as it could. The sandflats stretched away to the southwest for sixteen miles with not a settlement, not a farm but Redcliff's. If Abe managed to strike that line of scent, it must take him to the point whence the horses had started.

Clear and glaring, with an almost indifferent air, the sun rose to their left.

And suddenly they saw the wagon-box of the sleigh sticking out of the snow ahead of them.

Abe stopped, handed Bill the lines, and got out. Mike followed. Nobody said a word.

The two men dug the tongue of the vehicle out of the snow and tried it. This was part of the old, burnt-over bush land south of the sandflats. The sleigh was tightly wedged in between several charred stumps which stuck up through the snow. That was the reason why the man had unhitched the horses and turned them loose. What else, indeed, could he have done?

The box was filled with a drift which, toward the tail-gate, was piled high, for there three bags of flour were standing on end and leaning against a barrel half-filled with small parcels the interstices between which were packed with mealy snow.

Abe waded all around the sleigh, reconnoitring; and as he did so, wading at the height of the upper edge of the wagonbox, the snow suddenly gave way beneath him; he broke in; the drift was hollow.

A suspicion took hold of him; with a few quick reaches of his arm he demolished the roof of the drift all about.

And there, in the hollow, lay the man's body as if he were sleeping, a quiet expression, as of painless rest, on his face. His eyes were closed; a couple of bags were wrapped about his shoulders. Apparently he had not even tried to walk! Already chilled to the bone, he had given in to that desire for rest, for shelter at any price, which overcomes him who is doomed to freeze.

Without a word the two men carried him to the cutter and laid him down on the snow.

Bill, meanwhile, had unhitched the horses and was hooking them to the tongue of the sleigh. The two others looked on in silence. Four times the horses sprang, excited because Bill tried to make them pull with a sudden twist. The sleigh did not stir.

"Need an axe," Mike said at last, "to cut the stumps. We'll get the sleigh later."

Mike hitched up again and turned the cutter. The broken snowdrifts through which they had come gave the direction.

Then they laid the stiff, dead body across the floor of their vehicle, leaving the side-doors open, for it protruded both ways. They themselves climbed up on the seat and crouched down, so as not to put their feet on the corpse.

Thus they returned to Abe Carroll's farm where, still in silence, they deposited the body in the granary.

That done, they stood for a moment as if in doubt. Then Bill unhitched the horses and took them to the stable to feed.

"I'll tell the woman," said Mike. "Will you go tell her father?"

Abe nodded. "Wait for breakfast," he added.

It was ten o'clock; and none of them had eaten since the previous night.

On the way to Altmann's place in the bush, drifts were no obstacles to driving. Drifts lay on the marsh, on the open sandflats.

Every minute of the time Abe, as he drove along, thought of that woman in the shack; the woman, alone, with six children, and with the knowledge that her man was dead.

Altmann's place in the bush looked the picture of peace and comfort: a large log-house of two rooms. Window frames and doors were painted green. A place to stay with, not to leave . . . .

When Abe knocked, the woman, whom he had seen but once in his life, at the sale where they had lost their possessions, opened the door — an enormously fat woman, overflowing her clothes. The man, tall, broad, with a long, rolling beard, now grey, stood behind her, peering over her shoulder. A visit is an event in the bush!

"Come in," he said cheerfully when he saw Abe. "What a storm that was!"

Abe entered the kitchen which was also dining and living room. He sat down on the chair which was pushed forward for him and looked at the two old people, who remained standing.

Suddenly, from the expression of his face, they anticipated something of his message. No use dissembling.

"Redcliff is dead," he said. "He was frozen to death last night on his way home from town."

The two old people also sat down; it looked as if their knees had given way beneath them. They stared at him, dumbly, a sudden expression of panic fright in their eyes.

"I thought you might want to go to your daughter," Abe added sympathetically.

The man's big frame seemed to shrink as he sat there. All the unctuousness and the conceit of the handsome man dwindled out of his bearing. The woman's eyes had already filled with tears.

Thus they remained for two, three minutes.

Then the woman folded her fat, pudgy hands; her head sank low on her breast; and she sobbed, "God's will be done!"

(1947)

Ethel Wilson
(1888—)

Ethel Wilson was born in Port Elizabeth, South Africa, and spent her early childhood in England. In 1898 she moved to Vancouver, British Columbia, to live with her maternal grandmother, and, with the exception of a few months spent in travelling abroad, she has lived in Vancouver ever since. In 1921 she married Dr. Wallace Wilson, who became a most distinguished physician. Dr. Wilson died in 1966.

It was not until 1937, when she was almost fifty, that Mrs. Wilson began to publish prose fiction, but she quickly established a reputation as a most sensitive craftsman. Ethel Wilson's novels have included *Hetty Dorval* (1947), *The Innocent Traveller* (1949), *The Equations of Love* (1952), *Swamp Angel* (1954) and *Love and Salt Water* (1956). Her short stories, including the one re-printed below, were collected in *Mrs. Golightly and Other Stories*, Macmillan, Toronto, 1961.

HURRY, HURRY!

When the mountains beyond the city are covered with snow to their base, the late afternoon light falling obliquely from the west upon the long slopes discloses new contours. For a few moments of time the austerity vanishes, and the mountains appear innocently folded in furry white. Their daily look has gone. For these few moments the slanting rays curiously discover each separate tree behind each separate tree in the infinite white forests. Then the light fades, and the familiar mountains resume their daily look again. The light has gone, but those who have seen it will remember.

As Miriam stood at the far point of Sea Island, with the wind blowing in from the west, she looked back towards the city. There was a high ground fog at the base of the mountains, and so the white flanks and peaks seemed to lie unsupported in the clear spring sky. They seemed to be unattached to the earth. She wished that Harry were with her to see this sight of beauty which passed even as she looked upon it. But Harry was away, and she had come for a walk upon the dyke alone with her dogs.

It was the very day in spring that the soldier blackbirds had returned from Mexico to the marshes of the delta. Just a few had come, but in the stubble fields behind the high dyke, and in the salt marshes seawards from the dyke, and on the shallow sea, and over the sea there were thousands of other birds. No people anywhere. Just birds. The salt wind blew softly from the sea, and the two terrier dogs ran this way and that, with and against the wind. A multitude of little sandpipers ran along the wet sands as if they were on wheels. They whispered and whimpered together as they ran, stabbing with their long bills into the wet sand and running on. There was a continuous small noise of birds in the air. The terriers bore down upon the little sandpipers. The terriers ran clumsily, sinking in the marshy blackish sand, encumbered as they ran. And the little sandpipers rose and flew low together to a safer sandbank. They whispered and wept together as they fled in a cloud, animated by one enfolding spirit of motion. They settled on their sandbank, running and jabbing the wet sand with their bills. The terriers like little earnest monsters bore down upon them again in futile chase, and again the whispering cloud of birds arose. Miriam laughed at the silly hopeful dogs.

Farther out to sea were the duck and the brant and the seagulls. These strutted on the marsh-like sands, or lay upon the shallow water or flew idly above the water. Sometimes a great solitary crane arose from nowhere and flapped across the wet shore. The melancholy crane settled itself in a motionless hump, and again took its place in obscurity among stakes and rushes.

Behind the dyke where Miriam stood looking out to sea was a steep bank sloping to a shallow salt water ditch, and beyond that again, inland, lay the stubble fields of Sea Island, crossed by rough hedges. From the fields arose the first song of the meadow lark, just one lark, how curious after winter to hear its authentic song again. Thousands of ducks disclosed themselves from the stubble fields, rising and flying without haste or fear to the sea.

Miriam called to the dogs and walked on along the narrow clay path at the top of the dyke. She delighted in the birds and the breeze and the featureless ocean. The dogs raced after her.

Clumps of bare twisted bushes were scattered along the edge of the path, some-times obscuring the curving line of the dyke ahead. In a bush a few early soldier blackbirds talked to each other. Miriam stood still to listen. "Oh-kee-*ree*," called a blackbird. "Oh-kee-*ree*," answered his mate. "Oh-kee-*ree*," he said. "Oh-kee-*ree*," she answered. Then the male bird flew. His red epaulettes shone finely. What a strange note, thought Miriam, there's something sweet and something very ugly. The soldier blackbird's cry began on a clear flute's note and ended in piercing sweetness. The middle sound grated like a rusty lock. As Miriam walked on between the twisted black bushes more soldier blackbirds called and flew. Oh-kee-*ree*! Oh-kee-*ree*! Sweet and very ugly.

Suddenly she saw a strange object. Below her on the left, at the edge of the salt water ditch, there was an unlikely heap of something. Miriam stopped and looked. This thing was about the size of a tremendous hunched cat, amorphous, of a rich reddish brown. It was a rich brown of a lump of rotted wood. Although it did not move, Miriam had instant warning that this creature was alive and had some mean-ing for her. She called the dogs, who came wagging. She leashed them and they went forward together. The dogs tugged and tugged. Soon they, too, looked down the bank at the strange object. In the brown mass something now moved. Miriam saw that the brown object was a large wounded hawk. The hawk was intensely aware of the woman and the dogs. As they paused, and then as they passed along the high dyke path, the hawk's head turned slowly, very slowly, to observe them. Its body was motionless. Its eyes were bright with comprehension. Miriam was glad that she had leashed the dogs. In another minute they would have descended on the hawk. One brown wing lay trailed behind the big bird, but with its sharp beak and tearing claws it would have mauled the terriers, and they would have tormented it. Miriam looked at the hawk and the hawk stared brightly at her. She wished that she could save the hawk from its lingering death on the marshes, but there was nothing she could do. Motionless, save for the slowly turning head, the great hawk followed them with intent gaze. Its eyes were bright with comprehension, but no fear. It was ready. The hawk made Miriam feel uneasy. She walked on faster, keeping the dogs still on the leash. She looked back. The hawk steadily watched her. She turned and walked on still faster.

One of the dogs suddenly growled and then both barked loudly. Round a thorn bush, hurrying towards her, came a man. In all their walks upon the dyke, Harry and she had never met another human being. Miriam was startled. She was almost afraid. The strange hawk. The strange man. The man stopped. He was startled, too. Then he hurried again toward her. Crowded on the narrow clayey path of the dyke stood Miriam and the two dogs, uncertain. The man came close to her and stopped.

"Don't go on," he said urgently, "don't go on. It isn't safe. There's a cougar. I'm going to a farmhouse. To warn them. Perhaps I can get a gun. Turn back. And keep your dogs on the leash," he said sharply.

"Oh," said Miriam, "you must be mistaken. There's never been a cougar on these islands. No, of course, I won't go on, though. I'll turn back at once. But you *must* be mistaken. A dog or even a coyote, but not a cougar!"

"It *is* a cougar," said the man vehemently, "did you never hear of the cougar that swam across from the North Shore last year? Well — I can't stop to argue — there *is* a cougar, I saw it. Beside the dyke. It's driven in by hunger, starving, I expect. Well?"

He looked at her. He held her eyes with his eyes.

"Oh," said Miriam, "of course, I won't go on. I should never have come! I'm so glad I met you. But it's extraordinary!" and she turned in haste.

The man paid her no further attention. He stepped down a bit from the path on to the steep grassy side of the dyke, and pushed past her and the restless dogs. He walked on very fast without another word. Miriam hurried after him along the narrow dyke path, the dogs impeding her as she hurried. This was like a bad dream. Hurry, hurry! I can't hurry.

She nearly ran along the slippery bumpy dyke path, past the brown heap of the wounded hawk whose bright eyes watched her, and past the straggly bushes where the soldier blackbirds flew from tree to tree and sang. She hurried along until she turned the curve of the dyke and saw again the mountains behind the city. The peaks now hung pink and gold in the cold spring sky. To the farthest range of the Golden Ears the sunset caught them. Miriam fled on. The leashed dogs ran, too, bounding and hindering her as she ran. She crossed the little footbridge that led to the lane that led to her car.

She had lost sight of the man a long time ago. He had hurried on to give the alarm. She had seen him stumbling down the steep dyke side and splashing across the salt water ditch to the stubble fields.

. . . Far behind them along the dyke the body of the young woman who had just been murdered lay humped beside the salt water ditch.

The man who had killed her reached the cover of the hedge, out of sight of that woman with the dogs. When he reached the cover of the hedge he began to run across the tussocky field, stumbling, half blind, sobbing, crying out loud.

(1961)

186

Morley Callaghan
(1903—)

Morley Callaghan, perhaps Canada's most distinguished novelist and probably its most skilful practitioner of the short story, was born and educated in Toronto and has lived there almost continuously. As a young reporter on the Toronto *Daily Star* he met and was encouraged by Ernest Hemingway, and after publishing his first novel, *Strange Fugitive* (1928), and his first book of short stories, *A Native Argosy* (1929), he spent a few months in Paris, renewing acquaintance with Hemingway and associating with such other expatriates as Scott Fitzgerald, Gertrude Stein, James Joyce and the young Canadian, John Glassco. The story reprinted below is the product of this brief sojourn in Paris; it should be compared with Glassco's account of the same period in his *Memoirs of Montparnasse* (1969).

Callaghan's many short stories — collected in *Morley Callaghan's Stories* (1959) — and his dozen or so novels, of which the best perhaps are *Such Is My Beloved* (1934), *They Shall Inherit the Earth* (1935) and *The Loved and the Lost* (1951), usually concern themselves, ironically and yet compassionately, with "outsiders", with those who do not fit into the established system or hierarchy.

The story which follows was first collected in *Now That April's Here and Other Stories*, Random House, New York, 1936, and is reprinted in *Morley Callaghan's Stories*, Macmillan, Toronto, 1959.

NOW THAT APRIL'S HERE

As soon as they got the money they bought two large black hats and left America to live permanently in Paris. They were bored in their native city in the Middle West and convinced that the American continent had nothing to offer them. Charles Milford, who was four years older than Johnny Hill, had a large round head that ought to have belonged to a Presbyterian minister. Johnny had a rather chinless faun's head. When they walked down the street the heads together seemed more interesting. They came to Paris in the late autumn.

They got on very quickly in Montparnasse. In the afternoons they wandered around the streets, looking in art gallery windows at the prints of the delicate clever unsubstantial line work of Foujita. Pressing his nose against the window Johnny said, "Quite a sound technique, don't you think, Charles?"

"Oh sound, quite sound."

They never went to the Louvre or the museum in the Luxembourg Gardens thinking it would be in the fashion of tourists, when they intended really to settle in Paris. In the evenings they sat together at a table on the terrace of the cafe, and clients, noticing them, began thinking of them as "the two boys." One night Fanny Lee, a blonde, fat American girl who had been an entertainer at Zelli's until she lost her shape, but not her hilarity, stepped over to the boys' table and yelled, "Oh, gee, look what I've found." They were discovered. Fanny, liking them for their quiet, well-mannered behavior, insisted on introducing them to everybody at the bar. They bowed together at the same angle, smiling so cheerfully, so obviously willing to be obliging, that Fanny was anxious to have them follow her from one bar to another, hoping they would pay for her drinks.

They felt much better after the evening with Fanny. Johnny, the younger one, who had a small income of $100 a month, was supporting Charles, who, he was sure, would one day become a famous writer. Johnny did not take his own talent very seriously; he had been writing his memoirs of their adventures since they were fifteen, after reading George Moore's "Confessions of A Young Man". George Moore's book had been mainly responsible for their visit to Paris. Johnny's memoirs, written in a snobbishly aristocratic manner, had been brought up to the present and now he was waiting for something to happen to them. They were much happier the day they got a cheaper room on Boulevard Arago near the tennis court.

They were happy at the cafés in the evenings but liked best being at home together in their own studio, five minutes away from the cafés. They lay awake in bed together a long time talking about everything that happened during the day, consoling each other by saying the weather would be finer later on and anyway they could always look forward to the spring days next April. Fanny Lee who really liked them was extraordinarily friendly and only cost them nine or ten drinks an evening. They lay awake in bed talking about her, sometimes laughing so hard the bed springs squeaked. Charles, his large round head buried in the pillow, snickered gleefully listening to Johnny making fun of Fanny Lee.

Soon they knew everybody in the Quarter, though no one knew either of them very intimately. People sitting at the café in the evening when the lights were on, saw them crossing the road together under the street lamp, their bodies leaning forward at the same angle, and walking on tiptoes. No one knew where they were going. Really they weren't going anywhere in particular. They had been sitting at the café, nibbling pieces of sugar they had dipped in coffee till Johnny said, "We're being seen here too much, don't you think, Charles?" And Charles said, "I think we ought to be seen at all the bars. We ought to go more often to the new bar." So they had paid for their coffee and walked over to a sidestreet bar paneled in the old English style, with a good-natured English bartender, and sat together at a table listening to the careless talk of five customers at the bar, occasionally snickering out loud when a sentence overheard seemed incredibly funny. Stan Mason, an ingenuous heavy drinker, who had cultivated a very worldly feeling sitting at the same bars every night, explaining the depth of his sophistication to the same people, saw the boys holding their heads together and yelled, "What are you two little goats snickering at?" The boys stood up, bowing to him so politely and seriously he was ashamed of himself and asked them to have a drink with him. The rest of the evening they laughed so charmingly at his jokes he was fully convinced they were the brightest youngsters who had come to the Quarter in years. He asked the boys if they liked Paris, and smiling at each other and raising their glasses together they said that architecturally it was a great improvement over America. They had never been in New York or any other large American city but had no use for American buildings. There was no purpose in arguing directly with them. Charles would simply have raised his eyebrows and glanced slyly at Johnny, who would have snickered with his fingers over his mouth. Mason, who was irritated, and anxious to make an explanation began talking slowly about the early block-like houses of the Taos Indians and the geometrical block style of the New York skyscrapers. For ten minutes he talked steadily about the Indians and a development of the American spirit. The boys listened politely, never moving their heads at all. Watching them, while he talked, Mason began to feel uncomfortable. He began to feel that anything he had to say was utterly unimportant because the two boys were listening to him so politely. But he finished strongly and said, "What do you think?"

"Do you really believe all that's important?" Charles said.

"I don't know, maybe it's not."

"Well, as long as you don't think it important," Johnny said.

At home the boys sat on the edge of the bed, talking about Stan Mason and snickered so long they were up half the night.

They had their first minor disagreement in the Quarter one evening in November with Milton Simpson, a prosperous, bright and effeminate young American business-man who was living in Paris because he felt vaguely that the best approach to life was through all the arts together. He was secretly trying to write, paint and compose pieces for the piano. The boys were at a small bar with a floor for dancing and an American jazz artist at the piano, and Simpson and his wife came in. Passing, Simpson brushed against Charles, who, without any provocation at all, suddenly pushed him away. Simpson pushed too and they stood there pushing each other. Simpson began waving his arms in circles, and the man at the piano threw his arms around Charles, dragging him away. Neither one of them could have hurt each other seriously and everybody in the room was laughing at them. Finally Simpson sat down and Charles, standing alone began to tremble so much he had to put his head down on the table and cry. His shoulders were moving jerkily. Then everybody in the room was sorry for Charles. Johnny, putting his arm around him, led him outside. Simpson, whose thin straight lips were moving nervously was so impressed by Charles's tears, that he and his wife followed them outside and over to the corner café where they insisted on sitting down with them at one of the brown oblong tables inside. Simpson bought the boys a brandy and his wife, who was interested in the new psychology began to talk eagerly to Charles, evidently expecting some kind of an emotional revelation. The boys finished their brandies and Simpson quickly ordered another for them. For an hour the boys drank brandies and listened patiently and seriously to Simpson, who was talking ecstatically because he thought they were sensitive, sympathetic boys. They only smiled at him when he excitedly called them "sensitive organisms." Charles, listening wide-eyed, was nervously scratching his cheek with the nail of his right forefinger till the flesh was torn and raw.

Afterwards, undressing slowly at home, Johnny said, "Simpson is such a bore, don't you think so, Charles?"

"I know, but the brandies were very good." They never mentioned the fight at the bar.

"It was so funny when you looked at him with that blue-eyed Danish stare of yours," Johnny said, chuckling.

"People think I expect them to do tricks like little animals when I look at them like that," Charles explained.

Naked, they sat on the edge of the bed, laughing at Simpson's eagerness to buy them brandies, and they made so many witty sallies they tired themselves out and fell asleep.

For two weeks they weren't seen around the cafés. Charles was writing another book and Johnny was typing it for him. It was a literary two weeks for both of them. They talked about all the modern authors and Johnny suggested that not one of them since Henry James had half Charles's perception or subtle delicacy. Actually Charles did write creditably enough and everything he did had three or four good paragraphs in it. The winter was coming on and when this literary work was finished they wanted to go south.

No one ever knew how they got the money to go to the Riviera for the winter. No one knew how they were able to drink so much when they had only Johnny's hundred dollars a month. At Nice, where Stan Mason was living, they were very cheerful and Mason, admiring their optimism because he thought they had no money, let them have a room in his apartment. They lived with him till the evening he put his ear against the thin wall and heard them snickering, sitting on the edge of the bed. They were talking about him and having a good laugh. Stan Mason was hurt because he had thought them bright boys and really liked them. He merely suggested next morning that they would have to move since he needed the room.

The boys were mainly happy in Nice because they were looking forward to returning to Paris in April. The leaves would be on all the trees and people would be sitting outside on the terraces at the cafés. Everybody they met in Nice told them how beautiful it was in Paris in the early spring, so they counted upon having the happiest time they had ever had together. When they did leave Nice they owed many thousand francs for an hotel bill, payment of which they had avoided by tossing their bags out the window at two o'clock in the morning. They even had a little extra money at the time, almost twenty dollars they had received from an elderly English gentleman, who had suggested, after talking to them all one morning, he would pay well to see the boys make a "tableau" for him. The old fellow was enthusiastic about the "tableau" and the boys had something to amuse them for almost two weeks.

They returned to Paris the first week in April. Now that April was here they had expected to have so much fun, but the weather was disagreeable and cold. This year the leaves were hardly on the trees and there was always rain in the dull skies. They assured each other that the dull days could not last because it was April and Paris was the loveliest city in the world in the early spring.

Johnny's father had been writing many irritable letters from England, where he was for a few months, and the boys decided it was an opportune time for Johnny to go and see him for a week. When he returned they would be together for the good days at the end of the month.

People were not very interested in Charles while Johnny was away. They liked him better when he was with Johnny. All week he walked around on tip-toe or sat alone at a corner table in the café. The two boys together seemed well mannered and bright, but Charles, alone, looked rather insignificant. Without thinking much about it he knew the feeling people had for him and avoided company, waiting impatiently for the days to pass, worrying about Johnny. He said to Stan Mason late one night, "I hope Johnny has enough sense not to pick up with a girl over in England."

"Why worry? Do it yourself now."

"Oh I do, too, only I don't take them as seriously as Johnny does. Not that I mind Johnny having a girl," he said, "only I don't want him to have a complicated affair with one."

The night Johnny returned to Paris they went around to all the bars and people, smiling, said "There go the two boys." They were happy, nervously happy, and Charles was scratching his cheek with his nail. Later on they wanted to be entirely alone and left the café district and the crowds to walk down the narrow side streets to the Seine while Johnny, chuckling, related the disagreeable circumstances of his visit to his father. His father had contended that he was a wastrel who ought to be earning his own living, and Johnny had jeeringly pointed out that the old man had inherited his money without having to work for it. They were angry with each other, and the father had slapped Johnny, who retaliated by poking him in the jaw. That was the most amusing part of the story the boys talked about, walking along the left bank of the Seine opposite the Louvre. Casually Johnny told about a few affairs he had had with cheap women in London, and Charles understood that these affairs had not touched him at all. It was a warm clear evening, the beginning of the real spring days in April and the boys were happy walking by the river in the moonlight, the polished water surface reflecting the red and white lights on the bridges.

Near the end of the month Constance Foy, whom the boys had known at Nice, came to Paris, and they asked her to live with them. She was a simple-minded fat-faced girl with a boy's body and short hair dyed red, who had hardly a franc left and was eager to live with anybody who would keep her. For a week the three of them were happy in the big studio. The boys were proud of their girl and took her around to all the bars, buying drinks for her, actually managing to do it on the hundred dollars a month. In the night time they were impartial and fair about Constance, who appeared to have all her enthusiasm for the one, who at the moment, was making love to her. But she said to Stan Mason one evening, "I don't know whether or not I ought to be there messing up that relationship."

"Aren't the three of you having a good time."

"Good enough, but funny things are happening."

The boys were satisfied till Charles began to feel that Johnny was making love to Constance too seriously. It was disappointing, for he had never objected to having her in the studio, and now Johnny was so obvious in his appreciation of her. Charles, having this feeling, was now unable to touch her at all, and resented Johnny's unabated eagerness for her. It was all the same to Constance.

Before the end of the month the two boys were hardly speaking to each other, though always together at the cafés in the evening. It was too bad for the days were bright and clear, the best of the April weather, and Paris was gay and lively. The boys were sad and hurt and sorry but determined to be fair with each other. The evening they were at the English bar, sitting at one of the table beer barrels, Charles had a hard time preventing himself crying. He was very much in love with Johnny and felt him slipping away. Johnny, his fingers over his mouth, sometimes shook his head but didn't know what to say.

Finally they left the bar to walk home. They were going down the short, quiet street leading to the Boulevard.

"What are you going to do about Constance," Charles said.

"If it's all the same to you I'll have her to myself."

"But what are you going to do with her?"

"I don't know."

"You'd let a little tart like that smash things," Charles said, shaking his hand at Johnny.

"Don't you dare call her a tart."

"Please, Johnny, don't strike at me."

But Johnny who was nearly crying with rage swung his palm at Charles, hitting him across the face. Stan Mason had just turned the corner at the Boulevard, coming up to the bar to have a drink, and saw the two of them standing there.

"What's wrong?" he said.

"I begged him, I implored him not to hit me," Charles said.

"Oh, I hit him, I hit him, I hit him, what'll I do?" Johnny said, tears running down his cheeks.

They stood there crying and shaking their heads, but would not go home together. Finally Charles consented to go with Stan to his hotel and Johnny went home to Constance.

Charles stayed with Mason all week. He would not eat at all and didn't care what he was drinking. The night Mason told him Johnny was going back to America, taking Constance with him, he shook his head helplessly and said, "How could he hit me, how could he hit me, and he knew I loved him so much."

"But what are you going to do?"

"I don't know."

"How are you going to live?"

"I'll make enough to have a drink occasionally."

At the time, he was having a glass of Scotch, his arm trembling so weakly he could hardly lift the glass.

The day Johnny left Paris it rained and it was cold again, sitting at the café in the evening. There had been only one really good week in April. The boys always used to sit at the cafés without their hats on, their hair brushed nicely. This evening Charles had to go home and get his overcoat and the big black hat he had bought in America. Sitting alone at his table in the cool evening, his overcoat wrapped around him, and the black hat on, he did not look the same at all. It was the first time he had worn the hat in France.

(1936)

Hugh MacLennan
(1907 —   )

A native of Cape Breton Island in Nova Scotia, Hugh MacLennan was educated as a classical scholar at Dalhousie, Oxford and Princeton universities. For ten years after obtaining his Ph.D. from Princeton in 1935 he taught Latin and History at Lower Canada College in Montreal. Since 1951 he has been a member of the Department of English at McGill University in Montreal.

MacLennan's first novel, *Barometer Rising*, appeared in 1941, and he has since published five other novels and four volumes of essays. His best novels have probably been *Two Solitudes* (1945), a study of Anglo-French relations in Canada, and *Each Man's Son* (1951), a study of life in his native Cape Breton. His essays reveal his strong interest in Canadian national development and in the natural environment of this country.

The essay which follows is selected from *Scotchman's Return and Other Essays*, Macmillan, Toronto, 1960.

CONFESSIONS OF A WOOD-CHOPPING MAN

Pleasure, profit and beauty from a single afternoon's exercise — what more could a puritan ask, especially when the profit will not be reaped till next year, and the beauty harvested for years to come. As for the pleasure, merely to be alive on an Indian summer afternoon in my part of the country is as close to heaven as my imagination extends.

After the first frost has turned ferns to brown dust and the birds have flocked south, the woods around my house in the country are filled with the living presence of silence. My feet crunch outrageously in the dry undergrowth as I make my way to the heart of the grove. My jeans are stiff with ancient sweat and my jersey is out at the elbows, the red paint has long ago been rubbed off the bow of my Swedish saw and my axe blade, several ounces lighter than when I bought it nine years ago, is honed sharp enough to sever a hair on my forearm. Looking up to the sky through the leaf-patterns I shame my environment by the academic thought that this scene is the equal of Sainte-Chapelle, but the comparison lasts only a few seconds. A hardwood copse in the Eastern Townships of Quebec in Indian summer can be compared to nothing else on this earth, being itself an absolute. By some recurring good fortune I am here; I am here with the axe, the saw, the wedge and the determination to alter the landscape a little. It is a moment that involves every aspect of the slow change in my whole view of life over the past decade and a half.

I was born and raised in a part of Canada where nobody is able to change the landscape. Along the Atlantic coast of Nova Scotia you grow up with the conviction that everything in nature here is as it is forever, and that man, living with the shifting immutability of the ocean and the unshifting immutability of granite rocks, can never dominate his fate, never play artist with nature, but must take life and the world as he finds them. The glacier that set the mould of the Nova Scotia coast (and the coast set the mould of the Nova Scotian character) so denuded the rocks of topsoil that for evermore only a spruce will thrive there. From childhood I accepted the belief that summer, spring and fall are much the same. One is grateful for a spruce if it is the only tree one really knows, but since any spruce is much the same as any other, and since no spruce ever changes its colours, the trees of my childhood helped the granite and the ocean to confirm me in the belief that nature can neither be altered nor improved.

It took me a good many years to respond to the soft luxuriance of the Eastern Townships, where the eye, the ear and the sense of smell are played upon gently and with subtle variations. It took me no time at all, however, to learn that here the landscape can and must be altered from time to time because it is continually altering itself to your disadvantage. A house in the country for summer living must be tied to the earth by close plantings of shrubs and trees, to give protection from the winds and to take away its aspect of being a brash intruder. But a maple sapling grows eight feet a year in this rich, rainy land, and a small fir that looks like an incipient Christmas tree when you transplant it soon becomes a dense screen breeding swarms of blackflies. Where there was one butternut there is soon a grove, and within a decade the pasture in which your house was built has been taken over by a stand of maples, oaks, poplars, wild cherries, honey locusts, old appletrees, hornbeams, birches, beeches and even some stray pines. Their roots are now under your cottage, their branches are joined over your roof, and they have made your home as dark as an animal's den.

The year I bought my house, I cut away every cedar, pine and spruce that crowded it. This was an act with a double meaning for me. I intended to let the sun filter down through the branches of the great hardwoods farther back, and I also needed a symbol of emancipation from the stern acceptance of my youth, I suppose.

"You'll feel naked without some kind of protection, won't you?" said a neighbour. "Now there's only the garden and the lawn between you and the road."

He meant that *he* would; I felt as though cobwebs had been swept from a dirty window. What good to keep other people from looking in, if at the same time I was prevented from looking out? Anyway I live high on a hill away from the village, on a dirt road that leads to nowhere, and the passers-by are few and friendly. Since my land slopes at a twenty-five degree angle and the road is below the house, I can overlook any activity on the road and let my eye take in a view that extends for ten miles over a deep lake indented with bays that lap the feet of thrusting hills. I can look across wind-blown farms and red pine headlands and the shining roofs of new cattle barns.

I began to cut in order to get sun and air into the house and I continued to cut in order to get sun and air into the surrounding woods. The second year I was mildly surprised to discover that the wood I cut had saved me many dollars. Then I bought a lot across the road and down the hill to protect our view. But the view gradually disappeared behind a wall of rapidly growing trees. They were a fine mixture of greens in summer and an unbelievable blend of colours in the fall, but living with them in front of me was like living behind a seventy-foot hedge.

So, over the years, those rapidly growing trees have given a pattern to my life in much the same way that his rotating wheat fields pattern the life of the farmer. Come the fall and I must get to work on them.

I have a neighbour who thinks it a crime to cut any oak, but what do you do if you have two oaks within six feet of one another? I run my hand over the smooth, olive-green trunk and feel the hard muscles inside the bark. An oak, especially a young one, feels human when your hand strokes it. But more than any tree in the forest, the oak needs room to grow. Its roots spread wide and lie close to the surface of the earth. I look up at this pair and see that they have grown like basketball players, tall, thin and not much good for anything else but growing tall and thin. Their lowest branches are at least twenty-five feet above the ground, since it was always dark in here before I got busy cutting out the saplings, and the trees had to thrust high in order to reach the life-giving sun. I feel the trunks of both and decide that the spindlier one must go, to give the other a chance to fulfil the destiny of an oak.

So I go down on both knees, set the saw at the trunk of the victim and get to work. In such a close-grained tree the opening made by the slim saw-blade is almost invisible once the saw has buried itself in the trunk. White dust spurts out, to become brown as the blade reaches the darker heart of the tree. Then comes the crack — hard, solid, vibrating up the entire length of the trunk and echoing through the silent copse. There is a shiver, a twitch in the pinky-brown plumage, a moment of hesitation. As I stand up and watch, one hand on the trunk, the tree nods in the direction I had intended it to fall, then goes down in a swooshing, stately plunge. There is a flash of scarlet as a maple is brushed on the way down. Inevitably the oak comes to rest at an angle, its cascading upper branches caught by the interlocking branches of neighbouring trees.

In the new silence I consider my next move. A fallen tree, even one as modest as this, creates a sizable wreckage. I think of Mr. Gladstone, who used to slay giant oaks, Royal Navy oaks, to relieve his emotions. When Disraeli was extraordinarily witty or the Queen ordinarily rude, another oak on the estate of the Grand Old Man was doomed to fall. And then there was the labour of cleaning up the mess, a job that I know from experience must have taken days. So far as I can discover from my reading, the Prime Minister gave little thought to this aspect of forestry. He was able to sate his aggressions and stalk off, sweaty under the armpits but with his Victorian waistcoat still in place, while humbler men took over the long task of trimming the oak, sawing its trunk into logs, splitting them and trundling them into the woodshed. Humbler men without the need to sublimate a libido must have stacked and burned Mr. Gladstone's slash.

Perhaps the psychiatrist who lives below me on his own tree-enclosed acreage, hearing the crash of my falling oak, thinks I am ridding myself of aggressions, too. He may even think I am slaying a father-image. But no matter what he thinks, my oak has merely been severed at the base, it has not been transformed into cord-wood.

It was cold last night. It was colder still at six this morning when I peered out at the thermometer and saw that the mercury stood at twenty-seven degrees. When I got out of bed at eight and built a fire there was still rime on the lawn. The day was fine and clear, but it was so cold my fireplace consumed ten logs before one o'clock. This year a short cord sells at seven dollars, a long cord at anything from fifteen to twenty depending on what kind of wood it contains. No matter what my woodpile represents to a psychologist, it gives me an intense pleasure to use it for warmth, even though (as the countrywoman remarked yesterday when she came in to clean the house) it takes a lot of sweat to build a woodpile.

I think, sometimes, that Mr. Gladstone missed the best part of tree-cutting. Each fallen tree presents its own problems, and the man who walks off and leaves them is as bad a tree-butcher as the one who murders a copse with a power saw. This oak of mine is entangled with two other trees and of course the simplest thing to do is cut them both down so that all three are prone. But the tree supporting the oak on the left is a rowan, a fugitive from an old garden, probably, and under no circumstances, under absolutely none, will I cut a rowan tree in my own woods. The other is a rock maple, a tree which still fills me with wonder and joy because it was scarce in Nova Scotia and in England almost non-existent. I always have a twinge of conscience when I cut down a maple. But here the maples grow like weeds and this particular one is so close to the rowan it will rob it of nutriment as both try to grow. So the maple goes, and the crack of its fall echoes over the hill.

Still the oak is suspended; when the maple went, its weight was taken by more stuff beyond. There is nothing for it but to cut the oak down to size in the only way left. I start sawing the trunk in eight-foot lengths, each cut about four and a half feet above the ground, which is as high as I can drive the saw. With the entire tree exerting hundreds of pounds of pressure on the saw blade, I must use the wedge. And this means that for the rest of the afternoon these two trees, the oak and the maple, are going to keep me busy.

Towards sunset the logs are piled and split and fragrant, the slash dragged off into a great angular pile to dry and await my pleasure on a future moist day. I come out of the copse and look to see what effect my work has made on the landscape. A little, and the beginning of a lot, because a splendid butternut has now been uncovered and must be given its chance. With that poplar out of the way the sun will slant deeply into the copse and I will have the beginnings of a woodland nave. A forest without sun is like a church without God; I reflect that the thought is corny, but I don't care. Disposing of the poplar will put no burden on my conscience. Along with a ragged spruce, it exists to be destroyed, for if the axe doesn't get to it the insects will, and after the insects will come the flickers and the pileated woodpeckers. Tomorrow afternoon's work is now planned, and it, in turn, will lead to the work of the day after and the day after that. Carving out the raw material of a forest to create a civilized wood is like making a picture or writing a book. One vista suggests another and there is no absolute end to it in a country like ours. But when the season's cutting is over after Thanksgiving, and I go muscle-bound back to the city, I feel as Melville did when he finished *Moby Dick*, as pure as the lamb.

(1960)

Sinclair Ross
(1908 —   )

Born near Prince Albert, Saskatchewan, Sinclair Ross has spent most of his adult life as a bank clerk with the Royal Bank of Canada, mainly in Winnipeg and at the bank's head office in Montreal. He is the author of three novels, *As For Me and My House* (1941), *The Well* (1958), and *Whir of Gold* (1970), and a number of short stories. He has now retired from the bank, and is living in Greece. In all his works, he is concerned with the psychological effects of isolation and alienation.

The story which follows appeared first in *Queen's Quarterly* in 1938 and was reprinted in *The Lamp at Noon and Other Stories* by Sinclair Ross, McClelland and Stewart, Toronto, 1968.

THE LAMP AT NOON

A little before noon she lit the lamp. Demented wind fled keening past the house: a wail through the eaves that died every minute or two. Three days now without respite it had held. The dust was thickening to an impenetrable fog.

She lit the lamp, then for a long time stood at the window motionless. In dim, fitful outline the stable and oat granary still were visible; beyond, obscuring fields and landmarks, the lower of dust clouds made the farmyard seem an isolated acre, poised aloft above a sombre void. At each blast of wind it shook, as if to topple and spin hurtling with the dust-reel into space.

From the window she went to the door, opening it a little, and peering toward the stable again. He was not coming yet. As she watched there was a sudden rift overhead, and for a moment through the tattered clouds the sun raced like a wizened orange. It shed a soft, diffused light, dim and yellow as if it were the light from the lamp reaching out through the open door.

She closed the door, and going to the stove tried the potatoes with a fork. Her eyes all the while were fixed and wide with a curious immobility. It was the window. Standing at it, she had let her forehead press against the pane until the eyes were strained apart and rigid. Wide like that they had looked out of the deepening ruin of the storm. Now she could not close them.

The baby started to cry. He was lying in a homemade crib over which she had arranged a tent of muslin. Careful not to disturb the folds of it, she knelt and tried to still him, whispering huskily in a singsong voice that he must hush and go to sleep again. She would have liked to rock him, to feel the comfort of his little body in her arms, but a fear obsessed her that in the dust-filled air he might contract pneumonia. There was dust sifting everywhere. Her own throat was parched with it. The table had been set less than ten minutes, and already a film was gathering on the dishes. The little cry continued, and with wincing, frightened lips she glanced around as if to find a corner where the air was less oppressive. But while the lips winced the eyes maintained their wide, immobile stare. 'Sleep,' she whispered again. 'It's too soon for you to be hungry. Daddy's coming for his dinner.'

He seemed a long time. Even the clock, still a few minutes off noon, could not dispel a foreboding sense that he was longer than he should be. She went to the door again—and then recoiled slowly to stand white and breathless in the middle of the room. She mustn't. He would only despise her if she ran to the stable looking for him. There was too much grim endurance in his nature ever to let him understand the fear and weakness of a woman. She must stay quiet and wait. Nothing was wrong. At noon he would come—and perhaps after dinner stay with her awhile.

Yesterday, and again at breakfast this morning, they had quarrelled bitterly. She wanted him now, the assurance of his strength and nearness, but he would stand aloof, wary, remembering the words she had flung at him in her anger, unable to understand it was only the dust and wind that had driven her.

Tense, she fixed her eyes upon the clock, listening. There were two winds: the wind in flight, and the wind that pursued. The one sought refuge in the eaves, whimpering, in fear; the other assailed it there, and shook the eaves apart to make it flee again. Once as she listened this first wind sprang inside the room, distraught like a bird that has felt the graze of talons on its wing; while furious the other wind shook the walls, and thudded tumbleweeds against the window till its quarry glanced away again in fright. But only to return—to return and quake among the feeble eaves, as if in all this dust-mad wilderness it knew no other sanctuary.

Then Paul came. At his step she hurried to the stove, intent upon the pots and frying-pan. 'The worst wind yet,' he ventured, hanging up his cap and smock. 'I had to light the lantern in the tool shed, too.'

They looked at each other, then away. She wanted to go to him, to feel his arms supporting her, to cry a little just that he might soothe her, but because his presence made the menace of the wind seem less, she gripped herself and thought, 'I'm in the right. I won't give in. For his sake, too, I won't.'

He washed, hurriedly, so that a few dark welts of dust remained to indent upon his face a haggard strength. It was all she could see as she wiped the dishes and set the food before him: the strength, the grimness, the young Paul growing old and hard, buckled against a desert even grimmer than his will. 'Hungry?' she asked, touched to a twinge of pity she had not intended. 'There's dust in everything. It keeps coming faster than I can clean it up.'

He nodded. 'Tonight, though, you'll see it go down. This is the third day.'

She looked at him in silence a moment, and then as if to herself muttered broodingly, 'Until the next time. Until it starts again.'

There was a dark resentment in her voice now that boded another quarrel. He waited, his eyes on her dubiously as she mashed a potato with her fork. The lamp between them threw strong lights and shadows on their faces. Dust and drought, earth that betrayed alike his labour and his faith, to him the struggle had given sternness, an impassive courage. Beneath the whip of sand his youth had been effaced. Youth, zest, exuberance—there remained only a harsh and clenched virility that yet became him, that seemed at the cost of more engaging qualities to be fulfilment of his inmost and essential nature. Whereas to her the same debts and poverty had brought a plaintive indignation, a nervous dread of what was still to come. The eyes were hollowed, the lips pinched dry and colourless. It was the face of a woman that had aged without maturing, that had loved the little vanities of life, and lost them wistfully.

'I'm afraid, Paul,' she said suddenly. 'I can't stand it any longer. He cries all the time. You will go, Paul—say you will. We aren't living here—not really living—'

The pleading in her voice now, after its shrill bitterness yesterday, made him think that this was only another way to persuade him. He answered evenly, 'I told you this morning, Ellen; we keep on right where we are. At least I do. It's yourself you're thinking about, not the baby.'

This morning such an accusation would have stung her to rage; now, her voice swift and panting, she pressed on, 'Listen, Paul—I'm thinking of all of us—you, too. Look at the sky—what's happening. Are you blind? Thistles and tumbleweeds—it's a desert. You won't have a straw this fall. You won't be able to feed a cow or a chicken. Please, Paul, say we'll go away—'

'Go where?' His voice as he answered was still remote and even, inflexibly in unison with the narrowed eyes and the great hunch of muscle-knotted shoulder. 'Even as a desert it's better than sweeping out your father's store and running his errands. That's all I've got ahead of me if I do what you want.'

'And here—' she faltered. 'What's ahead of you here? At least we'll get enough to eat and wear when you're sweeping out his store. Look at it—look at it, you fool. Desert—the lamp lit at noon—'

'You'll see it come back. There's good wheat in it yet.'

'But in the meantime—year after year—can't you understand, Paul? We'll never get them back—'

He put down his knife and fork and leaned toward her across the table. 'I can't go, Ellen. Living off your people—charity—stop and think of it. This is where I belong. I can't do anything else.'

'Charity!' she repeated him, letting her voice rise in derision. 'And this—you call this independence! Borrowed money you can't even pay the interest on, seed from the government—grocery bills—doctor bills—'

'We'll have crops again,' he persisted. 'Good crops—the land will come back. It's worth waiting for.'

'And while we're waiting, Paul!' It was not anger now, but a kind of sob. 'Think of me—and him. It's not fair. We have our lives, too, to live.'

'And you think that going home to your family—taking your husband with you—'

'I don't care—anything would be better than this. Look at the air he's breathing. He cries all the time. For his sake, Paul. What's ahead of him here, even if you do get crops?'

He clenched his lips a minute, then, with his eyes hard and contemptuous, struck back, 'As much as in town, growing up a pauper. You're the one who wants to go, it's not for his sake. You think that in town you'd have a better time—not so much work—more clothes—'

'Maybe—' She dropped her head defencelessly. 'I'm young still. I like pretty things.'

There was silence now—a deep fastness of it enclosed by rushing wind and creaking walls. It seemed the yellow lamplight cast a hush upon them. Through the haze of dusty air the walls receded, dimmed, and came again. At last she raised her head and said listlessly, 'Go on—your dinner's getting cold. Don't sit and stare at me. I've said it all.'

The spent quietness in her voice was even harder to endure than her anger. It reproached him, against his will insisted that he see and understand her lot. To justify himself he tried, 'I was a poor man when you married me. You said you didn't mind. Farming's never been easy, and never will be.'

'I wouldn't mind the work or the skimping if there was something to look forward to. It's the hopelessness—going on—watching the land blow away.'

'The land's all right,' he repeated. 'The dry years won't last forever.'

'But it's not just dry years, Paul!' The little sob in her voice gave way suddenly to a ring of exasperation. 'Will you never see? It's the land itself—the soil. You've plowed and harrowed until there's not a root of fibre left to hold it down. That's why the soil drifts—that's why in a year or two there'll be nothing left but the bare clay. If in the first place you farmers had taken care of your land—if you hadn't been so greedy for wheat every year—'

She had taught school before she married him, and of late in her anger there had been a kind of disdain, an attitude almost of condescension, as if she no longer looked upon the farmers as her equals. He sat still, his eyes fixed on the yellow lamp flame, and seeming to know her words had hurt him, she went on softly, 'I want to help you, Paul. That's why I won't sit quiet while you go on wasting your life. You're only thirty—you owe it to yourself as well as me.'

He sat staring at the lamp without answering, his mouth sullen. It seemed indifference now, as if he were ignoring her, and stung to anger again she cried, 'Do you ever think what my life is? Two rooms to live in—once a month to town, and nothing to spend when I get there. I'm still young—I wasn't brought up this way.'

'You're a farmer's wife now. It doesn't matter what you used to be, or how you were brought up. You get enough to eat and wear. Just now that's all I can do. I'm not to blame that we've been dried out five years.'

'Enough to eat!' she laughed back shrilly. 'Enough salt pork—enough potatoes and eggs. And look—' Springing to the middle of the room she thrust out a foot for him to see the scuffed old slipper. 'When they're completely gone I suppose you'll tell me I can go barefoot—that I'm a farmer's wife—that it's not your fault we're dried out—'

'And what about these?' He pushed his chair away from the table now to let her see what he was wearing. 'Cowhide—hard as boards—but my feet are so calloused I don't feel them any more.'

Then he stood up, ashamed of having tried to match her hardships with his own. But frightened now as he reached for his smock she pressed close to him. 'Don't go yet. I brood and worry when I'm left alone. Please, Paul—you can't work on the land anyway.'

'And keep on like this? You start before I'm through the door. Week in and week out—I've troubles enough of my own.'

'Paul—please stay—' The eyes were glazed now, distended a little as if with the intensity of her dread and pleading. 'We won't quarrel any more. Hear it! I can't work—I just stand still and listen—'

The eyes frightened him, but responding to a kind of instinct that he must withstand her, that it was his self-respect and manhood against the fretful weakness of a woman, he answered unfeelingly, 'In here safe and quiet—you don't know how well off you are. If you were out in it—fighting it—swallowing it—'

'Sometimes, Paul, I wish I was. I'm so caged—if I could only break away and run. See—I stand like this all day. I can't relax. My throat's so tight it aches—'

With a jerk he freed his smock from her clutch. 'If I stay we'll only keep on all afternoon. Wait till tomorrow—we'll talk things over when the wind goes down.'

Then without meeting her eyes again he swung outside, and doubled low against the buffets of the wind, fought his way slowly toward the stable. There was a deep hollow calm within, a vast darkness engulfed beneath the tides of moaning wind. He stood breathless a moment, hushed almost to a stupor by the sudden extinction of the storm and the stillness that enfolded him. It was a long, far-reaching stillness. The first dim stalls and rafters led the way into cavern-like obscurity, into vaults and recesses that extended far beyond the stable walls. Nor in these first quiet moments did he forbid the illusion, the sense of release from a harsh, familiar world into one of peace and darkness. The contentious mood that his stand against Ellen had roused him to, his tenacity and clenched despair before the ravages of wind, it was ebbing now, losing itself in the cover of darkness. Ellen and the wheat seemed remote, unimportant. At a whinny from the bay mare, Bess, he went forward and into her stall. She seemed grateful for his presence, and thrust her nose deep between his arm and body. They stood a long time motionless, comforting and assuring each other.

For soon again the first deep sense of quiet and peace was shrunken to the battered shelter of the stable. Instead of release or escape from the assaulting wind, the walls were but a feeble stand against it. They creaked and sawed as if the fingers of a giant were tightening to collapse them; the empty loft sustained a pipelike cry that rose and fell but never ended. He saw the dust-black sky again, and his fields blown smooth with drifted soil.

But always, even while listening to the storm outside, he could feel the tense and apprehensive stillness of the stable. There was not a hoof that clumped or shifted, not a rub of halter against manger. And yet, though it had been a strange stable, he would have known, despite the darkness, that every stall was filled. They, too, were all listening.

From Bess he went to the big grey gelding, Prince. Prince was twenty years old, with rib-grooved sides, and high, protruding hipbones. Paul ran his hand over the ribs, and felt a sudden shame, a sting of fear that Ellen might be right in what she said. For wasn't it true—nine years a farmer now on his own land, and still he couldn't even feed his horses? What, then, could he hope to do for his wife and son?

There was much he planned. And so vivid was the future of his planning, so real and constant, that often the actual present was but half felt, but half endured. Its difficulties were lessened by a confidence in what lay beyond them. A new house— land for the boy—land and still more land—or education, whatever he might want.

But all the time was he only a blind and stubborn fool? Was Ellen right? Was he trampling on her life, and throwing away his own? The five years since he married her, were they to go on repeating themselves, five, ten, twenty, until all the brave future he looked forward to was but a stark and futile past?

She looked forward to no future. She had no faith or dream with which to make the dust and the poverty less real. He understood suddenly. He saw her face again as only a few minutes ago it had begged him not to leave her. The darkness round him now was as a slate on which her lonely terror limned itself. He went from Prince to the other horses, combing their manes and forelocks with his fingers, but always it was her face before him, its staring eyes and twisted suffering. 'See Paul—I stand like this all day. I just stand still—My throat's so tight it aches—'

And always the wind, the creak of walls, the wild lipless wailing through the loft. Until at last as he stood there, staring into the livid face before him, it seemed that this scream of wind was a cry from her parched and frantic lips. He knew it couldn't be, he knew that she was safe within the house, but still the wind persisted in a woman's cry. The cry of a woman with eyes like those that watched him through the dark. Eyes that were mad now—lips that even as they cried still pleaded, 'See, Paul—I stand like this all day. I just stand still—so caged! If I could only run!'

He saw her running, pulled and driven headlong by the wind, but when at last he returned to the house, compelled by his anxiety, she was walking quietly back and forth with the baby in her arms. Careful, despite his concern, not to reveal a fear or weakness that she might think capitulation to her wishes, he watched a moment through the window, and then went off to the tool shed to mend harness. All afternoon he stitched and riveted. It was easier with the lantern lit and his hands occupied. There was a wind whining high past the tool shed too, but it was only wind. He remembered the arguments with which Ellen had tried to persuade him away from the farm, and one by one he defeated them. There would be rain again—next year or the next. Maybe in his ignorance he had farmed his land the wrong way, seeding wheat every year, working the soil till it was lifeless dust—but he would do better now. He would plant clover and alfalfa, breed cattle, acre by acre and year by year restore to his land its fibre and fertility. That was something to work for, a way to prove himself. It was ruthless wind, blackening the sky with his earth, but it was not his master. Out of his land it had made a wilderness. He now, out of the wilderness, would make a farm and home again.

Tonight he must talk with Ellen. Patiently, when the wind was down, and they were both quiet again. It was she who had told him to grow fibrous crops, who had called him an ignorant fool because he kept on with summer fallow and wheat. Now she might be gratified to find him acknowledging her wisdom. Perhaps she would begin to feel the power and steadfastness of the land, to take a pride in it, to understand that he was not a fool, but working for her future and their son's.

And already the wind was slackening. At four o'clock he could sense a lull. At five, straining his eyes from the tool shed doorway, he could make out a neighbour's buildings half a mile away. It was over—three days of blight and havoc like a scourge—three days so bitter and so long that for a moment he stood still, unseeing, his senses idle with a numbness of relief.

But only for a moment. Suddenly he emerged from the numbness; suddenly the fields before him struck his eyes to comprehension. They lay black, naked. Beaten and mounded smooth with dust as if a sea in gentle swell had turned to stone. And though he had tried to prepare himself for such a scene, though he had known since yesterday that not a blade would last the storm, still now, before the utter waste confronting him, he sickened and stood cold. Suddenly like the fields he was naked. Everything that had sheathed him a little from the realities of existence: vision and purpose, faith in the land, in the future, in himself—it was all rent now, stripped away. 'Desert,' he heard her voice begin to sob. 'Desert, you fool—the lamp lit at noon!'

In the stable again, measuring out their feed to the horses, he wondered what he would say to her tonight. For so deep were his instincts of loyalty to the land that still, even with the images of his betrayal stark upon his mind, his concern was how to withstand her, how to go on again and justify himself. It had not occurred to him yet that he might or should abandon the land. He had lived with it too long. Rather was his impulse still to defend it—as a man defends against the scorn of strangers even his most worthless kin.

He fed his horses, then waited. She too would be waiting, ready to cry at him, 'Look now—that crop that was to feed and clothe us! And you'll still keep on! You'll still say "Next year—there'll be rain next year"!'

But she was gone when he reached the house. The door was open, the lamp blown out, the crib empty. The dishes from their meal at noon were still on the table. She had perhaps begun to sweep, for the broom was lying in the middle of the floor. He tried to call, but a terror clamped upon his throat. In the wan, returning light it seemed that even the deserted kitchen was straining to whisper what it had seen. The tatters of the storm still whimpered through the eaves, and in their moaning told the desolation of the miles they had traversed. On tiptoe at last he crossed to the adjoining room; then at the threshold, without even a glance inside to satisfy himself that she was really gone, he wheeled again and plunged outside.

He ran a long time—distraught and headlong as a few hours ago he had seemed to watch her run—around the farmyard, a little distance into the pasture, back again blindly to the house to see whether she had returned—and then at a stumble down the road for help.

They joined him in the search, rode away for others, spread calling across the fields in the direction she might have been carried by the wind—but nearly two hours later it was himself who came upon her. Crouched down against a drift of sand as if for shelter, her hair in matted strands around her neck and face, the child clasped tightly in her arms.

The child was quite cold. It had been her arms, perhaps, too frantic to protect him, or the smother of dust upon his throat and lungs. 'Hold him,' she said as he knelt beside her. 'So—with his face away from the wind. Hold him until I tidy my hair.'

Her eyes were still wide in an immobile stare, but with her lips she smiled at him. For a long time he knelt transfixed, trying to speak to her, touching fearfully with his fingertips the dust-grimed cheeks and eyelids of the child. At last she said, 'I'll take him again. Such clumsy hands—you don't know how to hold a baby yet. See how his head falls forward on your arm.'

Yet it all seemed familiar—a confirmation of what he had known since noon. He gave her the child, then, gathering them up in his arms, struggled to his feet, and turned toward home.

It was evening now. Across the fields a few spent clouds of dust still shook and fled. Beyond, as if through smoke, the sunset smouldered like a distant fire.

He walked with a long dull stride, his eyes before him, heedless of her weight. Once he glanced down and with her eyes she still was smiling. 'Such strong arms, Paul—and I was so tired just carrying him . . . .'

He tried to answer, but it seemed that now the dusk was drawn apart in breathless waiting, a finger on its lips until they passed. 'You were right, Paul . . . .' Her voice came whispering, as if she too could feel the hush. 'You said tonight we'd see the storm go down. So still now, and a red sky—it means tomorrow will be fine.'

(1968)

Norman Levine
(1924—)

Born in Ottawa, Norman Levine was educated at the High School of Commerce there and at McGill University in Montreal. During World War II he served in England with the Royal Canadian Air Force. Since 1949 he has lived mainly in England, although he returned to Canada as a writer-in-residence at the University of New Brunswick for the academic year 1965-66. His present home is in St. Ives, Cornwall.

Levine is the author of a book of poems, *The Tightrope Walker* (1950), of a travelogue, *Canada Made Me* (1958), of two novels, *The Angled Road* (1952) and *From a Seaside Town* (1969), and of two books of short stories, *One Way Ticket* (1961) and *I Don't Want to Know Anyone Too Well and Other Stories* (1971).

The story which follows is from *One Way Ticket*, McClelland and Stewart, Toronto, 1961.

THE COCKS ARE CROWING

Until I was eighteen I spent my summer holidays at the family cottage on the banks of the Richelieu south of Montreal and six miles north of the American border. Two miles away is the French Canadian village of Ile Aux Noix. There is an island in the river, opposite the village, with a decaying fort and a moat with shallow water. Water lilies and a thin green scum cover the surface. During the last war the fort was used as an internment camp for aliens.

I imagine that until the road was built, during prohibition, the river was busy. But though the channel is still occasionally dredged and the red and black buoys that mark its passage are sometimes repainted, I have seen few riverboats go by. The only traffic now comes from the small hired boats with the sport fishermen. For alongside the channel the weeds are thick — so thick that sometimes I have been stopped, as the keel or the propeller become entangled.

The countryside is not exciting to look at. Even from the water. It is flat with a few isolated trees and farm fences. The farmers have small fields. They are all French Canadian. They grow wheat, corn, potatoes. Some have chickens and pigs. The two hotels along the bank shut in winter. They are there for the American businessmen who come down in the summer and fall to play cards, drink, and fish. For this part of the Richelieu has some of the best fishing I know. I've anchored by the red buoy, opposite the Grand Hotel, for muskelonge; trolled along the banks for pike; caught carp at night using a light and spearing them as they rose to the surface a few yards from the shore. There are also fine black bass and perch.

When I first knew the place it still hadn't been discovered by the tourist, although the signs were there — a cluster of stilt-cottages along the bank, nearer Montreal. And every spring afterwards, when I came down, the cluster of stilts grew and spread downwards to the border.

Until the arrival of the stilts the people by the river's bank lived in a few proud old cottages. The one my parents had was built by a priest — so village rumour said — who came from Rimouski to retire after he won a lottery. It was made out of wood, dark green with white trimmings, and a wide veranda went right around. The main highway was a quarter of a mile away. Between highway and cottage were empty, gentle sloping fields. And between cottage and river there was a raised walk of rough planks. In spring the water came up the cottage steps so that I could take out the dinghy, the canoe, or the rowboat from the shed and push it down a few yards to float it. In summer I had to push the boats through mud. By the time I reached the deep water the bottom and sides of my feet were covered with mud and bloodsuckers.

Two miles down from the cottage, towards the border, the river had taken a small bite out of the land and left a cove. The banks of this cove are lined with magnificent elms. Whenever I was fishing or sailing near here I could see the hulk of a great house almost completely hidden by the trees. It was the largest house not only along the river but, I imagine, between Montreal and Montpelier. Sometimes I had a glimpse of rough greystone, large windows, the wood a shiny black. I knew, as did everyone else around here, that the house belonged to the Dobells.

Like individual people I sometimes think that families also have a zenith to their lives. So many generations have to be sacrificed in the climb upwards for another to have that bright interval at the top. After which there are others to take the decline down. From what I have read, and what my parents told me, I would say the Dobells were at their peak in the early 1920's. Arthur Dobell, who now had the house, was of the fifth generation. He rarely occupied it. Usually he was photographed at his place in Bermuda, or in Palm Beach, or somewhere on the Riviera.

My first meeting with him was accidental. It was a hot August afternoon. I had taken out the sailboat with the drop-keel — which was a present for my sixteenth birthday from my father—and combined sailing across the river while at the same time trolling for pike. I let the line out, tied it to my big toe, and felt the pleasurable vibration of the spoon travelling through the water. Not far from the island I felt the bite. Then I saw him drift alongside. He looked like some seaweed with the sun shining on it. I had a spinner with three hooks. One of the hooks had got inside the edge of his jaw, through the flesh, and come out again. I could see the blue end of the hook clearly. I landed him and clubbed him to death. I didn't know how much he weighed. But when I held him, he stretched from the bottom of the boat up to my hip. Then the storm came. I had to tack several times to make any progress back. When the rain began I decided to shelter in the cove in front of the Dobell house.

Apparently he had watched me for he came running out. Helped me tie up, dismantle the mast, and brought me inside where I rang my parents. Then we stood by the large windows and watched the lightning over the river, and the rain. It didn't look like easing up so he suggested that I spend the night there.

I had changed my clothes. Wrapped myself up in one of his expensive dressing-gowns that had a silken Miami-Florida label sewn inside with his name, and sat in front of the fireplace. He had lit the set-logs and quickly they were blazing away. It was the most impressive fireplace I had seen. A cement roof and sides came out from the wall like a canopy and leaned into the room.

'My great-grandfather built it from pebbles in the cove,' he said quietly.

Thousands of small round bluish-green stones were set in the cement.

The butler came with hot cocoa. I sat there drying out, feeling warm, and looked around the room. At the heavy curtains; the large oil paintings on the wall of the dead Dobells; the heads of stuffed animals, all with the same brown sad eyes.

'How heavy was the fish?'

'I dunno. But it's the biggest pike I've ever caught. Do you want it?'

'No thanks.' And he smiled, a shy, understanding smile.

I was disappointed when I first saw him. He looked much smaller than his photographs, about five foot seven, slightly built. And his appearance was entirely commonplace, except for the blue eyes, the slender hands, the grey suède shoes. While he was speaking to you he gave you the feeling that you were the most important person present. And yet I felt a curious sense of detachment about him. Though I knew he was in his late thirties, he looked amazingly young. Money, I thought, had preserved him, like it did this house.

'Do you like music?'

'I can play the trumpet,' I said, 'not well.'

209

He went to the gramophone by the wall, lifted the lid until it locked in its hinges, took out a collapsible steel handle, wound it several times, then put on a record.

'Are you going to college?'

In the morning
In the evening
Ain't we got fun.

'No. Not till next year.'
'What will you study?'
'Medicine.'

The rent's unpaid, dear,
We haven't a sou.
But life was made, dear,
For me and for you.

'Isn't that Sir Nicholas Dobell —— ?'

I indicated the second-last oil on the wall. It was a rhetorical question — the Kipling face, the weak eyes looking through glasses, the high white collar — were familiar to me from photographs. Nicholas Dobell had, along with Charlie Conacher and Sweeney Schriner, been one of my schoolboy heroes. I knew he had lectured in surgery at McGill, then went on to a chair in Cambridge, and was knighted just before he died.

The record stopped.

'When you graduate,' he said, 'I hope you'll go and see something of this world. I don't think these boys did. Not until it was too late. It's not the same after thirty. You begin to look at things differently. And things begin to flatten out . . . .'

And again I felt that curious feeling of tenderness emanate from him and with it the sense that it was impersonal. It was the kind that one usually gets from a doctor.

For the rest of that summer I was often in this house. I went sailing in his yacht up and down the river. Sometimes we swam out to the white raft anchored in the middle of the cove and lay there and got brown. And sometimes I was with him for meals when the butler brought the food to one of the wicker-tables under the large striped beach umbrellas which were stuck like mushrooms on the lawns. He introduced me to various dishes. He taught me how to make a passable omelette. He taught me what little I know about wines. There was always a phonograph handy, portable ones on the yacht and in the house, which he would take out on to the lawns and keep playing records — they were only records of the twenties. It was in his library that I first came across Hemingway, Fitzgerald, and Faulkner. He taught me to drive his Plymouth coupé with the white tyres and we raced along the highway flashing by the empty fields, the slow river, the signs showing how many more miles it was to *Morgans*. On week-ends he took me into Montreal or Ottawa — and bought me a small present, usually a book — and then to one of his favourite restaurants, or to a country place by the Lakeshore. Meals with him were always an event.

I guess all of us have a favourite period in our lives. That summer was mine. It was

210

one of those times that now, looking back, I realize how much it influenced my life. What I sometimes tend to forget was just how easy it was to live it, without much thought. Although I did sometimes wonder — especially at dusk when I saw him on the lawns against the large house, a solitary figure watching the sun set over the river behind the trees — why someone as likeable and with so much money, had no visitors. I had the feeling that he only used Ile Aux Noix in the sense of a retreat. That away from it he was quite a different person. Certainly the impression of an irresponsible playboy created by the papers and gossip did not bear out in what I knew of him.

The next summer he was away. I received a postcard from Antibes in June. A month later another card came from St. Tropez. In the fall I went to McGill and began my pre-med. Then the war came. I joined the RCAF and went overseas. And I heard no more of Dobell. When the war ended I went back to McGill, got my degree, then took six months off and visited parts of Europe and Africa that Dobell had told me about.

I intended to practise in the east — but things didn't work out that way. And after a few stopping-off places in Northern Ontario, I found myself in Vancouver, which was very pleasant. For ten years now I have built up a fairly successful practice, married, have a son and daughter, friends, and a fair amount of cash to do the things I want to do. Then last summer something curious happened.

I became homesick for the east. At thirty-four, with youth definitely over and middle-age relentlessly approaching, I found myself turning more and more to my roots and the friendships those bred. And though I have very close friends on the west coast I felt that I wanted to go back to the places and the people with whom I had the formative experiences of my youth. I seemed to have reached a point where I wanted to take a look backwards and sum up an epoch in my life, so as better to go forward. I felt a curious lack of completion. The momentum of youth was dying down without regenerating a new passion. And although I'm interested in medicine, I cannot say that it grips me totally.

So I flew back. Spent the first three days in Montreal. Montreal was a reassurance. It had not changed too much. Not along the parts of Sherbrooke Street I knew or walking along St. Catherine . . . .

The water still dripped from the gargoyles of Christ Church Cathedral and at noon the carillon at St. James's played its tin-penny tunes. At the corner of University the man who sold *The Star* and *The Gazette* (under the turning clock of the Bank of Montreal) looked, with age, even more like Ernest Hemingway. In Phillips Square the pigeons pecked at soaked bits of bread and in the pools of water the sharp reflections of Birks and Morgans, the statue of Edward VII, and the taxis on either side; while a Jehovah Witness stood with a copy of *Awake* in his hand. At night, the gay neon of the restaurants, the films, the delicatessens, the grey buses. And above them the three sweeping searchlights probing aimlessly through the low clouds. While at the end of each intersection the black shape of Mount Royal with the lit stubby cross on top.

. . . Except it was a different person now seeing this. And though I kept bumping into acquaintances, and bits and pieces of my past, there was the inevitable disappointment. I suddenly wanted to go back to Ile Aux Noix.

My father had sold the cottage just after mother died and had come out to Victoria. There was really only Dobell. I sent him a telegram in the off-chance that he

211

might be there. When I returned to the Mount Royal that evening there was one waiting: *Let Me Know When Arriving Chauffeur Will Meet Train — Arthur.*

The chauffeur who met me at St. Johns was new and had nothing of the servant about him. Although he wore the traditional dark double-breasted suit and chauffeur's cap — on him it looked a masquerade. He was stout, short, and slightly bow-legged. The face, although clean shaven, was swarthy. He looked like a well fed peasant. We talked on the drive in. I said he was new. 'A little over a year — You have pleasant journey — You are tired at end of day ——'

His English was full of copybook phrases, and he volunteered on his own that he was Hungarian. Outside. A few lights of farmhouses and lights by the river and patches of water in the fields lit up by the moon. I asked after Dobell. He appeared non-committal. 'He has waited to see you.'

He was waiting in that room with the oil paintings and the stuffed animal heads on the walls. I was prepared for the usual signs of old age, but not what appeared a different person. He was thinner, and this made him even smaller. His face was long and sallow, empty of any kind of expression. He rose to meet me, and his legs, bent at the knees, dragged across the floor. His hands hung near his chest like a pair of lifeless claws, and they shook. The left hand more than the other. When we grasped hands, there was no pressure in his. He said.

'It is good to see you.'

But there was no emotion in his face. All vitality seemed to be drained out of him. I must have talked to cover up my embarrassment. But he stopped me.

'I imagine this is a shock to you.'

The left hand began to tremble more than the other, and the right hand went over to steady it.

He still spoke quietly but the voice was coarse and less distinct. And looking at him I wondered if the brain was still active in the man and was only imprisoned by this shell of a body. I had, professionally, diagnosed as soon as I entered that Dobell had Parkinson's disease.

At supper, the chauffeur was also the butler; but Dobell hardly touched the food.

'Tell me what happened to you. I saw in the paper that you did graduate.'

I told him of the west, marriage, the family, wartime flying. He listened. But there were many silences. And there was an unhappy quality about the silences.

The cook was also the maid. She was also new. A German girl who spoke a shy English, in her twenties, pretty, with prominent cheekbones and high breasts.

I waited for him to tell me his story. But he didn't. Sometimes while I was talking the trembling hands forgetting to hold on to each other would creep up to the chest, and then he would remember and bring them down again.

The room hadn't changed. Except that his portrait was added to the others on the wall. It was painted the way I remembered him.

He appeared to be exhausted quickly, and we went to bed early. I had the same room as that first time. There were dried pussy-willows in the small ornamental brass vase on the dresser, and a picture of himself, as he used to look, on his yacht, with me beside him. In one corner were several of the portable phonographs, and stacks of old records.

I don't know what time it was when I woke up. My light was still on and the wind was blowing the curtain from the window. I heard a cock crowing. I looked at the window — it was dark outside — and saw my face in the glass. I waited, and heard it crow again. Only instead of coming from the outside it seemed to come from somewhere in the house.

I put on my dressing-gown and went out. There was a small night light on in the hall and I could see from the landing straight down to the large room with the paintings and stuffed animal heads. The room was in shadows except for a wedge of light from the door to the kitchen which was open. Then I saw the chauffeur come out of the shadow of a corner, in his bare feet and long winter underwear. He was shuffling in front of the cook, who also had her clothes disarranged, her hair loose, and who kept making furtive little gestures of trying to escape, while the chauffeur kept following. He continued to stalk, shuffling his legs, and holding his hands lifelessly up in front of his chest in a cruel parody of Dobell; then suddenly he leapt up, arms and legs flung out, and gave a crow of a cock.

Finally he cornered her — gave one more pathetic shuffle, then a vigorous crow — and hugging her to him like a bear, he lifted her off the ground. She immediately threw her arms around his neck, her legs fastened around his buttocks. Then he carried her inside the lighted door of the kitchen. I returned to my room, went back to bed, and listened as the clock in the house struck two.

In the morning I was awakened by a cock crowing not far from the window. It was the real thing this time, it sounded asthmatic. Then it was answered by another cock, some distance away. I dressed and went outside.

The morning had a fresh clean smell. The air cool. In front of the house leading to the elms and cove, the lawn was beautifully kept — the slugs moved like pieces of slow rubber across the cut grass — but where I remembered similar lawns on the sides and behind the house, there were chickens.

I watched the birds come running — heads forward, flapping wings, sometimes leaving the ground — as the chauffeur brought pails of food to the small, rough, wooden houses. While the roosters stood on the roofs of the houses, stretched up their necks magnificently, and crowed.

From the kitchen a nice smell of coffee and the cook greeted me shyly and asked if I would like three or four eggs with the bacon. Then the chauffeur returned.

'You like my hens? I ask Mister Dobell if I can have them. He say to me OK. In the back. We start in the back but soon they need more room. Now we have the sides.'

The cook said something in German to the chauffeur.

'You like a drive, sir. Mister Dobell never wake until mid-day?'

I suggested we drive down the river to where the cottage was.

There were stilts on either side of it, all deserted. The old road had not been mended and the car climbed and heeled and swung sideways as it went in and out of the large holes. I went down the gravel path. My parents' cottage looked shabby compared to the stilts. Two planks were missing in the raised walk. The grass had overgrown. The flagpole was no longer on the lawn by the mountain ash. I looked around and for a while it brought back sadly the happy time I had here. I peered inside one of the windows. Whatever furniture was there was draped in white sheets.

The chauffeur watched me.
'I used to live here,' I said.
'Once upon a time ago?'
'Yes.'
'You now come back?'
'No. I don't think I could, even if I wanted to.'
We drove back in silence. Passed the low fields. A few horses were grazing. A child stood on a haywagon. The wind lifted her skirt above her head. She waved in our direction. I waved back.

Back to the house, and a chicken squawked as it ran in front of the car. Dobell was sitting in a large chair on the flat stone porch looking out to the elms and the river. He was bundled up in a black winter coat, hands in a muff. From the kitchen I could hear the chauffeur and the cook talking in German. They had a radio on, and a girl with a husky voice sang about 'Real Love'.

The chickens were supposedly kept behind the wire fences, but some had come through holes, or over the top, and were invading the front lawn and the approaches to the river. I watched a honey-brown rooster head off a couple of hens then, as they settled down to peck at the earth, he nervously lifted his neck and crowed. And he was immediately answered from the other side of the house. And then another crowed even further away, before he replied.

Dobell sat there motionless.

A duck waded in the shallows. And across the river swallows became thick like carboned dust from a sharpened pencil. While in the marshes splashes of red flew slowly by, then settled black on the reeds.

Occasionally we spoke, but it was only small talk. Our thoughts remained and we had nothing to say, because there was nothing for either of us to discover in each other. I knew I would leave soon. And I also knew that I would not come back, except as a tourist.

(1961)

Margaret Laurence
(1926—   )

Margaret Laurence (née Wemyss) was born in Neepawa, Manitoba, and after graduating from United College (now the University of Winnipeg) in 1947, she accom-
panied her husband, a civil engineer, to West Africa and then England. She
has now returned to live in Canada. Her first novel, *This Side Jordan*
(1960), and the first collection of her short stories, *The Tomorrow Tamer
and Other Stories* (1963), as well as a travelogue, *The Prophet's Camel Bell*
(1963), are set in Africa, and deal with the conflict between the emerging
Africa and its colonial past, and the effect of this conflict upon individuals. She has since published three novels with Canadian settings,
featuring the small prairie town of Manawaka: *The Stone Angel*, *A Jest of
God* and *The Fire-Dwellers*. This town is also the locale of the eight short
stories collected under the title *A Bird in the House*. Mrs. Laurence has
also published a collection of Somali prose and poetry (in English trans-
lation) and a book on Nigerian drama. Her work is distinguished by its
combination of psychological, physical and social realism, and by its unob-
trusive use of symbolism.

The story which follows appeared first in the *Atlantic Advocate*, and is reprinted
in *A Bird in the House*, McClelland and Stewart Limited, Toronto, 1970.

THE LOONS

Just below Manawaka, where the Wachakwa River ran brown and noisy over the pebbles, the scrub oak and grey-green willow and chokecherry bushes grew in a dense thicket. In a clearing at the centre of the thicket stood the Tonnerre family's shack. The basis of this dwelling was a small square cabin made of poplar poles and chinked with mud, which had been built by Jules Tonnerre some fifty years before, when he came back from Batoche with a bullet in his thigh, the year that Riel was hung and the voices of the Metis entered their long silence. Jules had only intended to stay the winter in the Wachakwa Valley, but the family was still there in the thirties, when I was a child. As the Tonnerres had increased, their settlement had been added to, until the clearing at the foot of the town hill was a chaos of lean-tos, wooden packing cases, warped lumber, discarded car tyres, ramshackle chicken coops, tangled strands of barbed wire and rusty tin cans.

The Tonnerres were French halfbreeds, and among themselves they spoke a *patois* that was neither Cree nor French. Their English was broken and full of obscenities. They did not belong among the Cree of the Galloping Mountain reservation, further north, and they did not belong among the Scots-Irish and Ukrainians of Manawaka, either. They were, as my Grandmother MacLeod would have put it, neither flesh, fowl, nor good salt herring. When their men were not working at odd jobs or as section hands on the C.P.R., they lived on relief. In the summers, one of the Tonnerre youngsters, with a face that seemed totally unfamiliar with laughter, would knock at the doors of the town's brick houses and offer for sale a lard-pail full of bruised wild strawberries, and if he got as much as a quarter he would grab the coin and run before the customer had time to change her mind. Sometimes old Jules, or his son Lazarus, would get mixed up in a Saturday-night brawl, and would hit out at whoever was nearest, or howl drunkenly among the offended shoppers on Main Street, and then the Mountie would put them for the night in the barred cell underneath the Court House, and the next morning they would be quiet again.

Piquette Tonnerre, the daughter of Lazarus, was in my class at school. She was older than I, but she had failed several grades, perhaps because her attendance had always been sporadic and her interest in school-work negligible. Part of the reason she had missed a lot of school was that she had had tuberculosis of the bone, and had once spent many months in hospital. I knew this because my father was the doctor who had looked after her. Her sickness was almost the only thing I knew about her, however. Otherwise, she existed for me only as a vaguely embarrassing presence, with her hoarse voice and her clumsy limping walk and her grimy cotton dresses that were always miles too long. I was neither friendly nor unfriendly towards her. She dwelt and moved somewhere within my scope of vision, but I did not actually notice her very much until that peculiar summer when I was eleven.

"I don't know what to do about that kid," my father said at dinner one evening. "Piquette Tonnerre, I mean. The damn bone's flared up again. I've had her in hospital for quite a while now, and it's under control all right, but I hate like the dickens to send her home again."

"Couldn't you explain to her mother that she has to rest a lot?" my mother said.

"The mother's not there," my father replied. "She took off a few years back.

216

Can't say I blame her. Piquette cooks for them, and she says Lazarus would never do anything for himself as long as she's there. Anyway, I don't think she'd take much care of herself, once she got back. She's only thirteen, after all. Beth, I was thinking—what about taking her up to Diamond Lake with us this summer? A couple of months rest would give that bone a much better chance."

My mother looked stunned.

"But Ewen — what about Roddie and Vanessa?"

"She's not contagious," my father said. "And it would be company for Vanessa."

"Oh dear," my mother said in distress, "I'll bet anything she has nits in her hair."

"For Pete's sake," my father said crossly, "do you think Matron would let her stay in the hospital for all this time like that? Don't be silly, Beth."

Grandmother MacLeod, her delicately featured face as rigid as a cameo, now brought her mauve-veined hands together as though she were about to begin a prayer.

"Ewen, if that half-breed youngster comes along to Diamond Lake, I'm not going," she announced. "I'll go to Morag's for the summer."

I had trouble in stifling my urge to laugh, for my mother brightened visibly and quickly tried to hide it. If it came to a choice between Grandmother MacLeod and Piquette, Piquette would win hands down, nits or not.

"It might be quite nice for you, at that," she mused. "You haven't seen Morag for over a year, and you might enjoy being in the city for a while. Well, Ewen dear, you do what you think best. If you think it would do Piquette some good, then we'll be glad to have her, as long as she behaves herself."

So it happened that several weeks later, when we all piled into my father's old Nash, surrounded by suitcases and boxes of provisions and toys for my ten-month-old brother, Piquette was with us and Grandmother MacLeod, miraculously, was not. My father would only be staying at the cottage for a couple of weeks, for he had to get back to his practice, but the rest of us would stay at Diamond Lake until the end of August.

Our cottage was not named, as many were, "Dew Drop Inn" or "Bide-a-Wee," or "Bonnie Doon." The sign on the roadway bore in austere letters only our name, MacLeod. It was not a large cottage, but it was on the lakefront. You could look out the windows and see, through the filigree of the spruce trees, the water glistening greenly as the sun caught it. All around the cottage were ferns, and sharp-branched raspberry bushes, and moss that had grown over fallen tree trunks. If you looked carefully among the weeds and grass, you could find wild strawberry plants which were in white flower now and in another month would bear fruit, the fragrant globes hanging like miniature scarlet lanterns on the thin hairy stems. The two grey squirrels were still there, gossiping at us from the tall spruce beside the cottage, and by the end of the summer they would again be tame enough to take pieces of crust from my hands. The broad moose antlers that hung above the back door were a little more bleached and fissured after the winter, but otherwise everything was the same. I raced joyfully around my kingdom, greeting all the places I had not seen for a year. My brother, Roderick, who had not been born when we were here last summer, sat on the car rug in the sunshine and examined a brown spruce cone, meticulously turning it round and round in his small and curious hands. My mother and father toted the luggage from car to cottage, exclaiming over how well the place had wintered, no broken windows, thank goodness, no apparent damage from storm-felled branches or snow.

Only after I had finished looking around did I notice Piquette. She was sitting on the swing, her lame leg held stiffly out, and her other foot scuffing the ground as she swung slowly back and forth. Her long hair hung black and straight around her shoulders, and her broad coarse-featured face bore no expression — it was blank, as though she no longer dwelt within her own skull, as though she had gone elsewhere. I approached her very hesitantly.

"Want to come and play?"

Piquette looked at me with a sudden flash of scorn.

"I ain't a kid," she said.

Wounded, I stamped angrily away, swearing I would not speak to her for the rest of the summer. In the days that followed, however, Piquette began to interest me, and I began to want to interest her. My reasons did not appear bizarre to me. Unlikely as it may seem, I had only just realised that the Tonnerre family, whom I had always heard called half-breeds, were actually Indians, or as near as made no difference. My acquaintance with Indians was not extensive. I did not remember ever having seen a real Indian, and my new awareness that Piquette sprang from the people of Big Bear and Poundmaker, of Tecumseh, of the Iroquois who had eaten Father Brébeuf's heart — all this gave her an instant attraction in my eyes. I was a devoted reader of Pauline Johnson at this age, and sometimes would orate aloud and in an exalted voice, *West Wind, blow from your prairie nest; Blow from the mountains, blow from the west* — and so on. It seemed to me that Piquette must be in some way a daughter of the forest, a kind of junior prophetess of the wilds, who might impart to me, if I took the right approach, some of the secrets which she undoubtedly knew — where the whippoorwill made her nest, how the coyote reared her young, or whatever it was that it said in Hiawatha.

I set about gaining Piquette's trust. She was not allowed to go swimming, with her bad leg, but I managed to lure her down to the beach — or rather, she came because there was nothing else to do. The water was always icy, for the lake was fed by springs, but I swam like a dog, thrashing my arms and legs around at such speed and with such an output of energy that I never grew cold. Finally, when I had had enough, I came out and sat beside Piquette on the sand. When she saw me approaching, her hand squashed flat the sand castle she had been building, and she looked at me sullenly, without speaking.

"Do you like this place?" I asked, after a while, intending to lead on from there into the question of forest lore.

Piquette shrugged. "It's okay. Good as anywhere."

"I love it," I said. "We come here every summer."

"So what?" Her voice was distant, and I glanced at her uncertainly, wondering what I could have said wrong.

"Do you want to come for a walk?" I asked her. "We wouldn't need to go far. If you walk just around the point there, you come to a bay where great big reeds grow in the water, and all kinds of fish hang around there. Want to? Come on."

She shook her head.

"Your dad said I ain't supposed to do no more walking than I got to."

I tried another line.

"I bet you know a lot about the woods and all that, eh?" I began respectfully.

Piquette looked at me from her large dark unsmiling eyes.

"I don't know what in hell you're talkin' about," she replied. "You nuts or some-thin'? If you mean where my old man, and me, and all them live, you better shut up, by Jesus, you hear?"

I was startled and my feelings were hurt, but I had a kind of dogged perseverance. I ignored her rebuff.

"You know something, Piquette? There's loons here, on this lake. You can see their nests just up the shore there, behind those logs. At night, you can hear them even from the cottage, but it's better to listen from the beach. My dad says we should listen and try to remember how they sound, because in a few years when more cottages are built at Diamond Lake and more people come in, the loons will go away."

Piquette was picking up stones and snail shells and then dropping them again.

"Who gives a good goddamn?" she said.

It became increasingly obvious that, as an Indian, Piquette was a dead loss. That evening I went out by myself, scrambling through the bushes that overhung the steep path, my feet slipping on the fallen spruce needles that covered the ground. When I reached the shore, I walked along the firm damp sand to the small pier that my father had built, and sat down there. I heard someone else crashing through the undergrowth and the bracken, and for a moment I thought Piquette had changed her mind, but it turned out to be my father. He sat beside me on the pier and we waited, without speaking.

At night the lake was like black glass with a streak of amber which was the path of the moon. All around, the spruce trees grew tall and close-set, branches blackly sharp against the sky, which was lightened by a cold flickering of stars. Then the loons began their calling. They rose like phantom birds from the nests on the shore, and flew out onto the dark still surface of the water.

No one can ever describe that ululating sound, the crying of the loons, and no one who has heard it can ever forget it. Plaintive, and yet with a quality of chilling mockery, those voices belonged to a world separated by aeons from our neat world of summer cottages and the lighted lamps of home.

"They must have sounded just like that," my father remarked, "before any person ever set foot here."

Then he laughed. "You could say the same, of course, about sparrows, or chip-munks, but somehow it only strikes you that way with the loons."

"I know," I said.

Neither of us suspected that this would be the last time we would ever sit here together on the shore, listening. We stayed for perhaps half an hour, and then we went back to the cottage. My mother was reading beside the fireplace. Piquette was looking at the burning birch log, and not doing anything.

"You should have come along," I said, although in fact I was glad she had not.

"Not me," Piquette said. "You wouldn' catch me walkin' way down there jus' for a bunch of squawkin' birds."

Piquette and I remained ill at ease with one another. I felt I had somehow failed my father, but I did not know what was the matter, nor why she would not or could not respond when I suggested exploring the woods or playing house. I thought it was probably her slow and difficult walking that held her back. She stayed most of the time in the cottage with my mother, helping her with the dishes or with Roddie, but hardly ever talking. Then the Duncans arrived at their cottage, and I spent my days with Mavis, who was my best friend. I could not reach Piquette at all, and I soon lost interest in trying. But all that summer she remained as both a reproach and a mystery to me.

That winter my father died of pneumonia, after less than a week's illness. For some time I saw nothing around me, being completely immersed in my own pain and my mother's. When I looked outward once more, I scarcely noticed that Piquette Tonnerre was no longer at school. I do not remember seeing her at all until four years later, one Saturday night when Mavis and I were having Cokes in the Regal Café. The jukebox was booming like tuneful thunder, and beside it, leaning lightly on its chrome and its rainbow glass, was a girl.

Piquette must have been seventeen then, although she looked about twenty. I stared at her, astounded that anyone could have changed so much. Her face, so stolid and expressionless before, was animated now with a gaiety that was almost violent. She laughed and talked very loudly with the boys around her. Her lipstick was bright carmine, and her hair was cut short and frizzily permed. She had not been pretty as a child, and she was not pretty now, for her features were still heavy and blunt. But her dark and slightly slanted eyes were beautiful, and her skin-tight skirt and orange sweater displayed to enviable advantage a soft and slender body.

She saw me, and walked over. She teetered a little, but it was not due to her once-tubercular leg, for her limp was almost gone.

"Hi, Vanessa." Her voice still had the same hoarseness. "Long time no see, eh?"

"Hi," I said. "Where've you been keeping yourself, Piquette?"

"Oh, I been around," she said. "I been away almost two years now. Been all over the place — Winnipeg, Regina, Saskatoon. Jesus, what I could tell you! I come back this summer, but I ain't stayin'. You kids goin' to the dance?"

"No," I said abruptly, for this was a sore point with me. I was fifteen, and thought I was old enough to go to the Saturday-night dances at the Flamingo. My mother, however, thought otherwise.

"Y'oughta come," Piquette said. "I never miss one. It's just about the on'y thing in this jerkwater town that's any fun. Boy, you couldn' catch me stayin' here. I don' give a shit about this place. It stinks."

She sat down beside me, and I caught the harsh over-sweetness of her perfume.

"Listen, you wanna know something, Vanessa?" she confided, her voice only slightly blurred. "Your dad was the only person in Manawaka that ever done anything good to me."

I nodded speechlessly. I was certain she was speaking the truth. I knew a little more than I had that summer at Diamond Lake, but I could not reach her now any more than I had then. I was ashamed, ashamed of my own timidity, the frightened tendency to look the other way. Yet I felt no real warmth towards her — I only felt that I ought to, because of that distant summer and because my father had hoped she would be company for me, or perhaps that I would be for her, but it had not happened that way. At this moment, meeting her again, I had to admit that she repelled and embarrassed me, and I could not help despising the self-pity in her voice. I wished she would go away. I did not want to see her. I did not know what to say to her. It seemed that we had nothing to say to one another.

"I'll tell you something else," Piquette went on. "All the old bitches an' biddies in this town will sure be surprised. I'm gettin' married this fall — my boyfriend, he's an English fella, works in the stockyards in the city there, a very tall guy, got blond wavy hair. Gee, is he ever handsome. Got this real classy name. Alvin Gerald Cummings — some handle, eh? They call him Al."

For the merest instant, then, I saw her. I really did see her, for the first and only time in all the years we had both lived in the same town. Her defiant face, momentarily, became unguarded and unmasked, and in her eyes there was a terrifying hope.

"Gee, Piquette — " I burst out awkwardly, "that's swell. That's really wonderful. Congratulations — good luck — I hope you'll be happy — "

As I mouthed the conventional phrases, I could only guess how great her need must have been, that she had been forced to seek the very things she so bitterly rejected.

When I was eighteen, I left Manawaka and went away to college. At the end of my first year, I came back home for the summer. I spent the first few days in talking non-stop with my mother, as we exchanged all the news that somehow had not found its way into letters — what had happened in my life and what had happened here in Manawaka while I was away. My mother searched her memory for events that concerned people I knew.

"Did I ever write you about Piquette Tonnerre, Vanessa?" she asked one morning.

"No, I don't think so," I replied. "Last I heard of her, she was going to marry some guy in the city. Is she still there?"

My mother looked perturbed, and it was a moment before she spoke, as though she did not know how to express what she had to tell and wished she did not need to try.

"She's dead," she said at last. Then, as I stared at her, "Oh, Vanessa, when it happened, I couldn't help thinking of her as she was that summer — so sullen and gauche and badly dressed. I couldn't help wondering if we could have done something more at that time — but what could we do? She used to be around in the cottage there with me all day, and honestly, it was all I could do to get a word out of her. She didn't even talk to your father very much, although I think she liked him, in her way."

"What happened?" I asked.

"Either her husband left her, or she left him," my mother said. "I don't know which. Anyway, she came back here with two youngsters, both only babies — they must have been born very close together. She kept house, I guess, for Lazarus and her brothers, down in the valley there, in the old Tonnerre place. I used to see her on the street sometimes, but she never spoke to me. She'd put on an awful lot of weight, and she looked a mess, to tell you the truth, a real slattern, dressed any old how. She was up in court a couple of times — drunk and disorderly, of course. One Saturday night last winter, during the coldest weather, Piquette was alone in the shack with the children. The Tonnerres made home brew all the time, so I've heard, and Lazarus said later she'd been drinking most of the day when he and the boys went out that evening. They had an old woodstove there — you know the kind, with exposed pipes. The shack caught fire. Piquette didn't get out, and neither did the children."

I did not say anything. As so often with Piquette, there did not seem to be anything to say. There was a kind of silence around the image in my mind of the fire and the snow, and I wished I could put from my memory the look that I had seen once in Piquette's eyes.

I went up to Diamond Lake for a few days that summer, with Mavis and her family. The MacLeod cottage had been sold after my father's death, and I did not even go to look at it, not wanting to witness my long-ago kingdom possessed now by strangers. But one evening I went down to the shore by myself.

The small pier which my father had built was gone, and in its place there was a large and solid pier built by the government, for Galloping Mountain was now a national park, and Diamond Lake had been re-named Lake Wapakata, for it was felt that an Indian name would have a greater appeal to tourists. The one store had become several dozen, and the settlement had all the attributes of a flourishing resort — hotels, a dance-hall, cafés with neon signs, the penetrating odours of potato chips and hot dogs.

I sat on the government pier and looked out across the water. At night the lake at least was the same as it had always been, darkly shining and bearing within its black glass the streak of amber that was the path of the moon. There was no wind that evening, and everything was quiet all around me. It seemed too quiet, and then I realized that the loons were no longer here. I listened for some time, to make sure, but never once did I hear that long-drawn call, half mocking and half plaintive, spearing through the stillness across the lake.

I did not know what had happened to the birds. Perhaps they had gone away to some far place of belonging. Perhaps they had been unable to find such a place, and had simply died out, having ceased to care any longer whether they lived or not.

I remembered how Piquette had scorned to come along, when my father and I sat there and listened to the lake birds. It seemed to me now that in some unconscious and totally unrecognised way, Piquette might have been the only one, after all, who had heard the crying of the loons.

(1970)

Hugh Hood
(1928—)

Hugh Hood, a member of the Department of English at the University of Montreal, is the son of an English-speaking father and a French-speaking mother. Born and educated in Toronto, he obtained his Ph.D. in English Literature from the University of Toronto in 1955. His first book was a collection of short stories, *Flying a Red Kite*, and he has since published several novels and a book of essays. His most recent novel is *You Can't Get There from Here*, published in 1972.

 The story which follows is from *Flying a Red Kite*, Ryerson Press, Toronto, 1962.

FLYING A RED KITE

The ride home began badly. Still almost a stranger to the city, tired, hot and dirty, and inattentive to his surroundings, Fred stood for ten minutes, shifting his parcels from arm to arm and his weight from one leg to the other, in a sweaty bath of shimmering glare from the sidewalk, next to a grimy yellow-and-black bus stop. To his left a line of murmuring would-be passengers lengthened until there were enough to fill any vehicle that might come for them. Finally an obese brown bus waddled up like an indecent old cow and stopped with an expiring moo at the head of the line. Fred was glad to be first in line, as there didn't seem to be room for more than a few to embus.

But as he stepped up he noticed a sign in the window which said *Côte des Neiges — Boulevard* and he recoiled as though bitten, trampling the toes of the woman behind him and making her squeal. It was a Sixty-six bus, not the Sixty-five that he wanted. The woman pushed furiously past him while the remainder of the line clamoured in the rear. He stared at the number on the bus stop: Sixty-six, not his stop at all. Out of the corner of his eye he saw another coach pulling away from the stop on the northeast corner, the right stop, the Sixty-five, and the one he should have been standing under all this time. Giving his characteristic weary put-upon sigh, which he used before breakfast to annoy Naomi, he adjusted his parcels in both arms, feeling sweat run around his neck and down his collar between his shoulders, and crossed Saint Catherine against the light, drawing a Gallic sneer from a policeman, to stand for several more minutes at the head of a new queue, under the right sign. It was nearly four-thirty and the Saturday shopping crowds wanted to get home, out of the summer dust and heat, out of the jitter of the big July holiday weekend. They would all go home and sit on their balconies. All over the suburbs in duplexes and fourplexes, families would be enjoying cold suppers in the open air on their balconies; but the Calverts' apartment had none. Fred and Naomi had been ignorant of the meaning of the custom when they were apartment hunting. They had thought of Montreal as a city of the Sub-Arctic and in the summers they would have leisure to repent the misjudgment.

He had been shopping along the length of Saint Catherine between Peel and Guy, feeling guilty because he had heard for years that this was where all those pretty Montreal women made their promenade; he had wanted to watch without familial encumbrances. There had been girls enough but nothing outrageously special so he had beguiled the scorching afternoon making a great many small idle purchases, of the kind one does when trapped in a Woolworth's. A ball-point pen and a note-pad for Naomi, who was always stealing his and leaving it in the kitchen with long, wildly-optimistic, grocery lists scribbled in it. Six packages of cigarettes, some legal-size envelopes, two Dinky-toys, a long-playing record, two parcels of second-hand books, and the lightest of his burdens and the unhandiest, the kite he had bought for Deedee, two flimsy wooden sticks rolled up in red plastic film, and a ball of cheap thin string — not enough, by the look of it, if he should ever get the thing into the air.

When he'd gone fishing, as a boy, he'd never caught any fish; when playing hockey he had never been able to put the puck in the net. One by one the wholesome outdoor sports and games had defeated him. But he had gone on believing in them, in their curative moral values, and now he hoped that Deedee, though a girl, might sometime catch a fish; and though she obviously wouldn't play hockey, she might ski, or toboggan on the mountain. He had noticed that people treated kites and kite-flying as somehow holy. They were a natural symbol, thought Fred, and he felt uneasily sure that he would have trouble getting this one to fly.

The inside of the bus was shaped like a box-car with windows, but the windows were useless. You might have peeled off the bus as you'd peel the paper off a pound of butter, leaving an oblong yellow lump of thick solid heat, with the passengers embedded in it like hopeless breadcrumbs.

He elbowed and wriggled his way along the aisle, feeling a momentary sliver of pleasure as his palm rubbed accidentally along the back of a girl's skirt — once, a philosopher — the sort of thing you couldn't be charged with. But you couldn't get away with it twice and anyway the girl either didn't feel it, or had no idea who had caressed her. There were vacant seats towards the rear, which was odd because the bus was otherwise full, and he struggled towards them, trying not to break the wooden struts which might be persuaded to fly. The bus lurched forward and his feet moved with the floor, causing him to pop suddenly out of the crowd by the exit, into a square well of space next to the heat and stink of the engine. He swayed around and aimed himself at a narrow vacant seat, nearly dropping a parcel of books as he lowered himself precipitately into it.

The bus crossed Sherbrooke Street and began, intolerably slowly, to crawl up Côte des Neiges and around the western spur of the mountain. His ears began to pick up the usual melange of French and English and to sort it out; he was proud of his French and pleased that most of the people on the streets spoke a less correct, though more fluent, version than his own. He had found that he could make his customers understand him perfectly — he was a book salesman — but that people on the street were happier when he addressed them in English.

The chatter in the bus grew clearer and more interesting and he began to listen, grasping all at once why he had found a seat back here. He was sitting next to a couple of drunks who emitted an almost overpowering smell of beer. They were cheerfully exchanging indecencies and obscure jokes and in a minute they would speak to him. They always did, drunks and panhandlers, finding some soft fearfulness in his face which exposed him as a shrinking easy mark. Once in a railroad station he had been approached three times in twenty minutes by the same panhandler on his rounds. Each time he had given the man something, despising himself with each new weakness.

The cheerful pair sitting at right-angles to him grew louder and more blunt and the women within earshot grew glum. There was no harm in it; there never is. But you avoid your neighbour's eye, afraid of smiling awkwardly, or of looking offended and a prude.

"Now this Pearson," said one of the revellers, "he's just a little short-ass. He's just a little fellow without any brains. Why, some of the speeches he makes . . . I could make them myself. I'm an old Tory myself, an old Tory."

"I'm an old Blue," said the other.

"Is that so, now? That's fine, a fine thing." Fred was sure he didn't know what a Blue was.

"I'm a Balliol man. Whoops!" They began to make monkey-like noises to annoy

225

the passengers and amuse themselves. "Whoops," said the Oxford man again, "hoo, hoo, there's one now, there's one for you." He was talking about a girl on the sidewalk.

"She's a one, now, isn't she? Look at the legs on her, oh, look at them now, isn't that something?" There was a noisy clearing of throats and the same voice said something that sounded like "Shaoil-na-baig."

"Oh, good, good!" said the Balliol man.

"Shaoil-na-baig," said the other loudly, "I've not forgotten my Gaelic, do you see, shaoil-na-baig," he said it loudly, and a woman up the aisle reddened and looked away. It sounded like a dirty phrase to Fred, delivered as though the speaker had forgotten all his Gaelic but the words for sexual intercourse.

"And how is your French, Father?" asked the Balliol man, and the title made Fred start in his seat. He pretended to drop a parcel and craned his head quickly sideways. The older of the two drunks, the one sitting by the window, examining the passing legs and skirts with the same impulse that Fred had felt on Saint Catherine Street, was indeed a priest, and couldn't possibly be an impostor. His clerical suit was too well-worn, egg-stained and blemished with candle-droppings, and fit its wearer too well, for it to be an assumed costume. The face was unmistakably a southern Irishman's. The priest darted a quick peek into Fred's eyes before he could turn them away, giving a monkey-like grimace that might have been a mixture of embarrassment and shame but probably wasn't.

He was a little gray-haired bucko of close to sixty, with a triangular sly mottled crimson face and uneven yellow teeth. His hands moved jerkily and expressively in his lap, in counterpoint to the lively intelligent movements of his face.

The other chap, the Balliol man, was a perfect type of English-speaking Montrealer, perhaps a bond salesman or minor functionary in a brokerage house on Saint James Street. He was about fifty with a round domed head, red hair beginning to go slightly white at the neck and ears, pink porcine skin, very neatly barbered and combed. He wore an expensive white shirt with a fine blue stripe and there was some sort of ring around his tie. He had his hands folded flatly on the knob of a stick, round face with deep laugh-lines in the cheeks, and a pair of cheerfully darting little blue-bloodshot eyes. Where could the pair have run into each other?

"I've forgotten my French years ago," said the priest carelessly. "I was down in New Brunswick for many years and I'd no use for it, the work I was doing. I'm Irish, you know."

"I'm an old Blue."

"That's right," said the priest, "John's the boy. Oh, he's a sharp lad is John. He'll let them all get off, do you see, to Manitoba for the summer, and bang, BANG!" All the bus jumped. "He'll call an election on them and then they'll run." Something caught his eye and he turned to gaze out the window. The bus was moving slowly past the cemetery of Notre Dame des Neiges and the priest stared, half-sober, at the graves stretched up the mountainside in the sun.

"I'm not in there," he said involuntarily.

"Indeed you're not," said his companion, "lot's of life in you yet, eh, Father?"

"Oh," he said, "oh, I don't think I'd know what to do with a girl if I fell over one." He looked out at the cemetery for several moments. "It's all a sham," he said, half under his breath, "they're in there for good." He swung around and looked innocently at Fred. "Are you going fishing, lad?"

"It's a kite that I bought for my little girl," said Fred, more cheerfully than he felt.

"She'll enjoy that, she will," said the priest, "for it's grand sport."

"Go fly a kite!" said the Oxford man hilariously. It amused him and he said it again. "Go fly a kite!" He and the priest began to chant together, "Hoo, hoo, whoops," and they laughed and in a moment, clearly, would begin to sing.

The bus turned lumberingly onto Queen Mary Road. Fred stood up confusedly and began to push his way towards the rear door. As he turned away, the priest grinned impudently at him, stammering a jolly goodbye. Fred was too embarrassed to answer but he smiled uncertainly and fled. He heard them take up their chant anew.

"Hoo, there's a one for you, hoo. Shaoil-na-baig. Whoops!" Their laughter died out as the bus rolled heavily away.

He had heard about such men, naturally, and knew that they existed; but it was the first time in Fred's life that he had ever seen a priest misbehave himself publicly. There are so many priests in the city, he thought, that the number of bum ones must be in proportion. The explanation satisfied him but the incident left a disagreeable impression in his mind.

Safely home he took his shirt off and poured himself a Coke. Then he allowed Deedee, who was dancing around him with her terrible energy, to open the parcels.

"Give your Mummy the pad and pencil, sweetie," he directed. She crossed obediently to Naomi's chair and handed her the cheap plastic case.

"Let me see you make a note in it," he said, "make a list of something, for God's sake, so you'll remember it's yours. And the one on the desk is mine. Got that?" He spoke without rancour or much interest; it was a rather over-worked joke between them.

"What's this?" said Deedee, holding up the kite and allowing the ball of string to roll down the hall. He resisted a compulsive wish to get up and re-wind the string.

"It's for you. Don't you know what it is?"

"It's a red kite," she said. She had wanted one for weeks but spoke now as if she weren't interested. Then all at once she grew very excited and eager. "Can you put it together right now?" she begged.

"I think we'll wait till after supper, sweetheart," he said, feeling mean. You raised their hopes and then dashed them; there was no real reason why they shouldn't put it together now, except his fatigue. He looked pleadingly at Naomi.

"Daddy's tired, Deedee," she said obligingly, "he's had a long hot afternoon."

"But I want to see it," said Deedee, fiddling with the flimsy red film and nearly puncturing it.

Fred was sorry he'd drunk a Coke; it bloated him and upset his stomach and had no true cooling effect.

"We'll have something to eat," he said cajolingly, "and then mummy can put it together for you." He turned to his wife. "You don't mind, do you? I'd only spoil the thing." Threading a needle or hanging a picture made the normal slight tremor of his hands accentuate itself almost embarrassingly.

"Of course not," she said, smiling wryly. They had long ago worked out their areas of uselessness.

"There's a picture on it, and directions."

"Yes. Well, we'll get it together somehow. Flying it . . . that's something else

227

again." She got up, holding the note-pad, and went into the kitchen to put the supper on.

It was a good hot-weather supper, tossed greens with the correct proportions of vinegar and oil, croissants and butter, and cold sliced ham. As he ate, his spirits began to percolate a bit, and he gave Naomi a graphic sketch of the incident on the bus. "It depressed me," he told her. This came as no surprise to her; almost anything unusual, which he couldn't do anything to alter or relieve, depressed Fred nowadays. "He must have been sixty. Oh, quite sixty, I should think, and you could tell that everything had come to pieces for him."

"It's a standard story," she said, "and aren't you sentimentalizing it?"

"In what way?"

"The 'spoiled priest' business, the empty man, the man without a calling. They all write about that. Graham Greene made his whole career out of that."

"That isn't what the phrase means," said Fred laboriously. "It doesn't refer to a man who actually *is* a priest, though without a vocation."

"No?" She lifted an eyebrow; she was better educated than he.

"No, it doesn't. It means somebody who never became a priest at all. The point is that you *had* a vocation but ignored it. That's what a spoiled priest is. It's an Irish phrase, and usually refers to somebody who is a failure and who drinks too much." He laughed shortly. "I don't qualify, on the second count."

"You're not a failure."

"No, I'm too young. Give me time!" There was no reason for him to talk like this; he was a very productive salesman.

"You certainly never wanted to be a priest," she said positively, looking down at her breasts and laughing, thinking of some secret. "I'll bet you never considered it, not with your habits." She meant his bedroom habits, which were ardent, and in which she ardently acquiesced. She was an adept and enthusiastic partner, her greatest gift as a wife.

"Let's put that kite together," said Deedee, getting up from her little table, with such adult decision that her parents chuckled. "Come on," she said, going to the sofa and bouncing up and down.

Naomi put a tear in the fabric right away, on account of the ambiguity of the directions. There should have been two holes in the kite, through which a lugging-string passed; but the holes hadn't been provided and when she put them there with the point of an icepick they immediately began to grow.

"Scotch tape," she said, like a surgeon asking for sutures.

"There's a picture on the front," said Fred, secretly cross but ostensibly helpful.

"I see it," she said.

"Mummy put holes in the kite," said Deedee with alarm. "Is she going to break it?"

"No," said Fred. The directions were certainly ambiguous.

Naomi tied the struts at right-angles, using so much string that Fred was sure the kite would be too heavy. Then she strung the fabric on the notched ends of the struts and the thing began to take shape.

"It doesn't look quite right," she said, puzzled and irritated.

"The surface has to be curved so there's a difference of air pressure." He remembered this, rather unfairly, from high-school physics classes.

She bent the cross-piece and tied it in a bowed arc, and the red film pulled taut.

228

"There now," she said.

"You've forgotten the lugging-string on the front," said Fred critically, "that's what you made the holes for, remember?"

"Why is Daddy mad?" said Deedee.

"I'M NOT MAD!"

It had begun to shower, great pear-shaped drops of rain falling with a plop on the sidewalk.

"That's as close as I can come," said Naomi, staring at Fred, "we aren't going to try it tonight, are we?"

"We promised her," he said, "and it's only a light rain."

"Will we all go?"

"I wish you'd take her," he said, "because my stomach feels upset. I should never drink Coca-Cola."

"It always bothers you. You should know that by now."

"I'm not running out on you," he said anxiously, "and if you can't make it work, I'll take her up tomorrow afternoon."

"I know," she said, "come on, Deedee, we're going to take the kite up the hill." They left the house and crossed the street. Fred watched them through the window as they started up the steep path hand in hand. He felt left out, and slightly nauseated.

They were back in half an hour, their spirits not at all dampened, which surprised him.

"No go, eh?"

"Much too wet, and not enough breeze. The rain knocks it flat."

"O.K.!" he exclaimed with fervour. "I'll try tomorrow."

"We'll try again tomorrow," said Deedee with equal determination — her parents mustn't forget their obligations.

Sunday afternoon the weather was nearly perfect, hot, clear, a firm steady breeze but not too much of it, and a cloudless sky. At two o'clock Fred took his daughter by the hand and they started up the mountain together, taking the path through the woods that led up to the University parking lots.

"We won't come down until we make it fly," Fred swore, "that's a promise."

"Good," she said, hanging on to his hand and letting him drag her up the steep path, "there are lots of bugs in here, aren't there?"

"Yes," he said briefly — he was being liberally bitten.

When they came to the end of the path, they saw that the campus was deserted and still, and there was all kinds of running room. Fred gave Deedee careful instructions about where to sit, and what to do if a car should come along, and then he paid out a little string and began to run across the parking lot towards the main building of the University. He felt a tug at the string and throwing a glance over his shoulder he saw the kite bobbing in the air, about twenty feet off the ground. He let out more string, trying to keep it filled with air, but he couldn't run quite fast enough, and in a moment it fell back to the ground.

"Nearly had it!" he shouted to Deedee, whom he'd left fifty yards behind.

"Daddy, Dáddy, come back," she hollered apprehensively. Rolling up the string as he went, he retraced his steps and prepared to try again. It was important to catch a gust of wind and run into it. On the second try the kite went higher than before but as he ran past the entrance to the University he felt the air pressure lapse and saw the kite waver and fall. He walked slowly back, realizing that the bulk of the main building was cutting off the air currents.

"We'll go up higher," he told her, and she seized his hand and climbed obediently up the road beside him, around behind the main building, past ash barrels and trash heaps; they climbed a flight of wooden steps, crossed a parking lot next to L'Ecole Polytechnique and a slanting field further up, and at last came to a pebbly dirt road that ran along the top ridge of the mountain beside the cemetery. Fred remembered the priest as he looked across the fence and along the broad stretch of cemetery land rolling away down the slope of the mountain to the west. They were about six hundred feet above the river, he judged. He'd never been up this far before.

"My sturdy little brown legs are tired," Deedee remarked, and he burst out laughing.

"Where did you hear that," he said, "who has sturdy little brown legs?"

She screwed her face up in a grin. "The gingerbread man," she said, beginning to sing, "I can run away from you, I can, 'cause I'm the little gingerbread man."

The air was dry and clear and without a trace of humidity and the sunshine was dazzling. On either side of the dirt road grew great clumps of wild flowers, yellow and blue, buttercups, daisies and goldenrod, and cornflowers and clover. Deedee disappeared into the flowers — picking bouquets was her favourite game. He could see the shrubs and grasses heave and sway as she moved around. The scent of clover and of dry sweet grass was very keen here, and from the east, over the curved top of the mountain, the wind blew in a steady uneddying stream. Five or six miles off to the southwest he spied the wide intensely gray-white stripe of the river. He heard Deedee cry: "Daddy, Daddy, come and look." He pushed through the coarse grasses and found her.

"Berries," she cried rapturously, "look at all the berries! Can I eat them?" She had found a wild raspberry bush, a thing he hadn't seen since he was six years old. He'd never expected to find one growing in the middle of Montreal.

"Wild raspberries," he said wonderingly, "sure you can pick them dear; but be careful of the prickles." They were all shades and degrees of ripeness from black to vermilion.

"Ouch," said Deedee, pricking her fingers as she pulled off the berries. She put a handful in her mouth and looked wry.

"Are they bitter?"

"Juicy," she mumbled with her mouth full. A trickle of dark juice ran down her chin.

"Eat some more," he said, "while I try the kite again." She bent absorbedly to the task of hunting them out, and he walked down the road for some distance and then turned to run up towards her. This time he gave the kite plenty of string before he began to move; he ran as hard as he could, panting and handing the string out over his shoulders, burning his fingers as it slid through them. All at once he felt the line pull and pulse as if there were a living thing on the other end and he turned on his heel and watched while the kite danced into the upper air-currents above the treetops and began to soar up and up. He gave it more line and in an instant it pulled high up away from him across the fence, two hundred feet and more above him up over the cemetery where it steadied and hung, bright red in the sunshine. He thought flashingly of the priest saying "It's all a sham," and he knew all at once that the priest was wrong. Deedee came running down to him, laughing with excitement and pleasure and singing joyfully about the gingerbread man, and he knelt in the dusty roadway and put his arms around her, placing her hands on the line between his. They gazed, squinting in the sun, at the flying red thing, and he turned away and saw in the shadow of her cheek and on her lips and chin the dark rich red of the pulp and juice of the crushed raspberries.

(1962)

Mordecai Richler
(1931 —   )

A native of Montreal, and a former student at Sir George Williams University in that
city, Mordecai Richler has spent most of his adult life in Europe, though he has
returned recently to his native city. He has lived in Spain, the setting of
his first novel, *The Acrobats* (1954), and, for most of the last fifteen years, in
England. His later novels have included *Son of a Smaller Hero* (1955), *A Choice of
Enemies* (1957), *The Apprenticeship of Duddy Kravitz* (1959), *The Incomparable
Atuk* (1963), *Cocksure* (1968), and *St. Urbain's Horseman* (1971). He has also
written film scripts, essays and short stories and has edited the anthology *Canadian
Writing Today* (1969).

The story which follows appeared first in *The Tamarack Review*, and a modified
version is incorporated into *Cocksure*.

MORTIMER GRIFFIN, SHALINSKY, AND
HOW THEY SETTLED THE JEWISH QUESTION

I was, at the time, beginning my first scholastic year as a lecturer in English literature at Wellington College in Montreal. You've probably never heard of Wellington. It's a modest institution with a small student body. There's the Day College, comprised, for the most part, of students who couldn't get into McGill, and the Evening College, made up of adults, most of them working at full-time jobs and trying to get a college education after hours. I was responsible for two Evening College courses, English 112 (Shakespeare) and English 129 (The Modern Novel). Shalinsky registered for both of them.

Until my fourth lecture I was only aware of Shalinsky as a ponderous presence in the third row. My fourth lecture dealt with Franz Kafka and naturally I made several allusions to the distinctively Jewish roots of his work. Afterwards, as I was gathering my notes together, Shalinsky approached me for the first time.

'I want to tell you, Professor Griffin, how much intellectual nourishment I got out of your lecture tonight.'

'I'm glad you enjoyed it.'

I'm afraid I was in a hurry to get away that night. I was going to pick up Joyce at the Rosens'. But Shalinsky still stood before my desk.

His wisps of grey curly hair uncut and uncombed, Shalinsky was a small, round-shouldered man with horn-rimmed spectacles, baleful black eyes, and a hanging lower lip. His shiny, pin-striped grey suit was salted with dandruff round the shoulders. A hand-rolled cigarette drooped from his mouth, his eyes half-shut against the smoke and the ashes spilling unregarded to his vest.

'Why did you change your name?' he asked.

'I beg your pardon. Did you ask me why I changed my name?'

Shalinsky nodded.

'But I haven't. My name is Griffin. It always has been.'

'You're a Jew.'

'You're mistaken.'

Shalinsky smiled faintly.

'Really,' I began, 'what made you think — '

'All right. I'm mistaken. I made a mistake. No harm done.'

'Look here, if I were a Jew I wouldn't try to conceal it for a moment.'

Still smiling, blinking his eyes, Shalinsky said: 'There's no need to lose your temper, Professor *Griffin*. I made a mistake, that's all. If that's the way you want it.'

'And I'm not a professor, either. *Mr.* Griffin will do.'

'A man of your talents will be famous one day. Like . . . like I. M. Sinclair. A scholar renowned wherever the intelligentsia meet. Thanks once more for tonight's intellectual feast. Good night, Mr. Griffin.'

In retrospect, on the bus ride out to Hy and Eva Rosen's house, I found the incident so outlandishly amusing that I laughed aloud twice.

Joyce had eaten with the Rosens, and Eva, remembering how much I liked chopped liver, had saved me an enormous helping. I told them about Shalinsky, concluding with, '. . . and where he ever got the idea that I was Jewish I'll never know.' I had anticipated plenty of laughter. A witty remark from Hy, perhaps. Instead, there was silence. Nervously, I added: 'Look, I don't mean that I'd be ashamed . . . or that I was insulted that someone would think I was—Christ, you know what I mean, Hy.'

'Yes,' Hy said sharply. 'Of course.'

We left for home earlier than usual.

'Boy,' Joyce said, 'you certainly have a gift. I mean once you *have* put your foot in it you certainly know how to make matters worse.'

'I thought they'd laugh. God, I've known Hy for years. He's one of my best friends. He — '

'*Was*,' Joyce said.

'Look here,' I said, 'you don't seriously think that Hy thinks I'm an anti-semite?'

Joyce raised one eyebrow slightly — an annoying, college-girl habit that has lingered.

'Don't be ridiculous,' I said. 'Tomorrow, the day after, the whole thing will be forgotten, or Hy will make a joke of it.'

'*They* have an excellent sense of humour,' Joyce said, 'haven't they? There's Jack Benny and Phil Silvers and — '

'Oh, for Christ's sake!'

Two days later a copy of a magazine called *Jewish Thought* came in the mail. Attached was a printed note, WITH THE COMPLIMENTS OF THE EDITOR, and underneath, penned with a lavish hand, *Respectfully, J. Shalinsky*. It took me a moment or two to connect Shalinsky, the editor, with Shalinsky, my student. I began to flip through the pages of the little magazine.

The editorial, by J. Shalinsky, dealt at length with the dilemma of Jewish artists in a philistine community. The lead article, by Lionel Gould, B. COMM. (McGill), was titled 'On Being a Jew in Montreal West'. Another article, by I.M. Sinclair, M.D., was titled 'The Anti-Semite as an Intellectual: A Study of the Novels of Graham Greene'. There were numerous book reviews, two sentimental poems translated from the Yiddish, a rather maudlin Israeli short story, and, surprisingly, 'Stefan Zweig and J. Shalinsky: A Previously Unpublished Correspondence'.

That night, as soon as my Eng. 112 lecture was finished, Shalinsky loomed smiling over my desk. 'You got the magazine?' he asked.

'I haven't had time to read it yet.'

'If you don't like it, all you have to do is tell me why. No evasions, please. Don't beat around the bush.' Shalinsky broke off and smiled. 'I have something for you,' he said.

I watched while he unwrapped a large, awkward parcel. The string he rolled into a ball and dropped into his pocket. The brown wrapping paper, already worn and wrinkled, he folded into eight and put into another pocket. Revealed was an extremely expensive edition of colour plates by Marc Chagall.

'It occurred to me', he said, 'that a man so interested in Kafka might also find beauty in the art of Marc Chagall.'

'I don't understand.'

'Would you be willing', Shalinsky said, 'to write me a review, a little appreciation, of this book for the next issue of *Jewish Thought?*'

I hesitated.

'We pay our contributors, of course. Not much, but – '

'That's not the point.'

'And the book, it goes without saying, would be yours.'

'All right, Mr. Shalinsky. I'll do it.'

'There's something else. You have no lectures next Wednesday night. You are free, so to speak. Am I right?'

'Yes, but – '

'Next Wednesday night, Mr. Griffin, the Jewish Thought Literary Society will be meeting at my house. It is a custom, at these meetings, that we are addressed by a distinguished guest. I was hoping – '

'What would you like me to talk about?' I asked wearily.

'Kafka,' he said. 'Kafka and Cabbalism. Refreshments will be served.'

The address Shalinsky had given me was on St. Urbain Street. His house smelled of home-baked bread and spices. The livingroom, almost a hall once the double doors had been opened, was filled with folding chairs, all of them vindictively directed at the speaker's table. The walls were laden with enormous photographs of literary giants protected by glass and encased in varnished wooden frames. Tolstoi, a bearded scarecrow on horseback, glared at the refreshments table. Dostoyevsky and Turgenev, their quarrels forgotten, stood side by side. Opposite, Marcel Proust smiled enigmatically.

At dinner I was introduced to Shalinsky's wife and daughter. Mrs. Shalinsky was a round rosy-cheeked figure with a double chin. The daughter—plump, plum-cheeked Gitel Shalinsky — wore a peasant blouse laced tightly over a tray of milky bosom, and a billowy green skirt. Her thick black hair she wore in an upsweep; glittering glass ear-rings dripped from her cup-shaped ears. A wooden clasp, GRETA, rode one breast, and a rose the other. Throughout dinner Gitel never said a word.

I handed Shalinsky my twelve-hundred-word article on Chagall, titled — rather brightly, I thought — *The Myopic Mystic*. My editor pondered the piece in silence, waving his hand impatiently whenever his wife interrupted him, a frequent occurrence, with remarks like, 'Chew your meat, Jake,' and, in an aside to me, 'If I gave him absorbent cotton to eat, you think he'd know the difference?', and again, baring her teeth in a parody of mastication, 'Chew, Jake. *Digest.*'

Shalinsky read my article unsmilingly and folded it neatly in four.

'Is there anything the matter?' I asked.

'As an intellectual exercise your article is A-1, but –'

'You don't have to print it if you don't want to.'

'Did I say I wouldn't print it? No. But, if you'll let me finish, I had hoped it would be a little more from the soul. Take the title, for instance. *The Myopic Mystic,*' he said with distaste. 'Clever. Clever, Mr. Griffin. But no heart. Still, this is a fine article. I wouldn't change a word. Not for the world.'

The first of Shalinsky's guests arrived and he went into the livingroom with him. Mrs. Shalinsky excused herself, too, and so I was left alone with Gitel. 'Your father', I said, 'is quite an extraordinary man. I mean at his age to take university courses and edit a magazine – '

'*The Ladies' Home Journal,*' Gitel said. '*There's* a magazine for you. But *Jewish*

Thought. An eight-hundred-and-forty-two circulation, counting give-aways — that's no magazine.'

'Your father tells me he's printed work by S.M. Geiger. He's a very promising poet, I think.'

'Some poet. He comes up to here by me. Alan Ladd — there's another twerp. How long are you going to speak tonight?'

'I'm not sure.'

'Make it short, Morty. The blabbers never get invited back.'

Three-quarters of an hour after my lecture was supposed to have started, only twelve people, all middle-aged men, had turned up, though many more had been prepared for. 'It's the rain,' Shalinsky said. A half-hour later six more people had drifted into the livingroom: eight, if you counted the woman with the baby in her arms. Her name was Mrs. Korber. She lived upstairs and, in passing, I overheard her say to Mrs. Shalinsky, 'Tell Mr. Shalinsky it's no trouble. Harry and the boy will be here the minute *Dragnet* is finished.'

At that moment my jacket was given a fierce tug from behind. Whirling around, I was confronted by a small, wizened man with rimless glasses. 'I am I.M. Sinclair,' he said.

Retreating, I said: 'You're a doctor, I believe.'

'Like Chekhov.'

'Oh. Oh, I see.'

'I'm the only poet in Canada. Go ahead, laugh.' Then, as though he were composing on the spot, I.M. Sinclair said: 'I am an old man . . . an old man in a dry month- . . . waiting for rain.'

'You ought to write that down,' I said.

'I have burned better lines. We have a lot to talk about, Griffin. The moment in the draughty synagogue at smokefall . . . .'

I broke away just in time to see Harry and the boy arrive. Shalinsky quickly called the meeting to order. There were three of us at the speaker's table— Shalinsky, myself, and a thin man with a fat ledger open before him. Shalinsky gave me a fulsome introduction, and Harry's boy — a fourteen-year-old with a running nose — poked two grimy fingers into his mouth and whistled. The others applauded politely. Then, as Mrs. Korber fed her baby with a bottle, I began.

'Louder,' barked a voice from the back row.

So I spoke louder, elaborating on Kafka's difficulties with his father.

'What does he say?' somebody shouted. I waited while the man next to him translated what I had said into Yiddish. 'Nonsense,' his neighbour said. 'A Jewish education never harmed anybody.'

I rushed through the rest of my lecture, omitting half of it. A short question period was to follow. A Mr. Gordon was first.

'Mr. Griffin, my son is studying at McGill and he wishes to become a professor too. Now my question is as follows. How much can my Lionel expect to earn after five years?'

I had barely answered Mr. Gordon's question when a man in the back row began to wave his arm frantically.

'Yes,' Shalinsky said. 'What is it, Kaplan?'

Kaplan shot up from his seat. 'I move a vote of thanks to Mr. Griffin for his excellent speech. I also move no more questions. It's nearly a quarter to eleven.'

236

'Second both motions,' cried a little man with thick glasses. 'Segal. S,E,—no I—G,A,L. Get that in the minutes, Daniels.'

A moment later Shalinsky and I were abandoned on one side of the room. Everyone else crowded round the refreshments table. I asked for my coat. At the door, Shalinsky thanked me profusely for coming.

'It's you I ought to thank,' I said. 'I enjoyed myself immensely.'

'You see,' Shalinsky said, 'it's good to be with your own sometimes.'

'Just what do you mean by that?'

Shalinsky smiled faintly.

'Look, will you please get it through your head that I'm not Jewish.'

'All right, all right. I'm mistaken.'

'Good night,' I said, banging the door after me.

Joyce was waiting up for me in bed. 'Well,' she asked, 'how did it go?'

'Skip it.'

'What's wrong?'

'I don't want to talk about it, that's all.'

'I don't see why you can't tell me about it.'

I didn't answer.

'I mean you don't have to bite my head off just because I'm curious.'

'There's nothing to tell.'

'You've left a cigarette burning on the bureau.'

'Oh, for Christ's sake. It would be so nice not to have all my filthy little habits pointed out to me for once. I know there's a cigarette burning on the bureau.'

Retreating into the bathroom, I slammed the door after me. But even a bath failed to soothe my nerves. I lit a cigarette and lingered in the tub.

'What on earth are you doing in there?' Joyce shouted.

'Writing a book.'

'Isn't he witty?'

'And next time you use my razor on your blessed armpits, kiddo, I'll thank you to wash it and replace the blade.'

'Now who's pointing out whose filthy habits?'

I don't like mirrors. I make a point of never sitting opposite one in a restaurant. But tonight I had a special interest in studying my face.

'Mortimer!'

Mortimer, of course, could be a Jewish name.

'What are you doing in there?'

I'm a tall man with a long horse face. But my nose is certainly not prominent. Turning, I considered my face in profile. When I finally came out of the bathroom I asked Joyce: 'Would you say I had a Jewish face?'

She laughed.

'I'm serious, Joyce.'

'As far as I'm concerned,' she said, 'there's no such thing as a Jewish face.'

I told her about the lecture.

'If you want my opinion,' she said, 'you wouldn't mind Shalinsky's notion in the least if you weren't a sublimated anti-semite.'

'Thank you,' I said, switching off the light.

An hour later, sensing that I was still awake, Joyce turned to me in bed. 'I've been

237

thinking, darling. Look, if — now please don't get angry. But *if* you were Jewish — '

'*What?*'

'I mean, if you have got Jewish blood I'd love you just as — '

'Of all the stupid nonsense. What do you mean, *if* I'm Jewish? You've met my parents, haven't you?'

'All I'm saying is that if — '

'All right. I confess. My father's real name is Granofsky. He's a goddam defrocked rabbi or something. Not only that, you know, but my mother's a coon. She — '

'Don't you dare use that word.'

'Look, for the tenth time, if I had Jewish blood I would not try to conceal it. What ever made you think . . . ?'

'Well,' she said. 'You know.'

'Goddam it. I told you long ago that was done for hygienic reasons. My mother insisted on it. Since I was only about two weeks old at the time, I wasn't consulted.'

'O.K.,' she said. 'O.K. I just wanted you to know where I would stand if — '

'Look, let's go to sleep. I've had enough for one day. Tomorrow first thing I'm going to settle this matter once and for all.'

'What are you going to do?'

'I'm going to start a pogrom.'

'Some of your jokes', Joyce said, 'are in the worst possible taste.'

'Yes. I know. I happen to be cursed with what Hy calls a Goyishe sense of humour.'

The next morning I phoned Shalinsky.

'*Jewish Thought* here. Mr. Shalinsky is in Toronto. I'll have him get in touch with your office the minute he returns.'

'Shalinsky, it's *you.*'

'Ah, it's you, Griffin. I'm sorry. I thought it was Levite the printer. He usually phones at this hour on Thursday mornings.'

'Look, Shalinsky, I'd like you to come over here at three this afternoon.'

'Good.'

Taken aback, I said: 'What do you mean, *good*?'

'I was hoping you'd want to talk. Speaking frankly, I didn't expect it to happen so soon.'

'Just be here at three,' I said. 'O.K.?' And I hung up.

By the time Shalinsky arrived I had amassed all manner of personal documents — my army discharge papers, passport, driving license, McGill graduation certificate, marriage license, a Rotary Club public speaking award, my unemployment insurance card, vaccination certificate, Bo-lo Champion (Jr. Division) Award of Merit, three library cards, a parking ticket, and my bank book. On all these documents was the name Mortimer Lucas Griffin. Seething with suppressed anger, I watched as Shalinsky fingered each document pensively. He looked up at last, pinching his lower lip between thumb and index finger. 'Facts,' he said. 'Documents. So what?'

'So what? Are you serious? All this goes to prove that I was born a white Protestant male named Mortimer Lucas Griffin.'

'To think that you would go to so much trouble.'

'Are you mad, Shalinsky?'

238

'I'm not mad.' Shalinsky smiled, blinking his eyes against the smoke of his cigarette. 'Neither do I want to make problems for you.'

'What do I have to do to prove to you that I'm not Jewish?'

Shalinsky sifted through the papers again. 'And what about your father?' he
asked. 'Couldn't he have changed his name without you knowing it? I mean, this is
within the realm of possibilities, is it not?'

'Or my grandfather, eh? Or my great-grandfather?'

'You're so excited.'

'I'd take you to see my parents, but they're both dead.'

'I'm sorry to hear that. Please accept my condolences.'

'They died years ago,' I said. 'A car accident.'

'Is that so?'

'I suppose you think I'm lying?'

'Mr. Griffin, please.'

'You're ruining my life, Shalinsky.'

'I hardly know you.'

'Do me a favour, Shalinsky. Cut my courses. I'll be grateful to you for the rest of
my life.'

'But your lectures are marvellous, Mr. Griffin. A delight.'

'Some delight.'

'Why, some of your epigrams I have marked down in my notebook to cherish. To
memorize, Mr. Griffin.'

'I've got news for you, buster. They're not mine. I stole them from my professor
at Cambridge.'

'So what? Didn't Shakespeare, may he rest in peace, steal from Thomas Kyd? The
oral tradition, Mr. Griffin, is — '

'Shalinsky, I beg of you. If you won't quit my courses, then at least don't come
to classes. If you'll do that for me I promise to pass you first in the class.'

'Absolutely no.'

Emptied, undone, I collapsed on the sofa.

'You don't feel so hot?' Shalinsky asked.

'I feel terrible. Now will you please go.'

Shalinsky rose from his chair with dignity. 'One thing,' he said. 'Among all those
papers, no birth certificate. Why, I ask myself.'

'Will you please get the hell out of here, Shalinsky!'

My parents were very much alive. But I hadn't lied to Shalinsky because I was
afraid. There were my mother's feelings to be considered, that's all. You see, I was
born an indecent seven months after my parents' marriage. They never told me this
themselves. They always pre-dated the ceremony by a year, but once I accidentally
came across their marriage license and discovered their deception. Not a very scan-
dalous one, when you consider that they've been happily married for thirty-two
years now. But the secret of my early birth belonged to my parents and, to their
mind, had been carefully kept. There was something else. My father, a high-school
teacher all these years, had been a poet of some promise as a young man, and I
believe that he had been saving his money to go to Europe as soon as he graduated
from McGill. He met my mother in his senior year, alas. I was conceived—suspici-
ously close to the Annual Arts Ball, I put it—and they were married. (A shock to
their friends for, at the time, my mother was seeing an awful lot of Louis Cohen, a

famous judge today.) Next year, instead of Europe, my father enrolled for a teacher's course. I have always been tormented by the idea that I may have ruined their lives. So I was certainly not going to open a belated inquiry into the matter for Shalinsky's sake. Let him think I was Jewish and that I was afraid to show him my birth certificate. I knew the truth, anyway.

But as far as Shalinsky was concerned, so did he.

Beginning with my next lecture he contrived to make life a misery for me.

'It seems to be your contention — correct me if I'm wrong — that Kafka's strict Jewish upbringing had a crippling effect on the man. Would you say, then, that this was also true of Hemingway, who had a strict Catholic upbringing?'

Another day.

'I may have misinterpreted you, of course, but it seems to me that you place Céline among the great writers of today. Do you think it possible, Mr. Griffin, that anti-semitism goes hand in hand with literary greatness? Answer me that.'

Shalinsky filled all my dreams. He attacked me in alleys, he pursued me through mazes and, in a recurring nightmare he dragged me screaming into the synagogue to be punished for nameless iniquities. Many an afternoon I passed brooding about him. I saw myself being led up the thirteen steps to the hangman's noose, the despised strangler of Shalinsky, with—because of my ambiguous state — neither minister nor rabbi to comfort me. Because I was sleeping so badly, I began to lose weight, dark circles swelled under my eyes, and I was almost always in an unspeakable temper.

Fearful of Shalinsky, I cut *The Merchant of Venice* from Eng. 112.

'Ah, Mr. Griffin, a question please.'

'Yes, Shalinsky.'

'It seems to me that in our study of Shakespeare, may he rest in peace, we have so far failed to discuss one of the Bard's major plays, *The Merchant of Venice*. I wonder if you could tell me why.'

'Look here, Shalinsky, I do not intend to put up with your insolence for another minute. There are other problems besides the Jewish problem. This is not the Jewish Thought Literary Society, but my class in English 112. I'll run it however I choose, and damn your perverse Jewish soul.'

With that, and the sharper exchanges that were to come, my reputation as an anti-semite spread. Soon I found myself being openly slighted by other lecturers at Wellington. Several students asked to be released from my classes. It was rumoured that a petition demanding my expulsion was being circulated among the students with, I must say, huge success. Eventually, Joyce found out about it.

'Mortimer, this can't be true. I mean you didn't call Shalinsky a meddling Jew in class last week . . . ?'

'Yes, I did.'

'Is it also true, then, that you've stopped taking our newspapers from Mr. Goldberg because . . . you want to transfer our business to a Gentile store?'

'Absolutely.'

'Mortimer, I think you ought to see an analyst.'

'I'm crazy, eh?'

'No. But you've been overworking. I don't know what's come over you.'

'Is this Hy's idea?'

She looked startled.

'Come off it. I know you've been seeing Hy and Eva secretly.'

'Mortimer, how could you have written that article on Chagall for *Jewish Thought*?'

'What's wrong with it?'

'Did you have to call it 'A Jewish Answer to Picasso'? Hy's furious. He thinks that was so cheap of you. He — '

'I'll kill that Shalinsky. I'll murder him.'

Joyce, holding her hands to her face, ran into the bedroom. Three days later, when I sat down to the tiresome job of correcting the Eng. 129 mid-term essays, I was still in a rage with Shalinsky. But I swear that's not why I failed him. His essay on Kafka was ponderous, windy, and pretentious, and deserved no better than it got: F-minus. Unfortunately for me, Dean McNoughton didn't agree.

'Not only do I consider this failure unwarranted, Griffin, but frankly I'm shocked at your behaviour. For the past two weeks charges of the most alarming nature have been flooding my office. I've been in touch with your wife who tells me you've been over-working, and so I prefer not to discuss these charges for the present. However, I think you'd best take the second term off and rest. Hodges will take your courses. But before you go, I want you to mark this paper B-plus. I think Shalinsky's essay is worth at least that.'

'I'm afraid that's impossible, sir.'

Dean McNoughton leaned back in his chair and considered his pipe pensively. 'Tell me,' he said at last, 'is it true you offered to mark Shalinsky first in your class if he only stopped attending your lectures?'

'Yes, sir.'

'I'm afraid I have no choice but to mark this paper B-plus myself.'

'In that case I must ask you to accept my resignation.'

'Go home, man. Rest up. Think things over calmly. If after three weeks you still want to resign . . . .'

I started impatiently for the door.

'I don't understand you, Griffin. We're not prejudiced here. If you're Jewish, why didn't you say so at first?'

Pushing Dean McNoughton aside roughly, I fled the office.

Joyce wasn't home when I got there. All her things were gone, too. But she had left me a note, the darling. It said, in effect, that she could no longer put up with me. Perhaps we had never been right for each other. Not that she wished me ill, etc. etc. But all her instincts rebelled against sharing her bed with a fascist — worse, a Jewish fascist.

I don't know how Shalinsky got into the house. I must have left the door open. But there he stood above me, smiling faintly, a hand-rolled cigarette in his mouth.

'My wife's left me,' I said.

Shalinsky sat down, sighing.

'Joyce has left me. Do you understand what that means to me?'

Shalinsky nodded his head with ineffable sadness. 'Mixed marriages', he said, 'never work.'

241

All this happened two years ago, and I have married again since then. I don't earn nearly as much money in my new job, and at times it's difficult to live with my father-in-law, but next spring, God willing, we hope to rent an apartment of our own (not that I don't appreciate all he's done for us).

I don't see any of my old friends any more, but my new life offers plenty of rewards. I.M. Sinclair, for instance, composed a special poem for our wedding and read it after the rabbi's speech.

Lay your sleeping head, my love,
human on my faithless arm . . .

When the last issue of *Jewish Thought* appeared, imagine my delight when I read on the title-page: EDITED BY J. SHALINSKY AND M. GRIFFIN. Our circulation, I'm pleased to say, is rising steadily. Next year we hope to sell 1,500 copies of each issue. Meanwhile it's a struggle for Gitel and me. For me especially, as I am not yet completely adjusted to my new life. There are nights when I wake at three a.m. yearning for a plate of bacon and eggs. I miss Christmas. My father won't have anything to do with me. He thinks I'm crazy. Hy's another matter. He's phoned a couple of times, but I no longer have much use for him. He's an assimilationist. Last week my application for a teaching job with Western High School was turned down flatly — in spite of my excellent qualifications.

It's hard to be a Jew, you see.

(1968)

Alice Munro
(1931—)

Alice Munro was born in the small town of Wingham, Ontario, and began to publish short stories while she was a student at the University of Western Ontario. She married in 1951, and moved to Vancouver with her husband. She has published many short stories and one novel, *Lives of Girls and Women* (1971).

The story which follows was published first in *The Canadian Forum* and was reprinted in *The Dance of the Happy Shades*, Ryerson Press, Toronto, 1968.

SUNDAY AFTERNOON

Mrs. Gannett came into the kitchen walking delicately to a melody played in her head, flashing the polished cotton skirts of a flowered sundress. Alva was there, washing glasses. It was half-past two; people had started coming in for drinks about half-past twelve. They were the usual people; Alva had seen most of them a couple of times before, in the three weeks she had been working for the Gannetts. There was Mrs. Gannett's brother, and his wife, and the Vances and the Fredericks; Mrs. Gannett's parents came in for a little while, after service at St. Martin's bringing with them a young nephew, or cousin, who stayed when they went home. Mrs. Gannett's side of the family was the right side; she had three sisters, all fair, forthright and unreflective women, rather more athletic than she, and these magnificently outspoken and handsome parents, both of them with pure white hair. It was Mrs. Gannett's father who owned the island in Georgian Bay, where he had built summer homes for each of his daughters, the island that in a week's time Alva was to see. Mr. Gannett's mother, on the other hand, lived in half of the red brick house in a treeless street of exactly similar red brick houses, almost downtown. Once a week Mrs. Gannett picked her up and took her for a drive and home to supper, and nobody drank anything but grape juice until she had been taken home. Once when Mr. and Mrs. Gannett had to go out immediately after supper she came into the kitchen and put away the dishes for Alva; she was rather cranky and aloof, as the women in Alva's own family would have been with a maid, and Alva minded this less than the practised, considerate affability of Mrs. Gannett's sisters.

Mrs. Gannett opened the refrigerator and stood there, holding the door. Finally she said, with something like a giggle, "Alva, I think we could have lunch — "

"All right," Alva said. Mrs. Gannett looked at her. Alva never said anything wrong, really wrong, that is rude, and Mrs. Gannett was not so unrealistic as to expect a high-school girl, even a country high-school girl, to answer, "Yes, ma'am," as the old maids did in her mother's kitchen; but there was often in Alva's tone an affected ease, a note of exaggerated carelessness and agreeability that was all the more irritating because Mrs. Gannett could not think of any way to object to it. At any rate it stopped her giggling; her tanned, painted face grew suddenly depressed and sober.

"The potato salad," she said. "Aspic and tongue. Don't forget to heat the rolls. Did you peel the tomatoes? Fine — Oh, look Alva, I don't think those radishes look awfully attractive, do you? You better slice them — Jean used to do roses, you know the way they cut petals around — they used to look lovely."

Alva began clumsily to cut radishes. Mrs. Gannett walked around the kitchen, frowning, sliding her fingertips along the blue and coral counters. She was wearing her hair pulled up into a topknot, showing her neck very thin, brown and rather sun-coarsened; her deep tan made her look sinewy and dried. Nevertheless Alva, who was hardly tanned at all because she spent the hot part of the day in the house, and who at seventeen was thicker than she would have liked in the legs and the waist, envied her this brown and splintery elegance; Mrs. Gannett had a look of being made of entirely synthetic and superior substances.

"Cut the angel food with a string, you know that, and I'll tell you how many sherbet and how many maple mousse. Plain vanilla for Mr. Gannett, it's in the freezer — There's plenty of either for your own dessert — Oh, Derek, you monster!" Mrs. Gannett ran out to the patio, crying, "Derek, Derek!" in tones of shrill and happy outrage. Alva, who knew that Derek was Mr. Vance, a stockbroker, just remembered in time not to peer out the top of the Dutch door to see what was happening. That was one of her difficulties on Sundays, when they were all drinking, and becoming relaxed and excited; she had to remember that it was not permissible for her to show a little relaxation and excitement too. Of course, she was not drinking, except out of the bottoms of glasses when they were brought back to the kitchen — and then if it was gin, cold, and sweetened.

But the feeling of unreality, of alternate apathy and recklessness, became very strong in the house by the middle of afternoon. Alva would meet people coming from the bathroom, absorbed and melancholy, she would glimpse women in the dim bedrooms swaying towards their reflections in the mirror, very slowly applying their lipstick, and someone would have fallen asleep on the long chesterfield in the den. By this time the drapes would have been drawn across the glass walls of living room and dining room, against the heat of the sun; those long, curtained and carpeted rooms, with their cool colours, seemed floating in an underwater light. Alva found it already hard to remember that the rooms at home, such small rooms, could hold so many things; here were such bland unbroken surfaces, such spaces — a whole long, wide passage empty, except for two tall Danish vases standing against the farthest wall, carpet, walls and ceiling all done in blue variants of grey; Alva, walking down this hallway, not making any sound, wished for a mirror, or something to bump into; she did not know if she was there or not.

Before she carried the lunch out to the patio she combed her hair at a little mirror at the end of the kitchen counter, pushing curls up around her face. She retied her apron, pulling its wide band very tight. It was all she could do; the uniform had belonged to Jean, and Alva had asked, the first time she tried it on, if maybe it was too big; but Mrs. Gannett did not think so. The uniform was blue, the predominant kitchen colour; it had white cuffs and collar and scalloped apron. She had to wear stockings too, and white Cuban-heeled shoes that clomped on the stones of the patio — making, in contrast to the sandals and pumps, a heavy, purposeful, plebeian sound. But nobody looked around at her, as she carried plates, napkins, dishes of food to a long wrought-iron table. Only Mrs. Gannett came, and rearranged things. The way Alva had of putting things down on a table always seemed to lack something, though there, too, she did not make any real mistakes.

While they were eating she ate her own lunch, sitting at the kitchen table, looking through an old copy of *Time*. There was no bell, of course, on the patio; Mrs. Gannett called, "All right, Alva!" or simply, "Alva!" in tones as discreet and penetrating as those of the bell. It was queer to hear her call this, in the middle of talking to someone, and then begin laughing again; it seemed as if she had a mechanical voice, even a button she pushed, for Alva.

At the end of the meal they all carried their own dessert plates and coffee cups back to the kitchen. Mrs. Vance said the potato salad was lovely; Mr. Vance, quite drunk, said lovely, lovely. He stood right behind Alva at the sink, so very close she felt his breath and sensed the position of his hands; he did not quite touch her. Mr. Vance was very big, curly-haired, high-coloured; his hair was grey, and Alva found

245

him alarming, because he was the sort of man she was used to being respectful to. Mrs. Vance talked all the time, and seemed, when talking to Alva, more unsure of herself, yet warmer, than any of the other women. There was some instability in the situation of the Vances; Alva was not sure what it was; it might have been just that they had not so much money as the others. At any rate they were always being very entertaining, very enthusiastic, and Mr. Vance was always getting too drunk.

"Going up north, Alva, up to Georgian Bay?" Mr. Vance said, and Mrs. Vance said, "Oh, you'll love it, the Gannetts have a lovely place," and Mr. Vance said, "Get some sun on you up there, eh?" and then they went away. Alva, able to move now, turned around to get some dirty plates and noticed that Mr. Gannett's cousin, or whoever he was, was still there. He was thin and leathery-looking, like Mrs. Gannett, though dark. He said, "You don't happen to have any more coffee here, do you?" Alva poured him what there was, half a cup. He stood and drank it, watching her stack the dishes. Then he said, "Lots of fun, eh?" and when she looked up, laughed, and went out.

Alva was free after she finished the dishes; dinner would be late. She could not actually leave the house; Mrs. Gannett might want her for something. And she could not go outside; they were out there. She went upstairs; then, remembering that Mrs. Gannett had said she could read any of the books in the den, she went down again to get one. In the hall she met Mr. Gannett, who looked at her very seriously, attentively, but seemed about to go past without saying anything; then he said, "See here, Alva — see here, are you getting enough to eat?"

It was not a joke, since Mr. Gannett did not make them. It was, in fact, something he had asked her two or three times before. It seemed that he felt a responsibility ⌐for her, when he saw her in his house; the important thing seemed to be, that she should be well fed. Alva reassured him, flushing with annoyance; was she a heifer? She said, "I was going to the den to get a book. Mrs. Gannett said it would be all right — "

"Yes, yes, any book you like," Mr. Gannett said, and he unexpectedly opened the door of the den for her and led her to the bookshelves, where he stood frowning. "What book would you like?" he said. He reached toward the shelf of brightly jacketed mysteries and historical novels, but Alva said, "I've never read *King Lear*."

"*King Lear*," said Mr. Gannett. "Oh." He did not know where to look for it, so Alva got it down herself. "Nor *The Red and the Black*," she said. That did not impress him so much, but it was something she might really read; she could not go back to her room with just *King Lear*. She went out of the room feeling well-pleased; she had shown him she did something besides eat. A man would be more impressed by *King Lear* than a woman. Nothing could make any difference to Mrs. Gannett; a maid was a maid.

But in her room, she did not want to read. Her room was over the garage, and very hot. Sitting on the bed rumpled her uniform, and she did not have another ironed. She could take it off and sit in her slip, but Mrs. Gannett might call her, and want her at once. She stood at the window, looking up and down the street. The street was a crescent, a wide slow curve, with no sidewalks; Alva had felt a little conspicuous, the once or twice she had walked along it; you never saw people walking. The houses were set far apart, far back from the street, behind brilliant lawns and rockeries and ornamental trees; in this area in front of the houses, no one ever spent time but the Chinese gardeners; the lawn furniture, the swings and garden tables were set out on the back lawns, which were surrounded by hedges, stone walls, pseudo-rustic fences. The street was lined with parked cars this afternoon; from behind the houses came sounds of conversation and a great deal of laughter. In spite of the heat, there was no blur on the day, up here; everything — the stone and white stucco houses, the flowers, the flower-coloured cars — looked hard and glittering, exact and perfect. There was no haphazard thing in sight. The street, like an advertisement, had an almost aggressive look of bright summer spirits; Alva felt dazzled by this, by the laughter, by people whose lives were relevant to the street. She sat down on a hard chair in front of an old-fashioned child's desk — all the furniture in this room had come out of other rooms that had been redecorated; it was the only place in the house where you could find things unmatched, unrelated to each other, and wooden things that were not large, low and pale. She began to write a letter to her family.

— and the houses, all the others too, are just tremendous, mostly quite modern. There isn't a weed in the lawns, they have a gardener spend a whole day every week just cleaning out what looks to be perfect already. I think the men are rather sappy, the fuss they make over perfect lawns and things like that. They do go out and rough it every once in a while but that is all very complicated and everything has to be just so. It is like that with everything they do and everywhere they go.

Don't worry about me being lonesome and downtrodden and all that maid sort of thing. I wouldn't let anybody get away with anything like that. Besides I'm not a maid really, it's just for the summer. I don't feel lonesome, why should I? I just observe and am interested. Mother, of course I can't eat with them. Don't be ridiculous. It's not the same thing as a hired girl at all. Also I prefer to eat alone. If you wrote Mrs. Gannett a letter she wouldn't know what you were talking about, and I don't mind. *So don't!*

Also I think it would be better when Marion comes down if I took my afternoon off and met her downtown. I don't want particularly to have her come here. I'm not sure how maids' relatives come. Of course it's all right if she wants to. I can't always tell how Mrs. Gannett will react, that's all, and I try to take it easy around her without letting her get away with anything. She is all right though.

In a week we will be leaving for Georgian Bay and of course I am looking forward to that. I will be able to go swimming every day, she (Mrs. Gannett) says and—

Her room was really too hot. She put the unfinished letter under the blotter on the desk. A radio was playing in Margaret's room. She walked down the hall towards Margaret's door, hoping it would be open. Margaret was not quite fourteen; the difference in age compensated for other differences, and it was not too bad to be with Margaret.

The door was open, and there spread out on the bed were Margaret's crinolines and summer dresses. Alva had not known she had so many.

"I'm not really packing," Margaret said. "I know it would be crazy. I'm just seeing what I've got. I hope my stuff is all right," she said. "I hope it's not too — "

Alva touched the clothes on the bed, feeling a great delight in these delicate colours, in the smooth little bodices, expensively tucked and shaped, the crinolines with their crisp and fanciful bursts of net; in these clothes there was a very pretty artificial innocence. Alva was not envious; no, this had nothing to do with her; this was part of Margaret's world, that rigid pattern of private school (short tunics and long black stockings), hockey, choir, sailing in summer, parties, boys who wore blazers —

"Where are you going to wear them?" Alva said.

"To the Ojibway. The hotel. They have dances every weekend, everybody goes down in their boats. Friday night is for kids and Saturday night is for parents and other people — That is I *will* be going," Margaret said rather grimly, "if I'm not a social flop. Both the Davis girls are."

"Don't worry," Alva said a little patronizingly. "You'll be fine."

"I don't really like dancing," Margaret said. "Not the way I like sailing, for instance. But you have to do it."

"You'll get to like it," Alva said. So there would be dances, they would go down in the boats, she would see them going and hear them coming home. All these things, which she should have expected —

Margaret sitting cross-legged on the floor, looked up at her with a blunt, clean face, and said, "Do you think I ought to start to neck this summer?"

"Yes," said Alva. "*I* would," she added almost vindictively. Margaret looked puzzled; she said, "I heard that's why Scotty didn't ask me at Easter — "

There was no sound, but Margaret slipped to her feet. "Mother's coming," she said with her lips only, and almost at once Mrs. Gannett came into the room, smiled with a good deal of control, and said, "Oh, Alva. This is where you are."

Margaret said, "I was telling her about the Island, Mummy."

"Oh. There are an awful lot of glasses sitting around down there Alva, maybe you could whisk them through now and they'd be out of the way when you want to get dinner — And Alva, do you have a fresh apron?"

"The yellow is so too tight, Mummy, I tried it on — "

"Look, darling, it's no use getting all that fripfrap out yet, there's still a week before we go — "

Alva went downstairs, passed along the blue hall, heard people talking seriously, a little drunkenly, in the den, and saw the door of the sewing-room closed softly, from within, as she approached. She went into the kitchen. She was thinking of the Island now. A whole island that they owned; nothing in sight that was not theirs. The rocks, the sun, the pine trees, and the deep, cold water of the Bay. What would she do there, what did the maids do? She could go swimming, at odd hours, go for walks by herself, and sometimes — when they went for groceries, perhaps — she would go along in the boat. There would not be so much work to do as there was here, Mrs. Gannett had said. She said the maids always enjoyed it. Alva thought of the other maids, those more talented, more accommodating girls; did they really enjoy it? What kind of freedom or content had they found, that she had not?

She filled the sink, got out the draining rack again and began to wash glasses. Nothing was the matter, but she felt heavy, heavy with the heat and tired and uncaring, hearing all around her an incomprehensible faint noise — of other people's lives, of boats and cars and dances — and seeing this street, that promised island, in a harsh and continuous dazzle of sun. She could not make a sound here, not a dint.

She must remember, before dinner time, to go up and put on a clean apron.

She heard the door open; someone came in from the patio. It was Mrs. Gannett's cousin.

"Here's another glass for you," he said. "Where'll I put it?"

"Anywhere," said Alva.

"Say thanks," Mrs. Gannett's cousin said, and Alva turned around wiping her hands on her apron, surprised, and then in a very short time not surprised. She waited, her back to the counter, and Mrs. Gannett's cousin took hold of her lightly, as in a familiar game, and spent some time kissing her mouth.

"She asked me up to the Island some weekend in August," he said.

Someone on the patio called him, and he went out, moving with the graceful, rather mocking stealth of some slight people. Alva stood still with her back to the counter.

This stranger's touch had eased her; her body was simply grateful and expectant, and she felt a lightness and confidence she had not known in this house. So there were things she had not taken into account, about herself, about them, and ways of living with them that were not so unreal. She would not mind thinking of the Island now, the bare sunny rocks and the black little pine trees. She saw it differently now; it was even possible that she wanted to go there. But things always came together; there was something she would not explore yet — a tender spot, a new and still mysterious humiliation.

(1968)

Alden Nowlan
(1933—   )

A biographical note on Nowlan appears in the poetry section of this book.

In addition to his poems, Nowlan has written a number of short stories, most of which have been collected in the book *Miracle at Indian River*, Clarke Irwin, Toronto, 1968. Like his poems, his stories are mainly compassionate but ironic studies of the lives of poverty-stricken inhabitants of the rural areas of the province of New Brunswick. He has recently published a novel, *Various Persons Named Kevin O'Brien*, 1973, set in rural Nova Scotia.

The story which follows is from *Miracle at Indian River*.

ANOINTED WITH OILS

The day shift at the potato-chip plant quit at five o'clock. As soon as she reached her boarding house, Edith ran upstairs, lifted cologne-scented underwear from her dresser and took her pretty little blue frock from its hook in the closet. Then she whisked down to the bathroom, peeled off her clammy cotton uniform, unpinned her hairnet and got under the shower.

The first thin cloud of steam reeked of the frying oils that clung to her body. The plant was permeated with an odour like that of rancid butter. No matter how long she scrubbed her uniforms, there was always a whiff of that aroma when she took one of them from the closet. Her nostrils twitching in distaste, she rubbed fragrant soap between her hands, working up a lather. Sighing, she slid slippery palms down her legs. The steam took on a new scent: now it was as though she buried her face in roses.

She massaged salt out of her pores: the salt of the cooking fats and the salt of her sweat. Foaming rose-scented water danced on her shoulders and breasts.

In her first week at the Henderson boarding house, Edith had been too shy to bathe every night. Whenever she took a shower, Mrs. Henderson asked half-teasingly and half-inquisitively if she were preparing for a date. But she had grown bolder and now the bath was a ritual. As she towelled herself, she thought of what the preacher in the Pentecostal Chapel north of the creek said about being washed in the blood of the lamb. One became a new person. Well, she became a new person by washing in water. The rancid-butter-smelling Edith of the day shift was not the same person as the rose-scented Edith wriggling into a party dress . . . .

There was a loud knocking at the door. She heard Mrs. Henderson's voice, snide and querulous: "Don't take all night in there, Eddie. The other boarders will want to wash up before supper."

Oh, damn, Edith thought. Then she bit her lip as though she had said the word aloud. She had promised herself that she would stop swearing.

"I'm almost through."

Without replying, Mrs. Henderson shuffled back to the kitchen. Edith wadded up her soiled clothes and sprinted upstairs.

In her room she slipped on the wrist watch that she wore only in the evenings and on Sundays. The watch belonged to the rose-scented Edith. To have allowed the fat-reeking Edith to wear it would have been equivalent to lending it to a stranger. Impulsively she lifted her wrist and kissed the cool glass. The ticking was so soft that she could hear it only when the watch was pressed against her ear.

She sat down on the bed, being careful not to wrinkle her dress. Smiling, she reached out and took a little bottle from the dresser. She opened the bottle, held it close to her nose and sniffed. It was French perfume and she had bought it two months earlier with part of her first pay cheque. It had cost five dollars, leaving her with only four dollars and fifty cents after she had deducted the fifteen dollars that she paid Mrs. Henderson each week. She knew that she had been silly. But she loved rich, delicately scented things. Holding the bottle to the light, she wondered if it were evaporating. She had used none of it yet, but it seemed the level of the sparkling liquid was dropping. Or perhaps this was only her imagination. She sniffed again. It smelled of flowers she had never seen. She could close her eyes and inhale the fragrance of these flowers and imagine — oh, there were no words to convey what she could imagine.

"Supper's ready, Eddie!"

Lord, she hated to be called Eddie! That was her old name. Her mother's voice, spiteful or whining, Eddie. Her father's voice, crazy with rum or maudlin with contrition, Eddie.

"I'm coming right down!"

Carefully she screwed the cap on the little bottle and returned it to the dresser. Then she went downstairs to the dining room. The softness of the blue skirt, rustling against her legs, was like a caress.

Six persons sat at the table. Already, from observing other houses and from listening to the comments of her fellow boarders, Edith had learned that this was a shabby room and that the fare offered by Mrs. Henderson was coarse and meagre in comparison with that provided in local restaurants. But, sitting down to corned beef hash and apple sauce, she thought of how reassuring it was simply to know that meals were to be served at a specific time and place. In the shacks north of the creek there were never any real meals. Whenever anyone got hungry, he found whatever food there was and made himself a lunch.

As they always did, the male boarders, railway section hands and telephone linesmen, ate in silence. They were big, ruddy, awkward men and their jaws worked with the unhurried precision of champing horses. Edith was a little afraid of them.

"Anythin' goin' on at the plant today, Eddie?"

"Nothing that I know of," she said.

Mrs. Henderson scowled. "I heard somethin' today about Pattie Morrison and her husband. She works with you, don't she?"

"Yes, she works at the plant," Edith answered.

"You hear anything about Tim leavin' her?"

"No, I haven't heard anything about it," Edith said. Such scandals belonged to the shacks. And she wanted to escape from the shacks. She wanted to move into a world in which only married women had babies, and in which men and women stayed married forever.

"Eh," Mrs. Henderson muttered dubiously, turning back to her food.

Edith held her fork in her left hand, with the tines down, following the instructions in the etiquette book which she had bought at the drugstore. Someday, she thought, I'll get married and have a home of my own and we'll eat by candlelight and have finger bowls with little slices of lemon, like they do in the movies, and —

"You look real snappy tonight, Eddie."

Mr. Henderson winked at her from the other end of the table.

She supposed he was only trying to be kind and fatherly. But some men thought that just because a girl came from the shacks north of the creek . . . . Mr. Henderson wore a white shirt and a tie and his clean cheeks had been reddened by shaving lotion; she thought of her father with his week's growth of beard, his dirty undershirt and the old-fashioned drawers with the loops attached to his braces. The last time she saw her father he was standing in front of the drugstore: he was drunk and the schoolboys lounging on the steps were nudging one another and snickering at him. She was so ashamed she wanted to die. And he sensed that she was ashamed. He came so close she could smell the vanilla extract on his breath. "I won't shame yuh, Eddie," he whispered hoarsely. "Old Dad is gonna behave hisself. He ain't gonna shame yuh." And suddenly she pitied him and wished she could throw her arms around him and tell him it didn't matter. But she said nothing, and he turned unsteadily and lurched away . . . .

After supper she changed to shorts and a blouse and washed her uniform. The stale, greasy smell of the plant filled the bathroom like gas. She wished she could find another job. She thought enviously of the sales clerks at the dime store. They worked in cute little skirts and blouses and the store smelled of clean cotton and cellophane and perfume and candies. But the young manager looked like an actor in his flannel slacks and tweed jacket. She was scared to speak to him. And she supposed he hired only girls who had attended high school. She told herself that someday soon she would ask him. The worst he could do was say no. Then she realized that this wasn't true. He could do far worse than say no. He could smile and murmur his regrets while his eyes told her, as clearly as if he spoke, that she had been pitiably foolish to imagine that ignorant shack girls like her could obtain jobs in stores as grand as his.

She sighed and scrubbed the stink of the grease from her arms. She would have liked to take another shower, but she knew Mrs. Henderson would chide her about wasting all of the hot water, and besides, so Mrs. Henderson's eyes would ask, who but a crazy person took two baths in one day?

She brushed her teeth until her gums stung, then rubbed them with a bit of cotton dipped in peroxide. Returning to her room, she cleaned and filed her nails and brushed her hair as directed by the magazines: one hundred strokes, each one in, and out, and up.

Her calves and back ached after the long day on the packaging line. After brushing her hair, she put on her crisp, clean-smelling pyjamas and curled up in bed with a movie magazine. The stories she liked best told of the discoveries of great stars. A girl much like her would be sitting at a soda fountain or walking down the street and a millionaire producer returning from his vacation would see her and shout to his chauffeur, and — she shut her eyes, let the magazine fall, and hugged herself.

But stars had to be beautiful. And she was plain. Not ugly. Just plain. Her breasts were too small and her legs were too thin and her nose too long and her knees were rather knobby and . . . . She opened her eyes and picked up the magazine again.

"Eddie!"

Mrs. Henderson was shouting from the foot of the stairs.

"What is it?"

"Eddie!"

Oh damn, she's as deaf as a post, Edith thought. "What is it?" she yelled. "I hear you! What is it?"

"You're wanted on the telephone!"

Edith groaned. It was sure to be bad news. She could not remember a single time when it had not been bad news.

"I'm coming!" she shouted.

She got out of bed and put on her slippers and robe. Trembling, she trudged downstairs and into the kitchen.

Mrs. Henderson handed her the telephone and sat down. She'll hear every word I say, Edith thought bitterly. Drawing a deep breath, she spoke into the mouthpiece.

"Hello."

"Oh, Eddie, honey, it's so good to hear your voice! You don't know how good it

253

is to hear your voice!"

Her mother spoke in a high-pitched, plaintive whine. Edith could not recall ever having heard her mother speak in a normal conversational voice.

"What's wrong, Mama?" she asked wearily.

"It's your father, Eddie. Somethin' terrible has happened to your father."

Edith slumped and shut her eyes. "What is it, Mama? Is it an accident?" Her tone was almost hopeful. Of course she did not want him to be hurt. But if it were an accident, there would be no scenes and no disgrace —

"No, honey, I'd almost rather it was. I'd almost rather he was dead. He's in jail, honey! The Mounties came and took him to jail. I'm down at the courthouse, and —"

"Oh, good God!"

"Don't swear, Eddie. You remember what the Good Book says about swearin'."

"Oh, for Christ's sake, Mama, don't preach to me! Just tell me what happened."

Mrs. Henderson, in the background, made no attempt to disguise the fact that she was listening.

"He threatened a feller with a gun, honey. Of course the gun wasn't loaded. But the feller didn't know that and he called the Mounties and —"

"Oh, good God," Edith moaned again.

"I was wonderin' if you'd come down, honey. I'm down here at the courthouse, like I said. But I don't know nothin' about such things. I was wonderin' if you'd come down and talk to the Mounties."

"I don't know anything about it, Mama. There's nothing I can tell them."

"But it's your father, honey. We gotta try and help him."

"He got himself in. I guess he can get himself out."

"That's a terrible way to talk, Eddie. You sound downright heartless. You shouldn't oughta say such things to your mother, Eddie. Come down and sit with me, Eddie. Please, honey! I don't wanta be alone and all the other kids is too small to understand."

"You can't do anything, Mama. The best thing for you to do is to go home."

"Please, honey — "

"I'm tired, Mama. I'm going to bed."

Her mother's voice became louder, shriller. "Eh! After all I've done for you! You oughta be ashamed, Eddie! You oughta be ashamed!"

"I'm ashamed, Mama. You don't know how much I'm ashamed."

"Please, honey."

"I told you once, Mama: I'm going back to bed."

Edith slammed down the receiver. Mrs. Henderson stared.

"Anythin' wrong, Eddie?"

"No, nothin's wrong."

Dully, she realized that she had slipped and said nothin' rather than nothing. But that was unimportant. Even if her speech became flawless, she would still be a girl from the shacks.

"If there are any more calls for me, tell them I've gone to bed."

Without waiting for an answer Edith turned and headed for the stairs. As she climbed them, she supported herself against the bannister.

Still wearing her robe and slippers, she lay down on her rumpled bed. It had happened so quickly she could hardly believe she had actually talked with her mother. But it always happened quickly: she would spend weeks strengthening her dream and then, in a minute or two, her father or mother or someone else would explode it. Tomorrow everyone in the plant and everyone in the boarding house would know that her father was in jail. At the plant they thought her conceited. She could almost hear their jeering laughter: "She won't be so high and mighty now that her old man's in the jug."

She would run away. Tonight. But there was no money. She had wasted her money on clothes and perfume and a wrist watch. Next week she would start to save. She would save until she had enough money to buy a railway ticket to a place where they could never find her. She would change her name, and no one would ever suspect that she had been reared in a shack with a drunken jailbird for a father and a hallelujah-shouting fool for a mother. There, no one would torment her with sarcastic inquiries about her cousins who had babies at fifteen. There, she would not have to blush and stammer when persons asked her where she had been born. She could tell them anything she wished and they would have no way of knowing that she lied.

She sat up and removed her robe and pyjamas. Turning off the light, she drew the sheets over her head. The smell was there, faint but unmistakeable: the rancid butter stench of her naked body. She could bathe a hundred times a day and drench herself in perfumes, but so long as she worked at the chip plant that smell would not go away.

She felt an irrational urge to stretch out her hand and knock the little bottle of French perfume from the dresser. She hated herself for having bought it. Then, moving quickly so that she would not have time to think, she turned on the light and dressed. Five minutes later she was telephoning for a taxi to take her to the courthouse.

(1968)

255

Suggestions for Further Critical Reading

A. General Studies of English-Canadian Literature

Margaret Atwood, *Survival*, Toronto, 1972.

R.P. Baker, *English-Canadian Literature to the Confederation*, Cambridge and Toronto, 1920 (reprinted, New York, 1968).

E.K. Brown, *On Canadian Poetry*, Toronto, 1943.

W.E. Collin, *The White Savannahs*, Toronto, 1936.

Louis Dudek and Michael Gnarowski, eds., *The Making of Modern Poetry in Canada*, Toronto, 1967.

Wilfred Eggleston, *The Frontier and Canadian Letters*, Toronto, 1958.

D.G. Jones, *Butterfly on Rock*, Toronto, 1970.

Carl F. Klinck *et al.*, *Literary History of Canada*, Toronto, 1965.

E.A. McCourt, *The Canadian West in Fiction*, Toronto, 1949.

Eli Mandel, ed., *Context of Canadian Criticism*, Chicago, 1971.

Desmond Pacey, *Creative Writing in Canada*, revised edition, Toronto, 1962.

Desmond Pacey, *Ten Canadian Poets*, Toronto, 1958.

Desmond Pacey, *Essays in Canadian Criticism*, Toronto, 1969.

R.E. Rashley, *Poetry in Canada: The First Three Steps*, Toronto, 1958.

A.J.M. Smith, ed., *The Mask of Fiction*, Toronto, 1961.

A.J.M. Smith, ed., *The Mask of Poetry*, Toronto, 1962.

Norah Storey, ed., *The Oxford Companion to Canadian History and Literature*, Toronto, 1967.

Ronald Sutherland, *Second Image*, Toronto, 1971.

B. Studies of Individual Authors Represented in the Anthology

Earle Birney
Frank Davey, *Earle Birney*, Toronto, 1971.

Morley Callaghan
Brandon Conron, *Morley Callaghan*, Toronto, 1966.
Victor Hoar, *Morley Callaghan*, Toronto, 1969.

Bliss Carman
James Cappon, *Bliss Carman*, Toronto, 1930.
H.D.C. Lee, *Bliss Carman*, Boston, 1912.
Muriel Miller, *Bliss Carman: A Portrait*, Toronto, 1935.
Odell Shepherd, *Bliss Carman*, Boston, 1924.
Donald Stephens, *Bliss Carman*, New York, 1966.

Leonard Cohen
Patricia Morley, *The Immoral Moralists: Hugh MacLennan and Leonard Cohen*, Toronto, 1972.
Michael Ondaatje, *Leonard Cohen*, Toronto, 1970.

Frederick Philip Grove
Desmond Pacey, *Frederick Philip Grove*, Toronto, 1945.
Desmond Pacey, *Frederick Philip Grove*, Toronto, 1970.
Douglas Spettigue, *Frederick Philip Grove*, Toronto, 1969.
Margaret Stobie, *Frederick Philip Grove*, New York, 1973.
Ronald Sutherland, *Frederick Philip Grove*, Toronto, 1969.

A.M. Klein
Tom Marshall, *A.M. Klein*, Toronto, 1970.
Miriam Waddington, *A.M. Klein*, Toronto, 1970.

Archibald Lampman
Carl Y. Connor, *Archibald Lampman, Canadian Poet of Nature*, Montreal, 1929.
Michael Gnarowski, *Archibald Lampman*, Toronto, 1969.
Norman G. Guthrie, *The Poetry of Archibald Lampman*, Toronto, 1927.

Margaret Laurence
Clara Thomas, *Margaret Laurence*, Toronto, 1969.

Irving Layton
Eli Mandel, *Irving Layton*, Toronto, 1969.

Stephen Leacock

C.K. Allen, *Oh, Mr. Leacock*, Toronto, 1925.
Donald A. Cameron, *Faces of Leacock*, Toronto, 1967.
R.L. Curry, *Stephen Leacock, Humorist and Humanist*, New York, 1959.
Robertson Davies, *Stephen Leacock*, Toronto, 1970.
Elizabeth Kimball, *The Man in the Panama Hat*, Toronto, 1970.
David M. Legate, *Stephen Leacock*, Toronto, 1970.
Peter McArthur, *Stephen Leacock*, Toronto, 1923.

Hugh MacLennan

Peter Buitenhuis, *Hugh MacLennan*, Toronto, 1969.
Robert Cockburn, *The Novels of Hugh MacLennan*, Montreal, 1970.
Paul Goetsch, *Hugh MacLennan*, Toronto, 1973.
Alec Lucas, *Hugh MacLennan*, Toronto, 1970.
Patricia Morley, *The Immoral Moralists*, Toronto, 1972.
George Woodcock, *Hugh MacLennan*, Toronto, 1969.

E.J. Pratt

Carl F. Klinck and Henry W. Wells, *Edwin John Pratt: The Man and His Poetry*, Toronto, 1947.
David G. Pitt, *E.J. Pratt*, Toronto, 1969.
John Sutherland, *The Poetry of E.J. Pratt*, Toronto, 1956.
Milton Wilson, *E.J. Pratt*, Toronto, 1969.

James Reaney

Alvin A. Lee, *James Reaney*, New York, 1968.
Ross Woodman, *James Reaney*, Toronto, 1971.

Mordecai Richler

G. David Sheps, *Mordecai Richler*, Toronto, 1971.
George Woodcock, *Mordecai Richler*, Toronto, 1970.

Charles G.D. Roberts

James Cappon, *Roberts and the Influences of His Time*, Toronto, 1905.
James Cappon, *Charles G.D. Roberts*, Toronto, 1925.
W.J. Keith, *Charles G.D. Roberts*, Toronto, 1969.
Elsie Pomeroy, *Sir Charles G.D. Roberts: A Biography*, Toronto, 1943.

F.R. Scott and A.J.M. Smith

Peter Stevens, *The McGill Movement; A.J.M. Smith, F.R. Scott and Leo Kennedy*, Toronto, 1969.

Ethel Wilson

Desmond Pacey, *Ethel Wilson*, New York, 1968.